ADVANCE PRAISE FOR *SPYING ON DEMOCRACY* BY HEIDI BOGHOSIAN

"Modern life has a way of making us forget the deep political power of privacy. *Spying on Democracy* shakes that complacency, explaining how journalists, attorneys, political dissidents, religious groups, even children, are subject to ever new forms of surveillance in the name of convenience, marketing, and security. This book's great contribution is to remind us how government and private-sector control over information can have shocking implications for freedom and democracy."
—Alexandra Natapoff, author of *Snitching: Criminal Informants and the Erosion of American Justice*

"Heidi Boghosian's *Spying on Democracy* is the answer to the question 'If you're not doing anything wrong, why should you care if someone's watching you?' It's chock full of stories about how innocent people's lives were turned upside-down by public and private sector surveillance programs. But more importantly, it shows how this unrestrained spying is inevitably used to suppress the most essential tools of democracy: the press, political activists, civil rights advocates and conscientious insiders who blow the whistle on corporate malfeasance and government abuse."
—Michael German, former FBI agent and ACLU senior policy counsel

"It's about time someone reverses the spy lens and exposes the corporations and government agencies behind a new wave of surveillance. In *Spying on Democracy*, Heidi Boghosian draws on her extensive legal and activist experience to document a web of surveillance stretching between private industry and the state. It's a chronicle of rogue spy operations, but it's also a damning indictment of how our privacy rights are violated in ways that are shockingly legal. The material here is unsettling, but Boghosian's message is not that we should attempt to hide in the shadows; it's that we must be out front, loud, and on the side of the journalists and dissidents whose rights are most threatened."

—Will Potter, author of *Green Is the New Red: An Insider's Account of a Social Movement under Siege*

"*Spying on Democracy* puts a laser focus on a challenge faced by millions of Americans who, like me, took a solemn oath to defend the Constitution against all enemies, foreign and domestic. What does that oath require of us now, as most of our co-citizens nod an acquiescent 'yes' when New York Mayor Bloomberg (of 'stop-and-frisk' fame) tells us that, after the Boston bombing, 'our interpretation of the Constitution has to change'?

"The naïve 'but-I've-got-nothing-to-hide' reaction betrays how little most Americans know of history, and how willing they are to watch our Constitution shredded, 'as though from a box at the theater.' That is how

The First Amendment was designed to allow rebellion to remain as our heritage. The Constitution was designed to keep government off the backs of the people. The Bill of Rights was added to keep the precincts of belief and expression, of the press, of political and social activities free from surveillance. The Bill of Rights was designed to keep agents of government and official eavesdroppers away from assemblies of people.

—From Justice William O. Douglas's dissenting opinion (with Justice Thurgood Marshall concurring) in *Laird v. Tatum*, 408 U.S. 1 (1972)

Library of Congress Cataloging-in-Publication Data on file
ISBN: 978-0-87286-599-0
eISBN: 978-0-87286-603-4

City Lights Books are published at the City Lights Bookstore,
261 Columbus Avenue,
San Francisco, CA 94133.
www.citylights.com

SPYING ON DEMOCRACY

Government Surveillance, Corporate Power, and Public Resistance

Heidi Boghosian

Foreword by Lewis Lapham

Open Media Series | City Lights Books
San Francisco

Raimund Pretzel, a young German lawyer described (in his autobiographical book, *Defying Hitler*) the reaction in Germany after the parliament was burned down in 1933. It was Germany's 9/11, so to speak, after which (and you've heard the words a thousand times) 'everything changed!'

"Pretzel was there in Berlin to describe what he called the 'collective, limp collapse . . . the nervous breakdown' of the German people:

"'There are few things as odd as the calm, superior indifference with which we watched the beginnings of the Nazi revolution. . . . With sheepish submissiveness, the German people accepted that, as a result of the fire, each one of them lost what little personal freedom and dignity was guaranteed by the constitution, as though it followed as a necessary consequence. No one saw anything out of the ordinary in the fact that, from now on, one's telephone would be tapped, one's letters opened, and one's desk might be broken into.'

"Are we now 'Back to the Future'? Grateful applause for another young lawyer with the guts to tell it like it is. Let's hope Americans will read Heidi Boghosian's *Spying on Democracy* and learn from it. For, as Dr. King put it, 'There is such a thing as too late.'"

—Raymond McGovern, Veteran Intelligence
Professionals for Sanity

Contents

Acknowledgments

Friends and colleagues at the National Lawyers Guild are a constant source of inspiration. Many individuals gave feedback, including Lesley Alderman, Geoff Brady, Nora Eisenberg, Johanna Fernandez, Kris Hermes, Sarah Hogarth, Karen Menge, Rachel Rosnick, and Liz Templeton. Dan Gregor's assistance was invaluable.

My editor Greg Ruggiero taught me that a narrative needs more than "just the facts." From our first conversation aboard a train to Washington, D.C., his guidance has been gracious, his encouragement generous.

Marilyn and Varujan Boghosian appreciated the influence of corporations and the power of individual action as I learned after an incident involving a locked chain and the door of an unprincipled insurance company. Alice Wolff abetted an early fascination with spying.

Some books have ghostwriters. This one had a ghost thinker. Bill DiPaola's unstinting contributions of ideas and analysis about government and corporate surveillance were instrumental in shaping this compendium. I deeply appreciate his insights and ongoing collaboration.

FOREWORD
by Lewis Lapham

They that can give up essential liberty to obtain a little temporary safety deserve neither liberty nor safety.

—Benjamin Franklin

The evidence gathered by Heidi Boghosian on the following pages attests to the pathology of an American government so frightened by its own citizens that it classifies them as probable enemies. Suspicious of all forms of unlicensed expression, the custodians of the nation's conscience find the practice of democracy to be both uncivil and unsafe. Entirely too many people in the room or the parking lot who don't do what they're told, don't swallow their prescribed daily dosages of the think-tank swill slopped into their bowls by the wardens of the corporate security state.

Such people present the risk of having thoughts of their own, and therefore they must be carefully and constantly watched. How constantly and how carefully is the lesson embedded in *Spying on Democracy*. Before reading the book I knew that over the last fifty years the U.S. government had been stepping up its scrutiny of a populace that it chooses to regard as a mob. I had yet to appreciate the extent to which the computers have been programmed with the mind of a lunatic conspiracy theorist.

Heidi Boghosian shows the hydra-headed data banks to be targeted at all sectors of American society, at school-children and the mothers of school-children, at church congregations, credit card members, and Facebook friends, at everybody and anybody at work or at play with the tracking device otherwise known as a cell phone.

So intrusive is the surveillance that nobody leaves home without it. The clothes sold in both upscale and down-market retail outlets come with radio-frequency ID tags sewn into a stitch or a seam. Thousands of cameras installed in the lobbies of apartment and office buildings (also on roofs and in basements, in movie theaters and barbershops, in the eye sockets of the mannequins in department store windows) register and record the comings and goings of a citizenry deemed unfit to mind its own business. The corporate and political gentry distrust democratic government for its being by definition a work in progress, a never-ending argument between the inertia of things as they are and the energy inherent in the hope of things as they might become.

The country was founded by people willing to engage the argument. The Protestant dissenters arriving in the early seventeenth century on the shores of Massachusetts Bay brought with them little else except a cargo of contraband words. They possessed what they believed to be clear refutations of the lies told by the lords temporal and spiritual in Europe, and they settled the New England wilderness as an act of disobedience rooted in what they recognized as a "quarrel with Providence." Translated into the eighteenth-century language of secular politics, the quarrel resulted in the Declaration of Independence and a constitution predicated on James Madison's notion that whereas "in Europe charters of liberty have been granted by power," America would set the example of "charters of power granted by Liberty." The government established in Philadelphia in 1787 sought to ally itself with the ongoing discoveries of something new under the sun, with the ceaseless making and remaking not only of fortunes but also of laws. To a woman who had asked what the gentlemen had made of their deliberations, Benjamin Franklin is reported to have said, "A republic, Madam, if you can keep it."

The government enthroned in Washington in 2013 holds the view that the experiment with democracy has gone far enough, the upkeep of a republic more trouble than it's worth. Let too many freedoms wander around loose in the streets, and who knows when somebody will turn up with a guillotine, or a bomb. The reconfiguration of Madison's premise took shape during the prolonged Cold War with the Russians. How else to counter the threat of a paranoid offense unless with the fielding of an equally paranoid defense? The once-upon-a-time sons of liberty set to work replacing the antiquated U.S.

republic with what President Dwight Eisenhower recognized in 1956 as a "military-industrial complex" arming itself with weapons of every conceivable caliber and size, with a vast armada of naval vessels afloat on eight seas and seven oceans, with guidance systems as "infallible" as those deployed by the seventeenth-century Spanish Inquisition.

During the years 1947 to 1989, the constant reminder of next week's day of judgment provided the parties in power in Washington with justification for muffling the voices of dissent. Unpopular during even the happiest of stock market booms, dissent during times of war attracts the attention of the police. The parade marshals regard any breaking through the rope lines of consensus as unpatriotic and disloyal; the voicing of impolitic opinions comes to be confused with treason, civil liberties to be regarded as so much toxic waste. Nor do governments willingly relinquish charters of power seized under the pretext of apocalypse.

The loss of the Soviet threat in the 1990s brought forth as its replacement the war on drugs, a war waged not to defend the American people but to secure a perimeter around the majesty of the state. The terrorist attacks on New York and Washington on the morning of September 11, 2001, upgraded the war on drugs to a war against "all the world's evil," and by nightfall what was still left of the notion of a democratic republic framed on the premise of an argument had been suspended until further notice, cancelled because of rain. The barbarian was at the gates, civilization trembled in the balance, and now was not the time for any careless choice of word.

Nor is such a time anywhere foreseen by the national intelligence agencies that in the years since the fall of the World Trade Center have added to their payrolls 100,000 inquisitors both petty and grand, have appropriated upwards of $750 billion for military enhancements, and have enlisted the close collaboration of the data-mining engineers in what was once known as the private sector. The government's promotional literature describes the objective as "truth maintenance." To detect and classify each and every one of America's prospective enemies (terrestrial and extraterrestrial, real and imagined) high-speed computers sift through the electronic droppings of every human movement or expression—bank, medical, and divorce records, bookstore purchases, website visits and traffic violations, blood and urine samples, and so on. Connect the dots (all the names and places to all the dates and times), deploy "market-based techniques for avoiding surprises," and if all goes well, what comes up on the screen is an American democracy as safely and securely dead as a pheasant under glass.

Thus, apparently, the fond hope and eager expectation of the risk managers charged with the administration of the Department of Homeland Security, or with the command and control of a bank, an insurance company, a police precinct, or a congressional committee. The mission is the protection of property, not the preservation of the freedoms of the people. Royalist concentrations of wealth remain at liberty to do as they please—to poison rivers, cut down forests, charge cruel rates of interest, deny medical care, repudiate debt, eliminate species. Commonplace human beings, by nature untrustworthy, await instructions about where and how and when they walk the walk or talk the talk. Corporations dismiss employees for trafficking in ambiguous emails; no more than fifty people may assemble on the steps of Manhattan's City Hall. The FBI searches even small-scale street demonstrations for "anarchists" and "extreme elements," rounding up at random any participant deemed fit for a lesson in obedience. An arrest record discourages further experiments with the theory of free speech, and complicates the career plans for young and overly idealistic students obliged to meet the character requirements for admission to a prestigious university. Step out of line, my child, and you can say good-bye to the good hands people at Allstate and JPMorgan Chase.

When President Obama travels around the country to mouth the virtues of a government by the people, of the people, and for the people, the Secret Service sends advance scouts to set up "free speech areas" for the people who ask impolitic questions. Quarantined behind chainlink fences at a discreet distance from the presidential motorcade, the voices of protest remain out of earshot, the faces far enough away to avoid notice on the evening news. What is disheartening is the lack of objection on the part of a citizenry all too easily herded into the shelters of harmless speech and heavy law enforcement. Public opinion polls find the bulk of respondents willing to give up a generous percentage of their essential liberty in return for the shopping-mall measures of freedom (small and getting smaller) that they can still beg or borrow enough money to buy.

It's a poor trade. The well-being of a democratic republic depends less on the abundance of its cheap entertainment or the expense of its armies than on the capacity of its individual citizens to rely on their own thought. The big money never has much trouble drumming up smiles of prompt agreement, but democracy needs as many questions as its citizens can ask of their own stupidity and fear. We can't know what we're about, or whether we are telling ourselves too many lies, unless we can see and hear one another think out loud. Heidi Boghosian's *Spying on Democracy* suggests that dissent is what rescues democracy from a quiet death behind closed doors, and preserves for our society the constitutional right to its own name.

INTRODUCTION

Alexander the Great amassed an empire in the fourth century B.C. with innovations in military tactics and strategy that continue to be used today. Spy networks, including soldiers counting enemy camps at night to plan counterattacks, were essential to his maneuvers. But while Alexander used stealth tactics and reconnaissance against enemies at war, corporations and our government now conduct surveillance and militaristic counterintelligence operations not just on foreign countries but also on law-abiding U.S. citizens working to improve society. Bicycle-riding environmentalists in New York City, journalists raising awareness of flawed national security initiatives, and lawyers representing unpopular clients are but a few examples of individuals whose lives are subjected to monitoring, infiltration, and disruption once they are seen as a threat to corporate profits and government policies.

From the minute you wake up, your everyday activities are routinely subject to surveillance. Retailers capture consumer data and sell it to data aggregators, telecommunications companies hand over records of customer calls to government agencies, and personal data shared on social media platforms is readily available to businesses that may share it with the authorities.

Whether you are the head of the Central Intelligence Agency arranging a secret sexual encounter or an ordinary citizen shopping at Target, your interactions with others are under a staggeringly comprehensive network that tracks where you go, how long you stay, and what you browse, read, buy, and say. An intelligence-gathering infrastructure that commands access to, and control over, so much personal information is the hallmark of a totalitarian regime.

Historically, successful government spies are acclaimed as heroes, while those caught spying for the other side face harsh punishment, including execution. The lauded ones were masters of deception, betraying trusts and confidences to gain invaluable intelligence. In similar fashion, government and corporate authorities abuse trusting Americans by monitoring them around the clock and amassing their personal data. The more an individual draws attention to a corporate or government misdeed, the more that person is subject to intrusive observation.

This book documents the way relentless surveillance makes people in the United States less free. As government agencies shift from investigating criminal activity to preempting it, they have forged close relationships with corporations honing surveillance and intelligence-gathering techniques for use against Americans. By claiming that anyone who questions authority or engages in undesired political speech is a potential terrorist threat, this government-corporate partnership makes a mockery of civil liberties. The examples in these pages show how a free press, our legal system, activists, and other pillars of a democratic society—and even children—suffer as a consequence. As the assault by an alignment of consumer marketing and militarized policing grows, each single act of individual expression or resistance assumes greater importance. As individuals and communities, we need to dismantle this system if we are to restore and protect our civil liberties.

From Outrage to Complacency

Spying on Americans is not new. For almost all of the twentieth century, hysteria on the part of the Federal Bureau of Investigation and other government intelligence agencies fueled suspicion of domestic dissidents and ordinary citizens. Cold War fears under J. Edgar Hoover spawned counterintelligence programs to disrupt domestic peace groups and to discredit and neutralize public figures such as Martin Luther King Jr. and leaders of political movements such as the Puerto Rican Independence Party.

With revelations about covert spying in the 1970s, the public was galvanized in outrage and demanded investigations. In response, the FBI ended its covert counterintelligence programs. An era of regulation of political surveillance was launched, with Congress making permanent the House and Senate Intelligence Committees.

In 1976, Attorney General Edward H. Levi established guidelines limiting federal investigative power into the First Amendment activities of Americans.

Half a century later, reports of nationwide surveillance and First Amendment infringements elicit scant outcry, and hard-fought legal protections have been all but eliminated amid fears of terrorism. Beginning in 1981, Ronald Reagan reauthorized many of the domestic intelligence techniques that had been restricted just a decade earlier. After the 1995 attack on the Alfred P. Murrah Federal Building in Oklahoma City, Bill Clinton's Antiterrorism and Effective Death Penalty Act of 1996 authorized the targeting of individuals and groups for surveillance, not on the basis of acts they had allegedly committed, but on their "association" with other groups or individuals. Days after the 2013 Boston Marathon bombing, nearly one million residents sheltered in place as authorities locked down Boston during a high-profile hunt for one 19-year-old suspect. After arresting him and announcing that a public safety danger no longer existed, the Department of Justice nevertheless invoked a rarely used public safety exception to the Miranda obligation to inform suspects of their rights.

The opportunity to abolish any remaining impediments to domestic spying was laid at the feet of the George W. Bush administration after 9/11. FBI agents can now visit public places, attend public events, and install surveillance devices to gather information on individuals and organizations without any indication of criminal activity.

The Department of Homeland Security was created, providing a massive injection of funding to state and local police departments to identify terrorist threats, and bolstering an Internet surveillance apparatus. Federal and state agents access private databases and can search and monitor chat rooms, bulletin boards, and websites.

Government officials insist that mass surveillance makes us safer. In the absence of substantive national debate, most of the population—96 percent of which approves of public surveillance cameras, according to a 2009 Harris Poll survey—seems convinced of that assertion. The events following the Boston Marathon attack revealed to the world the extent to which individuals' movements are monitored and recorded from multiple angles. Lord & Taylor, the country's oldest high-end retail store, was among the many retailers that provided police investigators with tapes of individuals walking on surrounding sidewalks. When surveillance tapes help lead to the apprehension of criminal suspects in terrorism cases, as happened in Boston, lawmakers are quick to urge installation of even more monitoring devices. Exploiting public fears of terrorism, New York Republican representative Peter King praised surveillance cameras as a way to keep Americans safe from "terrorists who are constantly trying to kill us."

This convergence of government and business intelligence operations has created all the elements of an Orwellian mass surveillance network: a trusting and fearful public, a shift to preemptive policing justified by opportunistic citing of a nebulous enemy threat, domestic use of military equipment, and communications devices that provide direct portals into private transactions. Each component element is formidable. Together, they are a nightmare for democracy.

Normalizing Cultural Obedience through Surveillance

Every day you leave your home, your image is caught on surveillance cameras at least two hundred times, it is estimated. Little public debate has addressed the possible consequences of nearly continuous surveillance. Cameras monitor us while we shop, ride elevators, tour museums, stand in line at banks, use ATMs, or merely walk down streets, desensitizing us to unceasing observation and recording.

People growing up in the digital age may have a hard time imagining life without the self-consciousness and self-censorship prompted by today's surveillance state. Others may recall a time when the nation expressed outrage when its citizens were "bugged," trailed, or tracked. Today, only those living off the grid in rural areas of places such as Montana or Alaska are exempt from being monitored all the time. If they are determined to be "persons of interest," however, they too can be tracked down and monitored.

A new generation of advertisement-driven Americans is persuaded from an early age to buy cell phones, tablets, and computers with built-in monitoring capability. Disney and McDonald's, along with many other corporations, lure children into online worlds or amusement parks where personal information is collected in exchange for special rewards. At the same time, policymakers, quick to approve sweeping counterterrorism measures, have dismantled many levels of legal safeguards that evolved over time to protect individuals' civil liberties.

Normalization is the process by which we accept and take for granted ideas and actions that previously may have been considered shocking or taboo. Michel Foucault wrote that modern control over society may be accomplished by watching its members, and maintaining routine information about them. Foucault emphasized that Jeremy Bentham's eighteenth-century panopticon, a continuous surveillance model for prisoners who could not tell if they were being watched, exemplified an institution capable of producing what he called "docile bodies."

Distracted by the rush and convenience of information technology, few of us discern that opening a window into our personal transactions helps shape a culture of conformity and normalizes the nefarious business of domestic intelligence gathering.

Military Applications Turn Homeward
Spying on democracy at home is seamlessly connected to military intelligence and intervention abroad. The creation of the Department of Homeland Security and intelligence coordinating entities known as fusion centers encourages collaboration between branches of the United States military, a host of government agencies, and profit-

seeking corporations in collecting, storing, and acting on information about citizens.

Weapons of war used for national defense abroad are now being deployed against people at home. Military hardware such as drones, originally intended for tracking and killing enemy combatants in the battlefields of Iraq and Afghanistan, are now used on U.S. soil.

Seeking to avoid revenue loss from reduced military contracts, electronics and computer companies have expanded into new markets with equipment originally developed for military use. Although better known for calculators and other consumer electronics, companies such as Texas Instruments started out by selling computer and surveillance systems to governments. Increased sophistication of surveillance, identification, and networking technology (including ID cards, radio-frequency identification chips, data matching, biometrics, and various other systems) began to be used—for efficiency's sake—on such groups as immigrants, military personnel, and convicted offenders. Gradually they came to be employed more widely, often under pressure from manufacturers and their lobbyists, making it easier to conduct routine and widespread surveillance of broad segments of the population.

As military equipment is repurposed for domestic uses, more and more civilians are being classified as threats to national security. Domestic dissenters are no longer labeled "subversive" as they were in the 1970s. Now they are "terrorist" threats. Police used to photograph and videotape activists. Now they operate "Domain Awareness Systems" and roll "SkyWatch" mobile surveillance towers to public spaces on a daily basis. One such tower was used to monitor the Occupy movement's activities in New York's Zuccotti Park and remains a permanent fixture there, keeping tabs on those who come to the park to sit, talk, play, organize, and engage in free speech.

Over a decade after the 9/11 attacks, the government's methods for securing freedom are informed by little, if any, public debate about the consequences. Perpetual war, paid for on a credit card, threatens national security through economic debt and instability, thinning the lifeblood of democracy through the increasing intrusion of a surveillance state.

Civil Liberties Ceded to Consumerism and National Security

Political free speech isn't the only thing that triggers monitoring. Corporations no longer spy merely to protect or steal trade secrets. Ruffling corporate feathers can prompt not just surveillance but more aggressive reactions. Businesses spy to stop people from exposing them and holding them accountable for harmful environmental, financial, or labor practices. When environmental and animal rights advocates scored successes in bringing attention to harmful corporate policies, the FBI called them domestic terrorists. In an era when data is money, corporations are increasingly committing acts of infiltration and espionage against individuals, volunteer groups, and nonprofits that could hinder revenue or bring into question corporate reputations. The range of targets is wide and diverse. Lucrative intelligence-related contracts and equipment specifically designed to afford police easy access to customer information blur the lines between law enforcement charged with protecting the public and corporations seeking to profit from it.

The surveillance net ensnares once sacrosanct relationships. Attorney-client privilege—the ability to communicate freely in private with a lawyer—is now subject to monitoring, especially for individuals who have expressed views critical of corporations and government policies. Journalists who report on harmful or illegal actions by corporations or government agencies have their phone records subpoenaed in efforts to find confidential sources.

"Life, Liberty and the pursuit of Happiness"—the meaning of these hallowed words is undermined and challenged by the rise of the national security state. Our daily experience as Americans is, increasingly, less about freedom and more determined by credit reporting, consumerism, militaristic internal security, and the rise of corporate-government domination over what is left of the public space and the civic powers available to us within it. Supreme Court Chief Justice Earl Warren's observation in the 1967 case *United States v. Robel* rings true today: "It would indeed be ironic if, in the name of national defense, we would sanction the subversion of one of those liberties—the freedom of association—which make the defense of our nation worthwhile."[1]

Going Dark

The FBI began planning a multimillion-dollar secret surveillance unit in Quantico, Virginia, to invent new technologies to help government authorities eavesdrop on Internet and wireless communications as early as 2008. The Domestic Communications Assistance Center (also referred to as the National Domestic Communications Assistance Center) is to be staffed with agents from the U.S. Marshals Service and the Drug Enforcement Administration. Along with countless gigabytes of data afforded by wireless providers and social networks, it will house customized surveillance technologies targeting specific individuals and organizations.

The unit was originally conceived to combat a "going dark" problem. Going dark means that as communications shifted from telephones to the Internet, wiretapping became more difficult, with investigations encountering delays in executing court-authorized eavesdropping, as communications companies were not mandated to design backdoor ports of entry. The FBI told Congress that the problem was sufficient reason to expand the Communications Assistance for Law Enforcement Act (CALEA) of 1994. CALEA required telephone companies to design their systems so that law enforcement could eavesdrop when needed. The proposed expansion calls for a variety of computer programs to be designed with online communication capacities that will afford police similar backdoor means of entry.

The Department of Justice, in a funding request for

2013, noted that the Domestic Communications Assistance Center will facilitate sharing of expertise between federal, state, and local law enforcement agencies as well as telecommunications companies looking to centralize electronic surveillance.

Dismantling the Surveillance Infrastructure

In George Orwell's *1984*, the all-seeing state is represented by a two-way television set installed in each home. In our own modern adaptation, it is symbolized by the location-tracking cell phones we willingly carry in our pockets and the microchip-embedded clothes we wear on our bodies. For every way in which a microchip or cell phone might improve daily life, other sinister applications give big business and government authorities increased access to and power over our lives. The ubiquity of such devices threatens a robust democracy. Rather than advancing freedom and equality, inescapable surveillance enforces a form of authoritarianism that undermines both. It degrades the ability of members of society to challenge and organize against government and corporate injustices. The loss of cultural freedom stifles individual creativity and the unfettered community interaction necessary to keep power in check and to advance as an evolving society.

Constant surveillance influences how we live, connect, and learn. It impacts how we exercise freedom and contribute to democracy. As the state and big businesses increasingly monitor our lives, challenges to their authority are increasingly portrayed as a gateway activity to more ominous and intolerable threats. Political resistance, whistle-blowing, investigative journalism, and social and environmental advocacy of all kinds, by their very nature, question and challenge authority. They can now attract resources and responses associated with counterterrorism operations, as seen with the coordinated national repression of the nonviolent Occupy movement. An increasingly militaristic national climate, and the symbiotic corporate culture that profits enormously from it, are now virtually uncontested fixtures in the American experience.

As individuals, as communities, and as a society, we must dismantle the surveillance system if we are to protect and advance the basic conditions required to live our lives in real freedom. To accept anything less out of convenience or fear would be to embrace a grim and stunted future. For the more we accept that all kinds of information about us and our everyday lives is recorded, the more we succumb to the potential abuses of cyber-surveillance. In short, we run the risk of our civil liberties, to borrow the FBI's term, "going dark."

CHAPTER I

Trafficking Imagination in the Streets

New York City Police Commissioner Raymond W. Kelly has said that the helicopters in the New York City Police Department's aviation unit are essential for fighting terrorism. It was disconcerting, then, when an NYPD chopper equipped with an infrared camera hovered several hundred feet above lower Manhattan in October 2004. Hundreds of officers filled the streets, twenty buses stood by to transport prisoners and their property, and the deputy commissioner for counterterrorism was consulted, as was the department's organized crime unit.[1] Startled bystanders witnessed a series of fast-moving operations that ultimately cost the city millions of dollars in personnel, equipment, overtime, and legal settlements.

But it was not people plotting armed attacks or an even remotely equivalent danger that the authorities were tracking on that and several other days. The targets of the massive surveillance operation were merely New Yorkers on bicycles, sustainable energy advocates who imagine a cleaner, quieter, and healthier city through alternative and nonmotorized transportation. In the eyes of the police and partnering corporations, however, these individuals represented a significant threat.

Using Public Space for Community Activities
Like a festival on wheels, hundreds of bicyclists of all ages zigzagged through the congested streets of Manhattan. When they reached their destination—bustling Times Square—they quickly clustered together and, in an orchestrated display of exuberance and solidarity, lifted their bicycles high above their heads.

From the beginning to the end of the ride, scores of NYPD officers surrounded the bicyclists from virtually every angle: a helicopter in the air, and vans, bicycles, and scooters on the ground. This escort monitored the riders not only to capture faces on film but also to analyze the group's patterns and movements. As police officers leaned out of the windows of moving vehicles to video-record riders, they gave a public face to the previously covert practice of intelligence gathering. Video evidence turned over to the *New York Times* would later reveal that undercover officers posing as bicyclists had infiltrated the group.[2]

The story of the NYPD's hostile reaction to the monthly bicycling events called Critical Mass paints an unsettling portrait of how modern state tactics have evolved. Corporate and police interests, often enabled by the growing acceptance of surveillance, meet community activities with a threatening display of force. Critical Mass culture leans heavily toward a do-it-yourself,

Members of Time's Up join in a spontaneous Bike Bloc—a jubilant gathering similar to a Critical Mass—in New York's Union Square.
PHOTO: PETER MEITZLER

anticonsumerism, and antiauthoritarian ethic, which may help explain the police's heavy-handed tactics.

Monthly Critical Mass rides began in San Francisco in 1992 and quickly spread to more than three hundred cities around the world. Participants describe the ride as a fun way to increase sustainable transportation, make riders feel safer, and promote the joy of cycling. Many credit Critical Mass with raising awareness of alternatives to motorized transportation, and helping to double the number of bicycle commuters in New York City, in specific, between 2007 and 2011.[3]

Chris Carlsson, historian and often considered a Critical Mass "cofounder," frames its symbolic import: "Critical Mass has done much more than simply promote daily bicycling. It has challenged the organization of urban space, the prioritization of motorized transport over other uses, and the preponderant emphasis on commerce at the expense of public life outside of the narrow logic of buying and selling. Moreover, it has been an incubator space for countless relationships, organizations, and creative projects that have emerged in the new friendships forged rolling through the streets together in Critical Mass."[4]

And that prioritization of motorized transport is just what corporations rely on for profit. What better way for corporations to develop marketing strategies than to track individuals through automobile movements and generate consumer demographics as they drive from place to place? On foot or on a bicycle, citizens have greater freedom from monitoring and control than when in cars.

In New York, bicyclists represent a symbolic challenge to car culture. With fewer cars, not only would gas consumption plummet but insurance companies would lose profits; the state's income stream from registration fees, tags, titles, fuel-related costs, parking, and traffic tickets would wither. As in Amsterdam and other bicycle-friendly cities, people would interact more in quieter public spaces and would be unencumbered by tracking devices that may be built into automobiles.

It is thus not entirely surprising that for over a decade the New York City Police Department spent lavish amounts of time, personnel, and resources to monitor and disrupt the activities of individuals engaging in alternative transportation advocacy and bicycling events. Police tracked, arrested, assaulted, and infiltrated riders, devoting to the effort a level of resources usually reserved for terrorist threats. The travails of these individuals and groups underscore a simple truth: when bicycle riding is used for political expression and advocacy, authorities attempt to criminalize it. The more popular and independent such movements are, the likelier it is that state forces will engage in intimidating tactics to undermine or stop them. When members of a group know or even just suspect that they are under surveillance or infiltrated, democratic group dynamics are inexorably altered. In many cases, otherwise resilient groups may dissipate over time.

Corporations Co-opt a Grassroots Movement

After several fits and starts, and with great fanfare, in 2013 a public bicycle sharing program was launched in automobile-centric New York City. Hundreds of similar programs exist in cities around the world, providing free or affordable alternatives to motorized transportation. In New York, the initiative began with a fleet of six thousand bikes stationed at three hundred locations. As is standard practice, a catchy corporate name was bought. For $41 million, naming rights were awarded to the multinational financial services giant Citigroup, which runs Citibank—and Citibike was born. Another financial

Citi Bike hosted a series of demonstrations—this one at Tompkins Square Park—in 2012 to introduce New Yorkers about the bike share program sponsored by Citi (CitiBank) and MasterCard.
PHOTO: SHAWN G. CHITTLE

titan, MasterCard, gave $6.5 million. At a press conference announcing the program, Mayor Michael Bloomberg referred to it several times as "Citibank" instead of "Citibike." In introducing the bank's CEO, Vikram Pandit, the mayor said: "The person who I have the pleasure of introducing next hopes everyone confuses Citibike with Citibank."[5]

Both men heralded the bike-sharing program as an

important, entirely new, 24/7 transportation network, emphasizing that the bank was bringing a new level of sustainability to the city. But this upbeat conference and seemingly positive development rewrote a seminal chapter in history and credited the City of New York and its corporate partners for improvements won by the very residents who were once tracked as if they had learned how to ride bicycles in a terrorist training camp.

Citibike's blue bicycles serve as roving corporate advertisements, mobile reminders of the relentless assault against community use of public space. Yet when ordinary New Yorkers promote bicycle-friendly policies they are harassed by police, followed by helicopters, and subjected to clandestine and illegal surveillance.

As other examples in this book attest, police infiltration and disruption has the dual effect of splintering social networks while sometimes showcasing activist gains. In some instances, corporate and government alliances take credit for hard-fought achievements, brand them as their own, and allow corporations to reap the profits. Such was the case with bike sharing in New York City.

Law Enforcement "Obsessed with the Rides"

Government response to New York bicycle rides reveals how threatening community organizing can be to power structures. Critical Mass rides took place in Manhattan for a decade and were publicized by the grassroots environmental organization Time's Up and even the New York City Department of Transportation. By 2004, thousands of New Yorkers had participated in the events, attracting scant police response.

Police operations escalated markedly, however, as New York prepared for the 2004 Republican National Convention. It was a politically charged moment. Police Commissioner Ray Kelly and NYPD intelligence chief David Cohen "decided they would have to push beyond what many Americans and New Yorkers had come to think of as acceptable boundaries for police investigations of political groups."[6]

When Kelly was appointed commissioner in 2002, he made it a priority to weaken long-standing court-imposed restrictions on spying on political groups. In persuading a judge that "the entire resources of the NYPD must be available to conduct investigations into political activity and intelligence-related issues,"[7] he cleared the path for the Intelligence Division to "go out and find the groups, conduct surveillance, and penetrate them."[8] In the run-up to the Republican National Convention, detectives traveled to more than ten states "to hang out with the loosely organized anarchists, direct action provocateurs, libertarian clowns, conscientious protesters, and potential killers setting their sights on Madison Square Garden."[9] Such rhetoric reveals an open effort to propagate false associations between constitutionally protected political expression and criminal acts such as homicide.

Web-based organizing preceding the Convention had strong, often hyperbolic, critiques of corporate influence on society. Calls to "shut down the RNC," however, are afforded the same First Amendment protection as singing "God Bless America." Nonetheless, police warned residents that violent anarchists were coming to town, even releasing a list of specific individuals. They threatened hundreds of mass arrests and made good on that promise, engaging in often violent crackdowns on the monthly Critical Mass rides and on individual bicyclists in general. Police arrested nearly three hundred people at the August pre-RNC ride attended by more than five thousand. Arrests continued days later, and police proclaimed hundreds of bicycles to be "abandoned property" and carted them away in trucks, after using massive bolt cutters to break the locks securing them in place.

The tone of media coverage changed when reporters learned how much it was costing taxpayers to have the NYPD spend lavishly on actions that included infiltration, unlawful mass arrests, and police perjury. A *New York Times* editorial focusing on the disproportionate police resources devoted to Critical Mass commented: "The New York police, who deem Critical Mass an illegal parade and have drafted a law that would essentially ban it, have seemed obsessed with the rides since one coincided with the Republican National Convention in August 2004. . . . An amazing array of police resources— scooters, vans, unmarked cars, and helicopters—chase a quarry that looks like fish in a barrel. Police vehicles race the wrong way and on sidewalks, posing a greater public danger than the bikers."[11]

Police harassment of Critical Mass continued for at

least two years after the Republican National Convention. From fall 2004 until spring 2006 the NYPD arrested more than three hundred people, charging them with disorderly conduct and violation of newly created parade permit laws. Often police officials told the media that riders prevented emergency fire and medical vehicles from reaching their destination, when in fact bicyclists quickly moved out of the way when such vehicles approached.

Time's Up was a natural advocate for and active partner with Critical Mass. Founded in 1987, the New York–based nonprofit uses educational outreach and creative direct actions such as moonlight rides through Central Park and Polar Bear Rides to raise awareness of climate change and to promote what it calls a "less toxic" city.

Authorities engaged in covert spying on and infiltration of Time's Up in 2004 and for years after. Undercover police joined Time's Up rides and free events; hours after activities ended, they also attended social gatherings.[12] The aggressive ways in which the group was spied upon led many people to assert that surveillance was being used as an intimidation tactic. For years, members reported to the executive director that police vans were parked around-the-clock in front of the organization's street-level space. More than twenty photos of suspected undercover police officers were taped to the refrigerator of Time's Up's Houston Street headquarters with a hand-made sign cautioning: BE AWARE OF UNDERCOVER AGITATORS AND COINTELPRO-LIKE TACTICS."[13]

Revealing the extent to which it would thwart local community group efforts, in 2005 the city took the unusual step of initiating litigation against Time's Up, seeking to stop them from promoting their free rides and events unless they secured special event permits. The lawsuit asserted in part that without a permit, "it is unlawful to advertise the time and location of a meeting or group activity in a City park." Time's Up responded that the rides were spontaneous activities of many individuals and were not sponsored by any organization.[14]

The lawsuit threat loomed over the group, deterring many from attending events. A year after the suit was filed, a judge dismissed the city's request, writing that the rides did not fall under the city's examples of parades or programs necessitating permits and that "riding a bicycle on city streets is lawful conduct, as long as one observes the applicable traffic laws and rules."[15]

Monitoring a Moving Target

Time's Up founder and director Bill DiPaola noted that soon after the 2004 Republican National Convention, many community-based, volunteer-run groups splintered apart or disappeared altogether. He attributed their dissolution to members' awareness that they were under surveillance by authorities. "Critical Mass brought police spying out in the open. The NYPD decided that bicyclists needed to be stopped, but they had to adapt their spying tactics to a fast-moving target. That's when their spying techniques were exposed: police stood on street corners with cameras, rode SUVs with darkened windows, and used undercover agitators on bicycles. They even flew helicopters with infrared cameras that spied on people at night."[16]

With an eye to preserving this chapter of surveillance history, Time's Up members regularly photographed and videotaped the new roving surveillance, amassing hundreds of tapes of police encounters, including many that showed officers in vans monitoring and recording riders.

For years, New Yorkers involved with the rides could only guess the extent of surveillance. Their suspicions of NYPD spying, including deploying undercover officers to manipulate the outcome of bicycle rides, were ultimately validated. In 2012, the Associated Press obtained documents detailing that the police department's Intelligence Division attended and spied on Time's Up rides and events as late as 2008. The division also monitored the group's websites, added agents to email lists, and maintained intelligence files on its members.[17]

Police Perjury and Assaults of Cyclists

When government targeting of bicyclists was at its peak, on several occasions high-ranking plainclothes officers singled out riders, chasing and assaulting them. Bicyclists reported being pepper-sprayed and assaulted by uniformed and undercover police officers. Such actions were routinely covered up. One officer committed perjury by saying he had witnessed a traffic infraction when he had not, later claiming that his lieutenant had ordered him to testify falsely.

Brigitt Keller, executive director of the National Police Accountability Project, notes, "Attacks of bicyclists are an example of over-policing: The goal is not ensuring public safety, as officers are sworn to do, but silencing dissent and preserving the status quo. Time and time again we see police departments working at the behest of corporate interests with an ever expanding arsenal of new weaponry, unfettered surveillance, and bogus criminal charges that are later dropped in court."[18]

And that's just how events played out in New York. Videotape evidence exposed police assaults on bicyclists and police perjury, and to a certain extent undermined department credibility. I-Witness Video, a group that documented police interactions with protesters, discovered instances of police perjury and doctoring of video evidence by the District Attorney's office. Of 1,806 arrests at the RNC, the *New York Times* reported, an estimated four hundred were negated solely on the basis of video evidence that exonerated arrestees and exposed perjury by law enforcement agents.[19]

After city officials denied assembly permits to cyclists for the February 2006 Critical Mass ride, the commander of Patrol Borough Manhattan South, Assistant Chief Bruce Smolka, operating in plainclothes, grabbed a rider off her bicycle by the chain she wore around her waist and pushed her to the ground.[20] Hundreds witnessed the incident, and the photograph became emblematic of "over-policing" of riders. Smolka physically assaulted females on at least two other occasions. A (non-bicycle-related) federal lawsuit settled in 2007 for $150,000 alleged that the borough commander kicked Cynthia Greenberg in the head as he tried to arrest her in 2003.[21] At the April 2005 Critical Mass, Smolka manhandled a woman walking with her bicycle, then was joined by other officers in pushing her into a police van.[22]

When Assistant Chief Smolka retired suddenly in 2007, hundreds of activists celebrated by proceeding to the Thirteenth Police Precinct with a marching band. Not surprisingly, a cadre of armed officers on scooters escorted them, and police ticketed some cyclists upon their departure.[23]

New York City taxpayers footed the bill for the host of wrongful arrests and injuries inflicted by the NYPD on Critical Mass riders. In 2010 the City settled a 2008 lawsuit for $965,000, representing the claims of eighty-three riders from September 2004 to January 2006. Awards ranged from $500 to $35,000 per person.[24]

The Legacy of Critical Mass
Chris Carlsson described Critical Mass's value for building community in the face of corporate domination: "Critical Mass has been surprisingly transformative in New York and everywhere it has appeared. It acts as an early antibody against the degraded environment of a choking city, while simultaneously re-animating a public sphere, a life outside of the regimentation of the state of emergency maintained as the new normal by the state and (even more militarized) police."[25]

It was precisely this outspoken assertion of public sensibility—a burst of energy that filled New York's streets and attracted thousands of others to join in—that the NYPD deemed a threat warranting years of targeted surveillance and disruption. Mass displays of resistance, especially positive ones with potential to gain momentum, pose a singular challenge to what Carlsson aptly identifies as a city literally constricted by automobiles.

Corporations claim credit for improvements such as a bicycle-sharing program in New York City, giving additional insight into the nature of government and corporate surveillance and control of citizens' movements. Other gains have been realized, but rarely are Critical Mass or Time's Up acknowledged for their efforts.

Bill DiPaola noted that "New York City's Critical Mass was by far one of the most successful campaigns in increasing the level of urban bicycling for commuting and recreation and also in pressuring the City to create a sustainable and safe infrastructure for pedestrians and bicyclists alike."[26] New York City added over 250 miles of bicycle lanes to its streets in 2006. Three years later Mayor Bloomberg announced the transformation of traffic lanes on Broadway in Times Square—known as the Crossroads of the World—into pedestrian plazas. Remapping the area to bar automobile traffic and to ease traffic congestion in midtown Manhattan was made permanent in 2011. And the very same spot where thousands of bicyclists converged during monthly rides and raised their bikes over their heads is now an automobile-free zone.

These improvements illustrate the ways community advocates such as Critical Mass bicycle riders can be a valuable force for positive change. The riders should be appreciated as such instead of being deemed criminal threats and subjected to surveillance and disruption.

In addition to downplaying the role that community-level advocacy plays in improving a city's transportation system, government surveillance in New York left another enduring legacy. It exposed police spying, the excessive amount of money spent on it, and the violence and impunity with which authorities might attack cycling enthusiasts and others if they are perceived as a threat to the status quo. What begins as surveillance quickly takes on the form of counterterrorism operations that include physical intimidation, infiltration, mass arrests, assault, and spurious associations with criminal violence. That's what happened with the community groups and social networks that spurned the corporate way of life.

CHAPTER 2

A Whopper, a Coke, an Order of Spies

Public awareness of and opposition to corporate malfeasance and unfair labor practices threaten both the profits and the carefully manufactured family-friendly images of multinational companies such as Burger King and Coca-Cola. Food and beverage giants fear citizens engaging in old-fashioned boycotts or educational campaigns that expose corporate practices, because such exposure can impact their earnings. To undermine and silence such criticism, corporations increasingly turn to surveillance of individuals and infiltration of organizations working to reveal inhumane, offensive, and in many cases criminal business practices.

Under Florida's unrelenting sun, migrant workers painstakingly handpick tomatoes that will be used as condiments on hamburgers and tacos at thousands of fast-food restaurants. Tomatoes represent a $600 million industry in the state and are staples in the chain restaurants Taco Bell, McDonald's, and Burger King.[1] Workers earn an average of $6,500 a year, receiving as little as forty to forty-five cents per thirty-two pounds of tomatoes picked.[2] These laborers have the highest rate of injuries from exposure to toxic chemicals of any workers in the United States. Their children suffer higher rates of malnutrition, dental disease, and pesticide exposure than those in the general population. When Mary Bauer, director of the Southern Poverty Law Center's Immigrant Justice Project, testified before Congress in 2008, she called the exploitation of farmworkers one of the major civil rights issues of our time.[3]

A community-based worker organization was formed in 1993 to challenge exploitive conditions in the produce industry. The Coalition of Immokalee Workers (CIW) launched several campaigns to draw attention to the plight of tomato harvesters. They organized a broad base of labor inspectors, farmworkers, students, law enforcement bodies, and other nonprofit organizations in their initiatives. Hunger strikes and work stoppages won several victories, including pay raises of up to 25 percent.

A few days before the 2008 Senate hearing on tomato pickers' working conditions, Amy Bennett Williams reported in Florida's *Fort Myers News-Press* that the paper had identified emails originating from Burger King's corporate headquarters in Miami as the source of threatening messages sent to Immokalee Workers and the Student/Farmworker Alliance.[4]

Burger King had hired Diplomatic Tactical Services (DTS), a corporate espionage, security, and intelligence-gathering firm, to infiltrate the Student/Farmworker Alliance. The Alliance was working with the Immokalee

Members of the Coalition of Immokalee Workers (CIW) celebrate a victory on behalf of farmworkers. PHOTO COURTESY COALITION OF IMMOKALEE WORKERS.

Workers to demand a living wage for migrant farmworkers, including those harvesting tomatoes for Burger King. Cara Schaffer, owner of DTS, posed as a student volunteer with the Alliance to spy for the burger company. Suspicious of Schaffer's enthusiasm to join in national strategy calls, activists conducted their own Internet-based research and found that Schaffer owned the private espionage firm.[5] Burger King's corporate leadership was not idle, either. Steven Grover, vice president for regulatory compliance, posted derogatory comments online about the Student/Farmworker Alliance.[6]

News of the spying incident did not put a dent in Burger King Corporation. The company reported earnings of $51 million in the April to June 2008 quarter, up from $36 million a year earlier.[7] In 2010, the multimillion-dollar 3G Capital global investment firm (a hedge fund) purchased Burger King Corporation. That same year, 3G Capital's managing partner, Pavel Begun, joined the board of AlarmForce Industries, provider of live two-way security related services to commercial and residential customers in Canada and parts of the United States.[8]

In addition to Burger King, Coca-Cola has engaged in spying on its critics. The beverage company's online "Human Rights Statement" says its reputation is built on trust and respect, and that it is committed to earning that trust "with a set of values that represent the highest standards of quality, integrity, excellence, compliance with the law and respect for the unique customs and cultures in communities" where they operate.[9]

Their practices indicate otherwise. Coca-Cola hired the private intelligence firm Strategic Forecasting Inc. (known as Stratfor) to investigate People for the Ethical Treatment of Animals (PETA). Correspondence between Coca-Cola senior manager Van Wilberding, formerly a special agent in the U.S. Army and a foreign service officer at the State Department, and Stratfor's Anya Alfano focused on the company's concern that PETA would be protesting at the 2010 Vancouver Winter Olympics. PETA had opposed the company's animal experimentation practices, which included lethal taste reception tests

People for the Ethical Treatment of Animals (PETA) was the subject of intelligence gathering by the security company Stratfor. PUBLIC DOMAIN PHOTO BY SVTCOBRA

in rats. Coca-Cola sent a list of questions to Stratfor, including how many PETA supporters were in Canada, how PETA branches in Canada and the U.S. were connected, and to what extent "non-PETA hangers-on (such as anarchists . . .) might get involved in protest actions.[10] In a later email, Stratfor's president of intelligence, Fred Burton, wrote, "The FBI has a classified investigation on PETA operatives. I'll see what I can uncover." [11]

A Culture of Corporate Spying on Social Advocacy
High-stakes corporate espionage is a familiar concept in pop culture. Portrayals of high-tech efforts to steal business secrets populate alarming news stories and entertaining film and TV thrillers. In real life, American businesses lose up to $300 billion annually on corporate theft.[12] The FBI and CIA acknowledged in 1996 that the problem was so huge they could not protect U.S. enterprises from corporate spying. As a result, businesses devote billions of dollars to spying on each other, often hiring former military agents with espionage training.

In addition to spying on their own staff members, corporations gather intelligence on citizens working for public health, environmental sustainability, economic justice, and corporate accountability. This is where they cross a line from strictly business-related spying into repression of constitutionally protected political expression. Intelligence gathering and monitoring by corporations can stifle public discussion on important health, safety, and quality-of-life issues. This in turn affects society as a whole, not just the specific individuals targeted by surveillance. Private companies aggressively seek out individuals working to improve conditions in ways similar to those employed by the Coalition of Immokalee Workers on behalf of tomato pickers. These corporations fear a new generation of informed advocates in the mold of Karen Silkwood, Ralph Nader, and Rachel Corrie, whose effectiveness inspires others to join in efforts to counter corporate assaults on the public interest.

In the 1960s and 1970s, private political espionage focused on the antinuclear movement and on consumer and environmental issues. Security departments of private utility companies such as Georgia Power spied on antinuclear activists and environmentalists and were in communication with the Department of Energy and the Nuclear Regulatory Commission's Intelligence Assessment Team.[13] The National Caucus of Labor Committees (NCLC), managed by Lyndon LaRouche Jr., began cooperating with local police, providing briefings on perceived political enemies. The NCLC provided intelligence and briefing documents to the New Hampshire state police in April 1977 on a Clamshell Alliance protest against the proposed nuclear power plant in Seabrook, New Hampshire, calling it a cover for terrorist activity.[14]

When General Motors was the largest corporation in the world, its chief executive officer, Charles Wilson, became the U.S. Secretary of Defense. His saying, "What was good for the country was good for General Motors," has an ominous ring in light of the company's unscrupulous tactics to silence an outspoken critic. In 1966 a young Ralph Nader, who had just written *Unsafe at Any Speed: The Designed-In Dangers of the American Automobile*, testified before Congress for the first time about unsafe practices plaguing the as yet mostly unregulated automobile industry. He accused car companies of sacrificing people's safety in the design of stylish cars. One model singled out for criticism was General Motors' Chevrolet Corvair. After Nader testified, General Motors deployed private investigators to spy on him and tap his phone in an effort to discredit him; it also sent women to approach him to attempt to entrap him in illicit relationships.[15] Nader sued the automotive giant for harassment and invasion of privacy. He prevailed, eliciting an opinion from New York State's highest court, the New York Court of Appeals, that expanded tort law to cover "overzealous surveillance."[16]

Big business campaigns against the efforts of concerned citizens became even more sophisticated when Nestlé hired public relations executive Rafael Pagan in 1981 to break the Nestlé infant formula boycott. Pagan developed a campaign to ensure corporate survival and to counter international efforts at regulation. The plan included "separating the 'fanatic' activist leaders from those who are 'decent and concerned' people, and stripping the activists from the moral authority they receive from their alliance with religious organisations." Similarly, Shell Oil drafted a 250-page corporate plan, the Neptune Strategy, with help from Pagan's firm, Pagan International (PI). The plan called for using informants and spies and preparing dossiers on leaders of the Shell boycott campaign.[17]

Corporate-Governmental Partnerships: From Backlash to 9/11

Government surveillance of U.S. citizens waned during the 1970s as a result of successful public campaigns against it. Passage of the Freedom of Information Act (FOIA) brought increased citizen access to information about government spying but did little to counter corporate spying. Immunities offer an additional layer of protection to corporations from lawsuits alleging violations of constitutional rights, making it easier to engage in surveillance and infiltration operations with impunity. Business leaders are among the first to acknowledge that they are not as hindered by the constitution as government agencies are. Referring to security for the 2004 Republican National Convention, Joseph Sordi, CEO of the Strategic Security Corporation, noted that contractors enjoy a higher level of freedom from oversight, and act on it: "Law enforcement agencies can be somewhat inhibited as to what they can and can't do by First Amendment rights and civil liberties, but as a private contractor, we are uninhibited by departmental bureaucracy and can maintain data bases of individuals."[18]

Federal agencies sought out partnerships with corporations with spying capabilities around the time the government's several counterintelligence programs (described in the next chapter) were exposed. From 1972 through 1977, the Law Enforcement Assistance Administration of the U.S. Department of Justice commissioned the Private Security Advisory Council to study the relationship between private security systems and public law enforcement, and to create programs and policies concerning private security "consistent with the public interest."[19] A multifaceted working relationship between public and for-profit policing grew over the next two decades.

The private sector partners with government and

local law enforcement agencies in developing technology to conduct extensive domestic surveillance. This is a mutually beneficial relationship: corporations make a substantial profit by contracting to create cutting-edge information and surveillance equipment, while state authorities expand their data-collection networks and capacity. Government officials benefit to the extent that corporate actions are subject to less scrutiny than government actions. Lucrative government contracts that enable the creation of sophisticated surveillance technology by corporations create tools that can be used by a range of actors, including intelligence gathering in furtherance of corporate profit at the expense of the public's welfare.

The end of the Cold War brought new opportunities for privately owned military and security companies to sell services and products to the state. Law enforcement authorities have claimed that to fight domestic threats such as terrorism they must engage in blanket infiltration and spying on U.S. citizens and civic organizations, often by contracting with private security companies. Local police departments routinely obtain millions of dollars before "National Special Security Events," such as the Democratic and Republican National Conventions.

Today, private-public ventures are openly celebrated. The U.S. Department of Justice states, "It is also important to partner with the private sector. This includes businesses that will be affected by the special event and private security."[20] In addition to noting the lack of "inhibitions" of private contractors, Strategic Security Corporation's

Sordi is up-front about their spying tactics. Describing plans leading up to the 2004 Republican National Convention, he wrote: "Providing a high level of security today is far more demanding than it was pre-9/11. Our company must depend on intelligence gathering [and] reconnaissance . . . a lot of our work was done before the RNC even took place. . . . My firm has in-depth data on the ring leaders of these [protest] groups."[21] It's worth noting that intelligence-gathering and reconnaissance initiatives occur pre-arrest and when no alleged crime has occurred, making even the characterization of "ring leaders" troubling.

At times corporations are overt about their spying partnerships. During the political convention, a Fujifilm blimp patrolled the skies over Manhattan. The NYPD insignia was displayed below the Fujifilm brand mark on the blimp, which had the ability to remain airborne for sixteen hours and provide a continuous stream of real-time images to ground command posts.

"Threat Assessment" Firms

In response to the increased post-9/11 demand to identify threats to corporate profits, a market for sophisticated, private spy agencies has arisen. Today, privacy and political dissent is threatened as much by private-sector spying as by government intrusion. Companies that specialize in "risk mitigation," also known as "threat assessment," are paid lavishly by other corporations to conduct domestic surveillance of people, organizations, and communities.

To promote its spy thriller Hunted, *Cinemax posted fake advertisements (touting the fictitious private security firm named ByzantiumSecurity.com) around Wall Street in 2012.* PHOTO: HEIDI BOGHOSIAN

These companies produce briefing documents that include names of ordinary people, advocates, organizers, legislators, and special interest groups; indeed their profitability depends on the identification of "threats." In this case, the term does not refer to hazards to safety, health, or the environment, but to anything that might hinder corporate earnings, including public awareness and educational campaigns.

Often the investigations seem deeply personal and out of proportion to the anticipated events. The Society of Toxicology (which promotes the use of animal testing) hired the risk-assessment firm Information Network Associates to create a threat analysis and intelligence briefing in 2008 on local citizens' groups in preparation for its annual meeting and "ToxExpo" in Seattle. The report included such details as who some of the people involved were dating. It ultimately warned merely that "there is a distinct possibility that animal rights activists will use this conference as an opportunity to stage demonstrations or protests, distribute literature, and otherwise promote their animal rights agenda." The firm assigned a "moderate" threat level to the event.[22]

Other corporations seek even more intrusive prying from their investigators. Jeremy Scahill of *The Nation* broke the story in 2010 that biotech giant Monsanto had hired subsidiaries of the private security firm Blackwater to spy on and infiltrate animal rights and environmental activists organizing against the biotech firm's practices. Using Total Intelligence Solutions and the Terrorism Research Center, Blackwater effectively served as the "intel arm" of Monsanto from 2008 to 2009, receiving payments estimated at $100,000 to $500,000.[23] Following an initial meeting between the two companies, Total Intelligence chair Cofer Black emailed other Blackwater executives that Monsanto's security manager, Kevin Wilson, "understands that we can span collection from internet, to reach out, to boots on the ground on legit basis protecting the Monsanto [brand] name. . . . Ahead of the curve info and insight/heads up is what he is looking for."[24] The company also discussed how Blackwater "could have our person(s) actually join [activist] group(s) legally."[25] Public disgust with the activities of Blackwater has driven the company to change its name twice (so far), first to Xe Services and then to Academi, the name it is using at the time of this writing.

Examples abound of private security firms using sophisticated spying techniques and planting infiltrators in advocacy groups. Brian McNary, director of global risk at Pinkerton Consulting and Investigations (formerly the Pinkerton National Detective Agency) works with financial firms internally to "identify, map and track" people at public gatherings and on social media sites.[26] Banks readied for Occupy demonstrations at the 2012 North Atlantic Treaty Organization summit in Chicago by sharing information with police from video surveillance, robots and officers in buildings, giving "a real-time, 360-degree" view of the demonstrations, according to McNary.[27]

Lawsuits have exposed some of the spying but rarely obtain relief for the people whose privacy has been violated by the monitoring, especially when the targets of spying have few financial resources to pursue protracted litigation. Greenpeace USA filed a lawsuit in 2011 against chemical company giants Dow Chemical and Sasol, and their public relations firms, Dezenhall Resources and Ketchum.[28] The lawsuit alleged that between 1998 and 2000 these companies hired the security agency Beckett

Brown International (BBI) to conduct surveillance on Greenpeace. At the time of the surveillance, Greenpeace was spearheading a campaign with communities in Lake Charles, Louisiana, battling dioxin poisons being emitted from a Sasol plant. Greenpeace was alerted to the undercover surveillance in 2008 by *Mother Jones* reporters who obtained documents on other organizations, including Friends of the Earth, GE Food Alert, the Center for Food Safety, and Fenton Communications.[29]

Greenpeace contends that BBI relied on subcontractors, including off-duty police officers from Baltimore and Washington, to trepass and to misappropriate trade secrets by accessing thousands of internal Greenpeace documents, including donor lists, financial reports, legal papers, and campaign strategy memos, as well as the personal credit card information, bank statements, and social security numbers of Greenpeace employees.

Dirty Tricks Redux

In early 2011, the loosely associated network of "hacktivists" known as Anonymous provided a glimpse into how private contractors engage in what came to be known as "dirty tricks" after the Nixon-era Watergate break-ins.

Anonymous hacked into and released tens of thousands of emails of technology security company HBGary Federal, which engages in classified work for the federal government,[30] and its sister company HBGary. The emails revealed alleged plans to engage in unlawful tactics to embarrass corporate critics, such as launching cyber-attacks and campaigns of disinformation, creating false social networking profiles, phishing emails, and intimidating donors to nonprofit groups and unions critical of its clients. Among the clients was the law firm Hunton & Williams, which represented Bank of America and the U.S. Chamber of Commerce; targeted people and organizations included Glenn Greenwald, U.S. Chamber Watch, Change to Win, Wikileaks, and the Center for American Progress. HBGary also proposed to Hunton & Williams that it work with Palantir Technologies and Berico Technologies to attack Wikileaks,[31] which was rumored to be preparing to release Bank of America emails. The firms planned to use malicious and intrusive software to steal private information. They also planned to disrupt internal group communication using social network sites and other social engineering tactics—counterterrorism techniques originally developed to combat violent organizations.[32]

A subtler but perhaps equally dirty trick is painting legitimate opposition as terrorism. In September 2010, news broke that the Pennsylvania Office of Homeland Security had contracted with a private company, the Institute of Terrorism Research and Response (ITRR), to monitor social advocacy groups and provide intelligence briefings on terrorist threats. Briefings were shared with approximately eight hundred law enforcement agencies and with dozens of private businesses ranging from natural gas drillers to the chocolate manufacturer Hershey.[33] While ITRR bulletins acknowledged that the groups had no history of violence or illegal activity, they repeatedly warned law enforcement of the risk of violence and property destruction to private "Pennsylvania assets" such as the "key commercial-resource" Lockheed Martin. Targets of surveillance included the Coalition of Immokalee Workers, Stop Huntingdon Animal Cruelty, the Yes Men, citizen conservation groups, immigration activists, and the Pittsburgh Film Festival.[34]

Corporate Immunity and Impunity

Police and private business have built a leviathan surveillance network that is less accountable than the federal government is to the citizenry at large. A two-year *Washington Post* investigation revealed that, under the banner of counterterrorism, approximately 1,931 private security companies and 1,271 government organizations are currently engaged in intelligence gathering.[35]

When improper gathering of data by corporations is revealed, the penalties are relatively insignificant. Some court settlements or regulatory fines appear to be no more than a slap on the wrist for industries that violate their customers' privacy, especially given that they admit they did so knowingly. In March 2012, for example, Google Inc. (with a net worth of approximately $200 billion) reached a $7 million settlement with thirty-seven states and the District of Columbia to destroy data it collected—in violation of the Federal Wiretap Statute—from its Street View project from 2008 to 2010.[36]

When Street View was created in 2007, vehicles were

IF YOU SEE SOMETHING,

SAY SOMETHING.

TELL A COP OR CALL 1-888-NYC-SAFE.

Stair risers at New York City's Brooklyn Bridge subway station display the DHS campaign slogan, "If You See Something, Say Something.™" The New York Metropolitan Transportation Authority created the campaign and licensed its use. PHOTO: HEIDI BOGHOSIAN

deployed around the United States (and later outside North America) to capture photographs of various locations, later melding them together to create 360-degree panoramas for Google Maps.[37] Unsecure Wi-Fi networks allowed personal information to be gathered, including email, text messages, user passwords, and Web browsing histories from residents of those states. The company later disclosed that the project's main engineer had written code to log the data. In 2010, authorities in Germany discovered how much information Google was picking up and notified the FTC and FCC.

The Federal Communications Commission, which is in charge of regulating interstate and international radio, television, wire, satellite, and cable communications, found no violation of law. It merely fined Google $25,000 for obstruction after the lead engineer who wrote the code invoked the Fifth Amendment. The thirty-seven states, the District of Columbia and the European Union pursued the breach of privacy challenge, which ultimately resulted in the settlement. In addition to destroying the data, Google agreed to launch an employee training program about protecting customers' personal information and create an educational campaign to teach the public about how to protect personal and financial information.[38] By joining forces with private information technology corporations, government authorities multiply their surveillance, enforcement, and compliance powers through an increased capacity to monitor and collect data on individuals and organizations considered "of interest" to national security or an obstacle to corporate profit. Although both sectors often acknowledge that the groups they spy on are peaceful, they nonetheless label them potential domestic terrorism threats. Through lucrative government contracts, or even just for their own intelligence operations, corporations amass and store a trove of personal information on individuals that is easily retrievable by other businesses, as well as state and military forces around the globe.

As surveillance surges, the targets are too often people who organize around urgent issues of global peace and justice, environmental protection, human rights, and the sustainability of the human race on this planet. When their free speech, networking, and movement organizing become casualties of spying and disruption, civic trust is undermined, vital political debates are stifled, and the societal consequences impact us all.

CHAPTER 3

Enemies at Home

The rise of corporate surveillance and covert operations against society builds on a long history of tension between the hallowed political liberties underpinning our nation's founding and the suspicion and intolerance with which powerful elites view their critics.

Domestic surveillance by the state is nearly as old as the nation itself. The Alien and Sedition Acts of 1798 were passed to guard against overthrow of the government by restricting forms of free speech considered to be political dissent. Throughout the country's history, spying on citizens has resurfaced with regularity, usually in response to perceived threats, large and small.

At the beginning of the twentieth century, many legislators identified a need for more federal capacity to conduct investigations. Before that, the Justice Department used detectives from the Secret Service, which was under the Treasury Department's jurisdiction. This arrangement had numerous drawbacks: investigations could not be confidential, and the agents who were available were not always of high caliber.[1] During a congressional recess in 1908, Attorney General Charles Joseph Bonaparte, grandnephew of Napoleon I, created an unnamed investigative bureau employing thirty-four special agents within the United States Department of Justice.[2] In 1909, Bonaparte's successor, George Wickersham, named it the Bureau of Investigation.[3]

Congressional opposition to political surveillance meant that, until World War I, the bureau was limited to enforcing laws concerning interstate crime, such as automobile theft and postal fraud. During and after the war, national hysteria about spies increased, fueled by several domestic bombings. In 1919, the home of A. Mitchell Palmer, one of Bonaparte's successors as attorney general, was damaged in one of these bombings. In response, Palmer created the General Intelligence Division (initially referred to as the Radical Division) within the Bureau of Investigation. A young J. Edgar Hoover was put in command of the new division and rounded up as many as ten thousand suspected "radicals" during the Palmer Raids of 1919 and 1920.

Hoover was promoted in 1924 to head the Bureau of Investigation, which later became the Federal Bureau of Investigation (FBI). The new attorney general, Harlan Fiske Stone, directed Hoover to focus FBI efforts during World War I on law enforcement rather than political surveillance. Local police departments quickly filled the resulting void with their own so-called "red squads." Throughout the 1920s and 1930s, red squads monitored industrial unions, communists, and other dissidents. In many places, such as New York City, they remained active for another half century.

In 1938 Hoover proposed centralizing espionage- and subversive-related investigations and giving the FBI exclusive jurisdiction over them, coordinating with the Military Intelligence Division and the Office of Naval Intelligence.[4] In November 1938, Roosevelt confidentially approved Hoover's plan to give the FBI jurisdiction over espionage investigations; he also ordered, without congressional authorization, an appropriation of $600,000 for emergency espionage.[5] As tensions about espionage grew, Hoover ordered the bureau's special agents to establish local communication with military intelligence.[6]

Though Roosevelt's directive was meant to deal with what he felt was a wartime emergency, Hoover deemed the emergency to be ongoing and continued it long after domestic hysteria about the threat of communism had subsided. Millions of Americans were subjects of FBI political dossiers resulting from surveillance of the Communist Party and every group the Bureau felt had ever sympathized with, been infiltrated by, or served as a front for the party.

From Early Private Spying to the 70 Percent

Private spying as we know it today had its roots in the labor unrest of the late nineteenth and early twentieth centuries when the Pinkerton National Detective Agency began supplying businesses with private guards, commonly referred to as "Pinkertons," to infiltrate and sabotage union-organizing drives, keep strikers and suspected unionists out of factories, and to recruit goon squads to intimidate workers. The best-known of these confrontations was the Homestead Strike of 1892 in which Henry Clay Frick called in Pinkerton guards to enforce Andrew Carnegie's strikebreaking measures at Carnegie Steel mills around Pittsburgh, which resulted in deaths on both sides. After the agency's practices were revealed during 1936 congressional hearings, the company moved away from spying on labor. Today the company operates as Pinkerton Consulting and Investigations, a division of the Swedish security company Securitas AB.

Cooperating with financial institutions and outsourcing intelligence—routine government practices today—have been used for decades. As part of its counterintelligence program, for example, the FBI targeted individuals and organizations providing support to certain members of the press. Banks routinely gave the bureau financial records for alternative newspapers and their subscribers.[7] In a span of seven years, from 1971 to 1978, the number of alternative publications declined from more than four hundred to sixty-five, the direct result of customer and printer harassment, infiltration, wiretaps, and bomb threats.[8]

Since 9/11, however, there has been a quantitative upsurge in the level of private- and public-sector coordination in intelligence gathering. The government relies on outsourcing to corporations to conduct intelligence functions. It's generally accepted that approximately 70 percent of the U.S. intelligence budget is allocated for private contractors.[9]

The CIA began to examine the issue of outsourcing intelligence to the private sector in the early 1990s. A supplemental appropriations bill for intelligence spurred the CIA to hire outside contractors in 1999. After 9/11, Congress dramatically increased funding for intelligence initiatives, which reached $44 billion in 2005. The Defense Intelligence Agency's Joint Intelligence Task Force Combating Terrorism swelled from eighty members before 9/11 to around 350 to 400 within two years or so.[10] Industry has profited handsomely on the commodity of terrorism. Computer Sciences Corporation (CSS) announced in 2007 that the Eagle Alliance—its joint venture with the $30 billion global defense and technology company Northrop Grumman Corporation—had entered into a $528 million three-year option to provide secure information technology for the National Security Agency (NSA).[11] CSS describes the Eagle Alliance as a "unique government/industry partnership" dedicated to supporting the NSA.[12]

Surveillance initiatives have created lucrative opportunities for technology corporations. In his book *The Shadow Factory* James Bamford describes the ways contractors thrive off NSA outsourcing of surveillance. Some of the businesses contracting for data-aggregator and other intelligence services include Booz Allen Hamilton Inc., Lockheed Martin, Schafer Corporation, Adroit Systems, CACI Dynamic Systems, Syntek Technologies, ASI

International, and SRS Technologies; from 2000 to 2008 Booz Allen's revenue grew to $4 billion annually, half of which comes from the government. In 2005, four government agencies spent $30 million on private-sector data-mining services used for intelligence-related purposes.[13]

Networks of Political Surveillance

Political surveillance rarely stops at gathering evidence of possible crimes: domestic spying historically lends itself to the disruption of organizations targeted for monitoring. From 1956 through 1971, the FBI's counterintelligence programs (collectively referred to as COINTELPRO) actively disrupted the lawful activities of thousands of individuals and organizations advocating for social change. In addition to a campaign to "neutralize" Martin Luther King Jr., for being an effective civil rights leader,[14] the FBI targeted the Puerto Rican Independence Party, admitting that it engaged in "tremendous[ly] destructive" tactics focused on twelve leaders of the movement. The bureau sought information about their families, personal affairs, "morals," and "weaknesses."[15] J. Edgar Hoover said that the Black Panther Party represented "the greatest threat to the internal security of the country," and launched a full-fledged campaign of surveillance, infiltration, harassment, and even assassination in an effort to destroy the party.

The FBI photographed individuals at protests in an effort to learn their identities and recruited thousands of ordinary Americans—from switchboard operators at aca-

Poor People's March demonstrators in Washington, D.C., in 1968. The Poor People's Campaign, organized by Dr. Martin Luther King Jr. and the Southern Christian Leadership Conference, was a target of COINTELPRO. PHOTO: LIBRARY OF CONGRESS

demic institutions to mail carriers—to listen in on antiwar faculty members and to watch for mail coming from antiwar organizations. Even Boy Scouts were taught to look out for others suspecting of being disloyal.[16]

The FBI was not alone in this effort. During the Cold War, several other state agencies, including the CIA, the IRS, the Secret Service of the Treasury Department, the Passport Office of the State Department, and the Immigration and Naturalization Service, compiled dossiers on political dissidents. Monitoring was mostly covert and thus prompted little public controversy or debate. Instead, public outrage over political surveillance focused on several congressional committees, such as the House Un-American Activities Committee and the McCarthy Commission. Ironically, the public largely condemned congressional investigations and believed that guarding the country should be left to the FBI.

The U.S. military also engaged in political surveillance. In 1970, attorney and former U.S. Army captain Christopher Pyle convinced more than one hundred former military intelligence agents to reveal publicly that they had spied on U.S. citizens. These declarations led to an investigation by the Subcommittee on Constitutional Rights, chaired by Senator Sam Ervin, and an ACLU lawsuit, *Laird v. Tatum*, charging that the army prevented its surveillance targets from exercising their rights of free speech and association. As a result of these public declarations and the ensuing investigation, the military ended its political surveillance program.[17]

A Break-In for Justice

On March 8, 1971, in a stealth move that laid bare a brazen government intent on silencing free speech and dissent, the Citizens' Commission to Investigate the FBI broke into the FBI's resident agency in Media, Pennsylvania. The raiders took approximately one thousand classified documents that showed aggressive spying and disruption of politically active groups and individuals. The files detailed the ways that FBI agents provoked U.S.

citizens to commit unlawful activities to justify harsh police responses, as well as the fact that they broke into the homes and offices of group members and used informants to provoke internal feuds.[18]

This exposé set in motion a reevaluation of the program's viability. Assistant Director Charles D. Brennan recommended to FBI Assistant Director William C. Sullivan that the program be disbanded "to afford additional security to our sensitive techniques and operations."[19] On the following day—April 28, 1971—Hoover officially terminated the COINTELPRO operations but left open the possibility that they could be resumed in the future. "Although successful over the years, it is felt that they should now be discontinued for security reasons because of their sensitivity."[20]

Congressional Intelligence Oversight Committees

Following the program's disbanding, in 1975 the Senate established the Select Committee to Study Government Operations with Respect to Intelligence Activities. Also known as the Church Committee, after its chair, Senator Frank Church, it confirmed the existence of long-standing and wide-ranging clandestine national surveillance, infiltration, and counterintelligence programs against the lawful activities of thousands of civil rights supporters and peace advocates between 1956 and 1971, "which had no conceivable rational relationship to either national security or violent activity."[21] The reports, it was stated, further "compel the conclusion that Federal law enforcement officers looked upon themselves as guardians of the status quo," citing examples of FBI actions targeting individuals and organizations solely due to criticism of government policy.[22]

The Church Committee's disclosures launched an era of government regulation to limit the practice of spying on individuals with unpopular political viewpoints. Congress made permanent the House and Senate Intelligence Committees, and in 1976, Ford's attorney general, Edward Levi, established guidelines limiting federal investigative power into First Amendment political, associational, and religious activities. The Levi guidelines put in place the tenet that investigations could only be initiated if "specific and articulable facts" indicated the existence of criminal activity. Under this policy, surveillance by the federal government was temporarily curtailed.

Federal Guidelines Crumble

The attorney general's protections would crumble within a decade. In 1981, President Ronald Reagan's Executive Order 12333 reauthorized many domestic intelligence-gathering techniques prohibited under the Levi guidelines.

Attorney General William French Smith further relaxed the Levi guidelines in 1983, allowing an investigation to be opened if a "reasonable indication" of criminal activity existed. Smith's guidelines also authorized "limited preliminary inquiries," an investigation permitting all types of police techniques except for wiretapping and

tampering with mail, and sanctioned government infiltration "for the purpose of influencing the activity of"
domestic political organizations when such activity is
"undertaken on behalf of the FBI in the course of a lawful
investigation."[23] Protections were weakened yet further
with passage of the Antiterrorism and Effective Death
Penalty Act of 1996, which authorized the targeting of
individuals and groups not on the basis of acts allegedly
committed but on their "association" with other groups
or individuals.[24]

The events of 9/11 and the USA PATRIOT Act created room to further roll back hard-won restrictions on
domestic spying. Vast new powers were given to state
authorities, including roving wiretaps, "sneak and peek"
search warrants, and increased use of national security
letters, which allow agencies such as the FBI to subpoena information on individuals in secret. None of these
measures requires the check of a court order.[25] (In March
2013, however, a federal judge in California invalidated a
law permitting the FBI to covertly access subscriber information from Internet and telecommunications providers without a warrant.)[26]

FBI guidelines on domestic spying were again
amended in 2002, this time by Attorney General John
Ashcroft.[27] Under the Ashcroft guidelines, federal agents
were authorized to visit public places and attend public
events to gather information on individuals and organizations without any previous indication of criminal activity—methods that were previously impermissible. The

changes to the guidelines also allow FBI agents to use private-sector databases and engage in searches and monitoring of chat rooms, bulletin boards, and websites, again without any evidence of possible criminal wrongdoing.

In October 2008, the guidelines were amended by Attorney General Michael Mukasey. They now permit FBI agents to commence investigations, absent factual indications that a person has done anything wrong, as long as the agents claim they are acting to protect national security, prevent crime, or gather foreign intelligence.[28] In addition to opening the door for practices such as racial profiling or civil liberties infringements, lenient guidelines may render criminal investigations less effective. ACLU attorney and former FBI agent Mike German explained, "When there aren't guidelines governing where the FBI should investigate, they tend to stray from people who we want them investigating. We don't want them wasting time and invading the privacy of completely innocent people. The guidelines were put in place to make sure that the FBI has some actual basis for suspecting somebody before they started using tools to investigate them. As an FBI agent for sixteen years I found that was actually a very effective way of making me focus my investigations on people who were actually doing bad things rather than people who were just saying things I didn't like, or . . . I didn't think what they were doing [was] right, but it wasn't illegal."[29]

German describes the increased options available to agents as intrusive. "They can do physical surveillance.

They can stand outside your house, follow you around 24/7, they can recruit an informant to go up and start engaging you under false pretenses to try to gather information. They can interview your neighbors, interview your employer," he said.[30]

Local Guidelines Crumble

Since the Church Commission, restrictions on spying by local police departments have also waxed and waned. Red squads continued to operate without interruption in many municipalities until citizens' groups and civil rights attorneys challenged them as recently as in the 1980s. At that time, lawsuits against political intelligence units in some cities led to municipal ordinances, guidelines, or consent decrees limiting political surveillance.[31] Consent decrees are judicial judgments that formalize agreements between parties in a lawsuit, in this context usually accords between police departments and individuals or groups that have been spied on. Although these new guidelines varied in form, each required specific information that criminal activity was under way before authorizing an investigation, particularly with respect to the targeting of First Amendment activities and undercover infiltration as an investigation technique.

But police departments had incentives and license to resume red squad tactics after 9/11. The specter of terrorism, right-wing rhetoric, increasingly conservative federal policymaking, and increased funding opportunities to shore up local antiterrorism efforts combined to restart local spying units. These incentives were compounded by immense pressure on the judiciary to reverse hard-won gains in protecting citizens' political liberties.

In New York City, police investigations of individuals or groups engaging in religious or political activities are governed by a 1985 consent decree that settled *Handschu v. Special Services Division*, a class action lawsuit brought in 1971 against the NYPD's undercover unit.[32] The consent decree forbids the NYPD from investigating political and religious organizations absent specific information linking the group to past criminal activity or to an imminent crime. It limited political investigations to one unit of the department, which was monitored by a special board to check for unconstitutional activities.

In Chicago in 2004, a court-mandated internal police audit obtained by the *Chicago Sun-Times* revealed that undercover officers had infiltrated five social justice organizations in the lead-up to major public gatherings in November 2002. The audit also showed that Chicago police had launched at least four other spying operations in 2003. Targeted groups included Not in Our Name, American Friends Service Committee, the Autonomous Zone, and Anarchist Black Cross. None of the surveillance resulted in criminal charges. The spying operations were initiated after a 2001 federal appellate court abolished restrictions contained in a 1982 consent decree from a lawsuit over spying on activists by the Chicago police in the 1960s and 1970s.[33] The court decision, along with the dissolution of other consent decrees across the nation, effectively ended more than a quarter century of restrictions on police spying, as other police agencies in the post-9/11 era eliminated or significantly weakened their guidelines governing political surveillance.[34]

In 2011 the City of Chicago settled with the ACLU and the American Friends Service Committee after the two organizations filed a petition in 2005 alleging that the city had violated individuals' First Amendment rights.[35]

With the dissolution of consent decrees and other limitations on government surveillance, spying has targeted entire groups of individuals based on their religious or political beliefs, as seen in the following examples of Muslims and anarchists.

Spying on Muslims

In a broad surveillance initiative, the New York Police Department monitored Muslim student groups at six City University of New York (CUNY) campuses between 2003 and 2006. Tellingly, the spying was not predicated on any evidence of criminal conduct. The Associated Press (AP) obtained documents showing that the NYPD deployed undercover officers at Baruch and Brooklyn Colleges and used police in its Intelligence Division Cyber Unit to monitor students at Brooklyn and Queens Colleges. The documents refer to the use of "secondary" undercover officers at City College of New York, Hunter, Queens, and LaGuardia Colleges who attended events organized by Muslim student groups.[36] Some CUNY personnel, according to the AP, might have made student records available to law enforcement in clear violation of the Federal Educational Rights and Privacy Act (FERPA), a violation punishable by the loss of federal university funding. The spying may also have violated a 1992 agreement between CUNY and the NYPD establishing that, except in cases of emergency, police "shall enter upon CUNY campuses, buildings and other property only upon the request or approval of a CUNY official."[37]

Such pervasive surveillance reinforces stereotypes that the entire Muslim community is criminally suspect. It also has a chilling effect on academic environments once students are aware that undercover officers have been, and may still be, on their campuses. Professor Johanna Fernandez, who teaches history at CUNY's Baruch College, said, "Aside from the illegality of engaging in racial profiling and spying on an entire Muslim community, the NYPD violated one of the most sacred tenets in the academy in a democratic society: the right to think, act, and learn in an environment free of repression and control. This spying represents a chilling reality for twenty-first-century students and activists alike, a transparent indication that over the course of the past three decades, U.S. domestic policies against its citizens have become increasingly similar to those of dictatorships around the world."[38]

The NYPD's spying on Muslims was not limited to student groups. An AP investigation in August 2011 uncovered documents outlining a vast spying operation in a host of Muslim community spaces, including mosques and even beauty salons.[39] Rather than investigating specific criminal acts, the NYPD program spread its feelers through an entire community.

The "Anarchist" Threat Justification

To justify surveillance of certain activists, law enforcement agencies around the country cite the need to protect against extremist threats, including a category they call "anarchists." Intelligence reports shared among law enforcement before National Special Security Events (NSSEs), for example, frequently refer to alleged plots by anarchists, including allegations that they are going to manufacture explosive devices or throw urine, feces, or acid at police.[40] Tabloid headlines at the 2004 Republican National Convention in New York warned readers that violent anarchists were coming to town, and after releasing a list of names of anarchists from around the country, officers from the NYPD Technical Assistance Response Unit (TARU) overtly photographed and followed protesters.

In August 2011, the FBI and the Department of Homeland Security issued a joint report suggesting that "anarchist extremists" were readying to engage in "violent and criminal tactics" to disrupt the Republican and Democratic national political conventions. The report said that activists in the past threw "Molotov cocktails, flaming torches, or acid-filled eggs at law enforcement," even though no instance of such existed from any NSSE over the previous fifteen years. As a result of the report, Tampa police publicized fears of an anarchist attack at a

Officers with cameras from the NYPD's Technical Assistance Response Unit followed a group of individuals onto subway cars at the 2004 Republican National Convention. PHOTO: STECKLEY LEE

press conference announcing that bricks and pipes had been found on a rooftop near so-called "anarchist graffiti" before the RNC; in Charlotte, news headlines proclaimed warnings of "anarchist extremists willing to use explosives at DNC," although no violence or even noteworthy protests took place at either political convention.[41]

A lawsuit on behalf of a student who attended an antiwar protest revealed that he had been described by law enforcement as a "known anarchist" and was followed and harassed by police due to that designation. The Washington State Patrol, the City of Aberdeen, and Grays Harbor County settled for $169,000 plus over $375,000 in legal fees in the case, which claimed that their officers engaged in political spying and harassment of Philip Chinn, a twenty-two-year-old antiwar activist.[42]

Court documents charge that police relayed an "attempt-to-locate" message describing Chinn's green Ford Taurus as carrying "three known anarchists," and further allege that Chinn was the subject of surveillance from the time he left his Olympia residence and headed for the Aberdeen protest on May 6, 2007. Assistant Chief Dave Timmons of the Aberdeen police admitted that his department had been alerted about Chinn through intelligence channels that include the military and other law enforcement agencies, and that detectives monitored Chinn and others to ascertain their plans. State troopers stopped and arrested Chinn, a student at Evergreen State College, in May 2007 on suspicion of drunken driving. He was on his way to an antiwar protest at the Port of Grays Harbor. Test results showed that Chinn had no alcohol or illicit substances in his system.[43]

"Your World Delivered"

AT&T has fulfilled its campaign slogan. Along with Verizon and BellSouth, the telecommunications giant has delivered records of millions of telephone calls to the National Security Agency (NSA). Despite several Justice Department Office of the Inspector General reports criticizing the practice and citing abuses of the USA PATRIOT Act, such data collection is authorized by legislation signed by both George W. Bush and Barack Obama.[44]

After 9/11, Bush authorized the NSA to monitor phone calls, emails, Internet activity, text messaging, and other communication involving any party the NSA believed to be outside the United States, even if the other end of the communication was within the United States, without a warrant or other express approval. This came after Congress passed the Authorization for Use of Military Force Act allowing the president to prevent future acts of terrorism through the use of force against anyone he determined had aided in the 9/11 attacks.[45]

The exact scope of the NSA surveillance program is classified, but several former officials and telecommunications workers provided information indicating that the program extends beyond monitoring those with suspected links to foreign terrorists. Perhaps the most significant disclosure came in 2005 when former AT&T technician Mark Klein shared documents revealing that AT&T had installed a fiber-optic splitter at its facility at 611 Folsom Street in San Francisco that "makes copies of all emails, Web browsing, and other Internet traffic to and from AT&T customers, and provides those copies to the NSA."[46]

Why do corporations routinely and readily hand over this information, often without legal justification and often giving more data than asked for? Litigation challenging these requests suggests that if businesses cared enough about customers' privacy to mount challenges to these requests, they might prevail. It is revelatory that, with an eye on the profit motive, no major corporations have bothered to do so. Given the technology industry's reliance on lucrative government contracts, their widespread acquiescence is not surprising.

There have been a few exceptions, with varying results. In May 2012, the micro-blogging service Twitter went to court to defend against prosecutors' efforts to access months of history from the account of Malcolm Harris. Prosecutors wanted to examine the tweets for indication that Harris, one of seven hundred individuals arrested on the Brooklyn Bridge in an Occupy march on October 1, 2011, might have been aware that police told demonstrators not to march across the bridge.[47] In September 2012, Twitter gave three months' worth of tweets to a Manhattan Criminal Court judge to avoid being held in contempt of court, but it vowed to continue fighting to keep them out of the prosecutor's hands.[48]

Major lawsuits against telecommunications companies have been directed at Cingular Wireless, BellSouth, Sprint, and MCI/Verizon, alleging that they invaded their customers' privacy by disclosing information to the government without a warrant. After the plaintiffs won important preliminary rulings, Congress passed and President George W. Bush signed the FISA Amendments Act of 2008, which granted immunity to telecommunications companies if the attorney general filed a certification that the assistance the company provided was pursuant to presidentially approved antiterrorist intelligence activity conducted between September 11, 2001, and January 17, 2007. As a result, these lawsuits were dismissed.

A small online provider also fought such invasions of privacy and secured success. Members of the queer activist network Bash Back disrupted a 2008 Sunday service at the conservative Mount Hope Baptist Church in Lansing, Michigan, to protest that church's antigay policies. Months later, Mount Hope and the Alliance Defense Fund, a reactionary Christian nonprofit organization, sued Bash Back and fifteen named activists to uncover protesters' identities. Riseup.net, a progressive provider of online communication tools, was the only email provider to challenge the subpoenas. Google turned over protesters' information without objection. Riseup's challenge was successful; federal judge Richard A. Jones ruled that Riseup did not have to turn over the records, finding that "the Users' First Amendment right to speak anonymously online outweighs Mount Hope's right to discovery."[49]

The Uncertainty of Who's Listening In

While there have been some modest successes in industry challenges to demands that providers turn over customers' personal information, legal challenges to the NSA warrantless wiretapping program have uniformly resulted in dismissals for lack of standing, meaning that the individuals bringing the suits could not prove with certainty that their communications had been monitored. Constitutional law professor and cooperating attorney Michael Avery argued the case of *CCR v. Bush*, a 2006 challenge to the wiretapping program. After the oral argument, Avery reflected that presidents who want to engage in electronic surveillance must obtain either judicial warrants or FISA warrants, or must follow the law that Congress has established. He noted, "If the president says that law is inadequate to meet the needs of the kind of surveillance that he wants to do today, then he should go to Congress and make some suggestions about how the law can be changed. We don't want to see the president and the executive branch of the government making all the decisions about who they're going to listen to and under what circumstances with no review by Congress and no review by the courts."[50]

Placing the Bush and Obama administrations' wiretapping program in context, Avery cited the Supreme Court's reaction to President Harry Truman's attempt at seizing the steel mills to prevent workers from going on strike so they could manufacture weapons and munitions for the war in Korea. Avery said, "Justice Jackson in his opinion in the steel seizure cases . . . said the same person is the head of the civilian government and the commander in chief so that there is civilian control over the military, not so that there is military control over civilian life. That's an important lesson that needs to be brought to this issue today."[51] (The case was dismissed for lack of standing in 2011.)

The ACLU sued the NSA in 2006 on behalf of a group of journalists, scholars, attorneys, and national nonprofit organizations that frequently communicate by phone and email with people in the Middle East. The plaintiffs in *Amnesty v. Clapper* suspected that the NSA was intercepting their communications and claimed this disrupted their ability to talk with sources, advise clients, locate witnesses, conduct scholarship, and engage in advocacy. In 2009 a New York judge dismissed the lawsuit ruling the plaintiffs could not state with certainty that they had been wiretapped. A federal appeals court reversed that ruling in 2011, and the Supreme Court heard oral arguments in 2012. In early 2013, the high court held, once again, that the plaintiffs lacked standing to challenge the warrantless wiretapping program.[52]

In *Al Haramain Islamic Foundation v. Obama*, the leadership and attorneys of the Islamic charity Al Haramain Foundation claimed they were subjected to warrantless wiretapping. This time, a secret and sealed government document had been inadvertently disclosed to the plaintiffs by the government. The case was dismissed in 2012 under the doctrine of sovereign immunity, which provides that the federal government may not be sued unless it waives its immunity or consents to a lawsuit.

The Electronic Frontier Foundation (EFF) filed the class action suit *Hepting v. AT&T* in 2006 on behalf of its customers for violating privacy law by collaborating with the NSA in warrantless wiretapping and data mining of communications of people in the United States.[53] A few months later more than fifty other lawsuits were filed against various telecommunications companies after a *USA Today* article confirmed the surveillance of communications and communications records. The cases were combined into a multidistrict litigation proceeding called

In re NSA Telecommunications Records Litigation.[54] When George W. Bush signed the FISA Amendments Act of 2008, immunity was given to telecommunications companies who cooperated with the government's request for surveillance. As a result, a judge dismissed *Hepting* in 2009. After the plaintiffs appealed the decision and submitted some of the issues to the Supreme Court, in October 2012 the court declined to hear the case.

In the 2008 case *Jewel v. NSA*, the EFF sued the NSA and other government agencies on behalf of AT&T customers to stop warrantless surveillance of their communications and records. The case includes evidence from three NSA whistle-blowers (William E. Binney, Thomas A. Drake, and J. Kirk Wiebe—all targets of the federal investigation into leaks to the *New York Times* resulting in initial news coverage about the wiretapping program) and former AT&T telecommunications technician Mark Klein showing that the company had routed copies of Internet traffic to a room in San Francisco controlled by the NSA.[56] After wending its way through the courts, with the Obama administration claiming immunity under the state secrets privilege, the matter was heard by the federal district court in San Francisco in December 2012.[57] At the time of this writing, a ruling in the case was still pending.

Technology's Creep

The authorities of the United States have a long history of spying on those who actively participate in the nation's democracy through free speech and other civic and community activities. Over the years, citizens and the judiciary have tried to rein in state surveillance by asserting First Amendment protections of free speech and Fourth Amendment protections against unreasonable searches and seizures. From the Palmer Raids through COINTELPRO, periods of perceived national emergency have typically eroded these protections. Today, a sprawling industry has mushroomed, financed by taxpayer money, ostensibly to protect the nation from terrorism and other threats. As this industry consolidates and grows, sophisticated surveillance technologies pose new threats to privacy and the right of association.

One such surveillance technology is biometrics. The FBI has been planning since 2011 to deploy a Next Generation Identification (NGI) Facial Recognition Program. According to documents obtained by the National Day Laborer Organizing Network at a meeting of the FBI's Criminal Justice Information Services Advisory Policy Board, the program should be fully operational in 2014 and is expected to contain at least 12 million searchable photographs. In addition to storing facial-recognition data, the NGI program will contain finger and palm prints, iris scans, and biographical information from more than 100 million Americans. Touted for its convenience, such as helping expedite routine doctor visits, palm-print scanners are installed in many hospitals. Gathering and storing individuals' biometric profiles and linking them to their personal data is yet another component of the corporate and state surveillance net.

In addition to technology advances, other social forces collude to make pervasive domestic surveillance easier to conduct on a scale unimaginable in earlier eras. Corporations exert pressure on law enforcement to counter perceived threats that vocal critics, an informed citizenry, and social networks pose to profits. The post-9/11 political climate has led to laws and practices that weaken constitutional protections and afford greater power to state authorities and multinational corporations to spy on democracy. The affordability and ease with which technology is able to delve deeper into the lives of more people, along with the eroding expectation of privacy that modern technology has wrought, combine to make spying a distasteful, but increasingly pervasive fixture of modern life.

CHAPTER 4

Always Deceptive, Often Illegal

The FBI's counterintelligence programs (COINTEL-PRO) brought shame to the reputation of the bureau, and for good reason. The covert and manipulative programs sought to destroy influential and effective leaders of civil rights and other political movements, as well as other politically active individuals, through a series of insidi-ous, immoral, and frequently illegal actions. Operations aimed at "neutralizing" critics of government policies in-cluded defamation, libel, assault, poisoning, entrapment, and even assassination. COINTELPRO illustrates the ease with which domestic intelligence initiatives can esca-late to warlike counterintelligence maneuvers, employed unlawfully and with total impunity, accountable to no branch of government.[1]

An FBI wiretap of the Black Panther Party head-quarters in 1970 revealed that actress Jean Seberg was pregnant, and not by French writer Romain Gary, her estranged husband. An FBI memo noted, "Jean Seberg has been a financial supporter of the BPP and should be neutralized. Her current pregnancy by [name deleted]

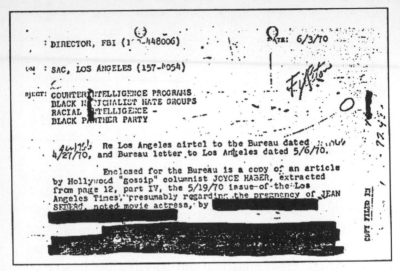

Exchange of information between FBI HQ and FBI Los Angeles, in plans to defame Jean Seberg. PUBLIC DOMAIN FBI FILE

while still married affords an opportunity for such effort."[2] In addition to giving money to the Panthers, Seberg had spoken out against U.S. war policies and racism. The bureau's leaks that she was carrying the child of a Panther resulted in news headlines such as A BLACK PANTHER'S THE PAPPY OF A CERTAIN FILM QUEEN'S EXPECTED BABY.[3] On August 7, Seberg tried to kill herself by taking an overdose of sleeping pills; on August 20 her baby was born prematurely and died. For the next several years, Seberg grew depressed, attempted suicide each year on the anniversary of her baby's death, and finally succeeded on August 20, 1979.[4]

Shortly before the Seberg rumors were spread, Black

Panther Party member Fred Hampton was assassinated in his bed by a coordinated group of agents from the FBI, Chicago Police Department, and a tactical unit of the Cook County, Illinois, State Attorney's Office. Fellow Panther Mark Clark was asleep in a chair in the living room and was shot in the heart. A rising leader of the party's Chicago chapter, Hampton, just a few hours before his premeditated murder on December 4, 1969, had taught a course at a local church. FBI informant William O'Neal (who had been Hampton's former bodyguard) provided details of the furniture layout in Hampton's apartment, including the location of his bed, to the bureau. When Hampton and others returned home from the church, the agent, O'Neal, prepared dinner and put secobarbitol into Hampton's drink so that he would not awaken during the raid. O'Neal later committed suicide after admitting his role in the assassination.[5]

Jean Seberg, Mark Clark, Fred Hampton, and William O'Neal died as the direct result of U.S. counterintelligence campaigns; Seberg's suicide was prompted by a rumor, Hampton's and Clark's death the result of premeditated criminal homicide, and O'Neal's demise likely due to guilt over his role in Hampton's murder. Although the FBI announced the formal end of COINTELPRO in 1971, the modern-day perpetual "war on terror" has revived the same kind of tactics employed during the Cold War days. Because counterintelligence is by definition covert, domestic spying incidents are difficult to document with certainty. Often the identity of an infiltrator or disrupter comes to light by accident, as when a peace activist read the obituary of a local Joint Terrorism Task Force agent and recognized the photograph as a man she had known as a fellow antiwar advocate, a role he had assumed for the job. In contrast to intelligence gathering and assessment, counterintelligence involves counteracting a perceived threat, often by deceptive and psychologically manipulative means. Tactics aimed at discrediting or neutralizing targets have deservedly earned the name "dirty tricks," and range in nature from the repugnant to the unlawful.

As in the 1950s and 1960s, it is still the case that when individual Americans or groups propose alternatives to corporate practices or criticize U.S. domestic and foreign policy, they may find themselves on the receiving end of infiltration, agents provocateurs, harassment, and attempts to manipulate members. Common practices include spreading disinformation and gossip about simple matters through emails and websites, establishing intimate relationships with activists, or entrapping them into actions the FBI will use as a basis for terrorism or conspiracy charges. Often, disinformation is shared with local and national media outlets.

Information occasionally surfaces that reveals glimpses of how non-intelligence groups, such as corporations, engage in warlike maneuvers. It continues to be standard practice for domestic counterintelligence tactics to include disrupting social justice organizations and maligning charismatic leaders and community groups.

Alexandra Natapoff outlines some of the problems with informant use in the political context in the book *Snitching: Criminal Informants and the Erosion of American Justice*. She writes that in addition to the chilling effect on free speech of infiltrators and agents provocateurs, "Infiltrating informants may get away with wrongdoing in exchange for their usefulness. They may finger the innocent or entrap others into behaving in ways that they otherwise would not. When they are exposed, they may undermine public perceptions of law enforcement legitimacy."[6]

Some police departments admit that undercover officers try to steer organizations into unlawful actions. The ACLU learned in 2006 that undercover officers in Oakland, California, had infiltrated an antiwar group. Deputy Chief Howard Jordan explained to the police board of review in recorded testimony how the Oakland Police Department could improve its intelligence-gathering efforts: "If you put people in there from the beginning, I think we'd be able to gather the information and maybe even direct them to something that we want."[7]

Fusion Centers

To better coordinate federal and local intelligence, secret and unregulated intelligence facilities known as fusion centers were formed during the period 2003–2007. In them, federal and local law enforcement work alongside military units and private security companies to collect personal data on Americans. The country's seventy-seven fusion centers act much the same as for-profit data aggregation companies (described in Chapter 10). They mine public databases and other sources to gain information related to spending habits, real estate transactions, and insurance claims. Little, if any, evidence exists that the extraordinarily expensive centers have streamlined intelligence or helped solve any crimes.

Thomas Cincotta, an attorney and former Civil Liberties Project director with the Massachusetts-based think tank Political Research Associates, says of the centers: "Officials everywhere have trumpeted more intense information-sharing with the private sector through 'partnerships.' It's not at all clear how tight the relationships are. Some fusion centers share threat bulletins with their 'partners' in critical infrastructure. Corporations are encouraged to share tips and leads on suspicious persons appearing outside their gates."[8] Cincotta notes that at some fusion centers, as in Washington State, officials have spoken of giving Boeing and Microsoft security clearances so they can participate more fully in the center's operations and meetings. He believes that centers share information on activists' identities with industry giants. "It's not clear what level of classified or 'terrorism' information is being shared with these partners," he says, "but I do not doubt that is occurring."[9]

Cincotta cites some of the problems inherent in the race to collect high volumes of data in the name of national security: "Counterterrorism has become a boondoggle and a way to fleece the American taxpayer—with very little to show for it in terms of success. None of the terrorism prosecutions since 9/11 has relied on computer-assisted analysts or high-tech systems tying together seemingly unconnected dots. Traditional low-tech detective work or aggressive use of informants has uncovered (and often instigated) the few domestic plots that have emerged."[10] Such investigations have been led by FBI Joint Terrorism Task Force members, not fusion centers. In fact, the U.S. Senate questioned fusion centers' relevance and noted their wastefulness in a 2012 report; its two-year investigation found that fusion centers yielded intelligence of "uneven quality . . . oftentimes shoddy, rarely timely,"[11] at a cost of somewhere between $289 million and $1.4 billion since 2003.[12]

A Multi-Year Stakeout

Significant allocation of resources to pursue perceived domestic terrorism threats is often ill-advised. With an early track record of incompetence, inadequate oversight, and redundancy, fusion centers may invent new domestic security threats to justify their existence and expense. Already, counterterrorism department resources are directed at monitoring peaceful civil advocacy, free events, and public protests. Scott Crow, from East Austin, Texas, attracted the attention of FBI counterterrorism agents who parked outside his home and monitored him on a daily basis for at least three years.[13] The surveillance began after Crow participated in a 2003 Greenpeace demonstration in Irving, Texas. (Crow was also mentioned in Texas activist investigations from 2001 to at least 2008.) Agents affixed a video camera to a telephone pole across from his house, and undercover officers and informants infiltrated meetings of political organizations. Crow's phone calls and emails were tracked and police rummaged through his garbage and may have served subpoenas on his bank and mortgage companies. They even asked the IRS to look at his tax returns. In response, an IRS employee pointed out that Crow earned only $32,000 a year, a sum not likely to impress a jury were he to be prosecuted.[14]

Agents Provocateurs

Police infiltration of groups that conduct advocacy, criticize government conduct, or organize protests is a slippery slope: surveillance allowed for criminal investigation can easily lead to unlawful actions. Infiltrators, for example, sometimes engage in illegal actions, such as partaking in acts of civil disobedience solely to maintain their cover, or spraying chemical weapons into a crowd, as described below. The actions are reported publicly, and peaceful protesters are vilified for the infiltrators' acts of criminal assault. A decision to use force by police officers, if based on false reports filed by infiltrators, is improper.[15]

Undercover police officers in 2010 infiltrated a meeting of School of the Americas Watch protesters before a November 2010 vigil outside of Fort Benning, Georgia. According to one organizer, five undercover officers took part in a workshop preparing for a blockade of Victory

Drive. The police joined in the actual blockade and later testified in court against the activists who were arrested along with bystanders and individuals leaving the demonstration site.

In an earlier case, an amateur video taken in 2001 shows two men in plainclothes, one with his face covered by a black ski mask, walking through the crowds at the Bush inauguration, assaulting and pepper-spraying protesters.[16] In response to litigation by the D.C.-based Partnership for Civil Justice (now the Partnership for Civil Justice Fund), the District of Columbia acknowledged that the men were on-duty undercover police officers on an intelligence detail. A D.C. City Council report on its investigation of the handling of demonstrations by the Metropolitan Police Department described the tape as showing "Investigator Cumba [whose] face is hidden by a black ski mask and a white hood . . . holding a can in his right hand. He is seen walking through the crowd, and he shoves someone out of his way to his left. In two series of shots he appears to hold the can and spray its contents at other persons in the crowd. . . . At no time is there any indication that the officer announced he was a police officer, as is required by department policy."[17]

Harrassment of Peaceful, Peace-Seeking "Enemies"
John Towery, a civilian employee of the Fort Lewis Force Protection Division in Washington State, struck up friendships with many peace activists. For at least two years, he posed as an activist with Port Militariza-

tion Resistance (PMR), a group in Washington opposing the Iraq and Afghanistan invasions. He gave information about planned protests to his supervisor, Thomas Rudd, who wrote threat assessments that local law enforcement officials used in harassment campaigns that included "preemptive arrests and physical attacks on peaceful demonstrations, as well as other harassment."[18] One individual was arrested so many times that his landlord evicted him.[19]

Towery admitted that he spied on and infiltrated PMR. He also targeted Students for a Democratic Society, the Olympia Movement for Justice and Peace, the Industrial Workers of the World, Iraq Veterans Against the War, an anarchist bookstore in Tacoma, and other groups. In November 2007, after Towery provided "intelligence" to the Olympia police commander suggesting that a group of women was going to block a convoy because they had discussed it during action-planning meetings, the women were arrested on the nonexistent charges of "attempted disorderly conduct."[20] In the words of the government agencies involved, they aimed to neutralize PMR through a pattern of false arrests and detentions, attacks on homes and friendships, and attempting to impede members from peacefully assembling and demonstrating anywhere, at any time. Harassment was systematic and pervasive. PMR participants were arrested not just locally but in other venues, including the Denver Democratic National Convention in 2008 and a San Francisco protest at which they were the only ones arrested.[21]

For the first time in U.S. history, a court found that civilians have a right to sue the military for violating their First and Fourth Amendment rights. The lawsuit, *Panagacos v. Towery*, was brought in 2009 by the Washington state activists whose group Towery had infiltrated. It names Towery, the army, the navy, the air force, the FBI, the CIA, and other law enforcement agencies.[22] The activists' attorney, Larry Hildes, explains the significance of the case: "We've known that the military has spied on antiwar movements many times in the past. What made this unusual is that our clients actually caught them, and through diligent research gathered enough hard evidence to prove it. I think the Court let this case proceed because in addition to spying, the Army set out to destroy PMR."[23]

As in the case of New York's Critical Mass bicycle rides, protracted infiltration and surveillance eventually drained a grassroots movement of much of its spirit. Hildes notes, "Through all of this, the Army did destroy PMR. It has not engaged in a major protest since 2009."[24] But as in New York, where citizen action helped establish bicycle lanes to make the city less dependent on cars, Olympian activists' efforts yielded some positive changes: the army no longer uses the civilian ports of Puget Sound to ship Strykers and other war materials to its wars in the Middle East, Central Asia, or anywhere else.

The *Towery* case revealed that today's military has continued to engage in COINTELPRO-type operations and shows the extent to which the lines between the military and civilian law enforcement have blurred. Forces now used against ordinary people engaged in free speech and protest include, increasingly, weapons and tactics used by the U.S. military for combat missions. At the same time, the military has taken on more and more civilian law enforcement duties, in Iraq, Afghanistan, and the United States, fomenting the armed and authoritarian degradation of civilian-based democracy and the public sphere. Military, corporate, and federal law enforcement is increasingly employed in local jurisdictions, often crippling the ability of local police forces to build trust among the public. This hinders local law enforcement and endangers people in vulnerable communities, who may be afraid of federal and military police and therefore may not report crimes, even if they are the victims.

The drift from passive intelligence gathering to offensive counterintelligence is one manifestation of the difference between civilian law enforcement principles and the military's exclusive focus on defeating perceived enemies through combat, propaganda, and covert operations. As Hildes says: "The role of civilian law enforcement, in theory, is to protect the public and the Constitution, [whereas] role of the military is to identify the enemy and neutralize them. . . . That is the military mindset, it is how they are trained, it is what they are sent to do. When the military starts identifying peaceful dissenters here as the enemy, God help us all. The Constitution and especially the First Amendment are up for grabs."[25] Of course, even civilian law enforcement is increasingly militarized in many respects, including the use of weaponry and the adoption of preemptive counterintelligence tactics.

Outed in an Obituary

When schoolteacher Camille Russell read an obituary in the August 31, 2003, *Fresno Bee*, she recognized a photo as that of Aaron Stoke, someone she knew from the antiwar group Peace Fresno. But the name in the death notice was Aaron Michael Kilner, and he was identified as a deputy sheriff in the Fresno County Sheriff's Department and a member of the antiterrorism team. For several months he had been attending Peace Fresno meetings, even taking minutes for the group, distributing fliers, and participating in street protests. He claimed he was not working because he had received a modest inheritance.

Russell and other Peace Fresno members asked local attorney Catherine Campbell to ask Fresno County Sheriff Richard Pierce why the group had been infiltrated. Pierce replied that the department did not have any files on Peace Fresno, but would not confirm whether Kilner had been directed to spy for the department, saying that the department was within its rights to visit or attend events open to the public for the purpose of detecting or preventing terrorist activities. After seeking additional information, in April 2004 the ACLU of Northern California filed a complaint with the California attorney general asking for disclosures about why the infiltration had been ordered.[26] Two months later, the attorney general's office opened an investigation. In February 2006, Attorney General Bill Lockyer confirmed that the Fresno County Sheriff's Department had sanctioned the infiltration even though no members of Peace Fresno had engaged in any criminal activity.[27]

Titans of Counterintelligence

Expansion of the New York City Police Department's counterintelligence division has been enabled in part by the nationwide tilt away from consent decrees limiting policy spying, described in Chapter 3.

When Ray Kelly became police commissioner in 2002, he decided he wanted to strip *Handschu* restrictions on political spying. In 2002 the NYPD asked the courts for greater freedom, and in 2003 the department won significant expansion of its surveillance powers. The court refused to eliminate the guidelines entirely, but relaxed them, freeing the NYPD of court oversight and the possibility of contempt of court charges for any future violations of the less restrictive guidelines. Even these were quickly violated, however; during arrests in February and March 2003 the NYPD regularly interrogated antiwar protesters about their political views. Upon learning this, *Handschu* lawyers asked the court to restore court oversight of the NYPD, thereby making police violations again punishable by the court.

While weakened guidelines still exist on paper in some jurisdictions, the rules usually contain such broad exceptions that police can conduct widespread spying. In

New York, the Modified *Handschu* Guidelines allow the NYPD intelligence chief, David Cohen, to authorize undercover investigations for up to four months, and investigations generally for up to one year. Instead of requiring that police have specific information indicating that a crime may be about to occur, the loosened guidelines require facts that would "reasonably indicate" a crime may occur in the future.[28]

As the public has learned, Kelly's move to loosen *Handschu* unleashed wide-ranging spying and infiltration campaigns not only on activists but also on entire communities, such as Muslims on college campuses, in their mosques, and in their neighborhoods.[29] In a February 2013 federal court filing, lawyers in the *Handschu* case sought to end the NYPD practice of creating dossiers on Muslim New Yorkers, asserting that the broad surveillance program violates even the weakened *Handschu* guidelines.[30] The attorneys also asked that an auditor be appointed by the court to monitor police compliance with the guidelines.

Funding Incentives for Spying and Counterintelligence

Federal law enforcement agencies have facilitated the surveillance of activists by local police through sweeping funding initiatives. A *US News & World Report* inquiry revealed that federal officials poured "hundreds of millions of dollars into once discredited state and local police intelligence operations."[31] As a result, police are expending large amounts of time and money to following ordinary Americans. "*US News* has identified nearly a dozen cases in which city and county police, in the name of homeland security, have monitored or harassed animal rights and antiwar protesters, union activists, and even library patrons surfing the Web."[32]

From 2003 to 2012, the Department of Homeland Security gave $35 billion in grants to help local governments prepare for terrorism and disasters.[33] One such program is the Urban Area Security Initiative (UASI), which has spent $7.144 billion from 2002 to 2012.[34] An analysis of the way funds have been spent during this period reveals that many grant applicants create assessments of risk where none exists. Local officials blatantly attempt to influence the risk assessments made by the DHS by focusing on worst-case scenarios to their communities, with members of Congress even chiming in to ask that funding be awarded to the areas they represent.[35] In California, the acting secretary of the state's Emergency Management Agency said, "We're always looking for creative ways to calculate risk," in order to "get the risk score as high as we can to get the funding."[36] One website for law enforcement officials, Lawofficer.com, suggests embellishing worst-case scenarios: "Tell them what they want to hear, and you stand a chance of getting a better score. Fear has always been a motivating factor in getting the government to spend its money."[37] Brian Cost, a police captain in Keene, New Hampshire, applied for a $285,933 DHS grant to purchase a BearCat tank. The grant application mentioned an annual Pumpkin Festival as a potential terrorist target. Keene police chief Kenneth Meaola said, "Do I think al-Qaeda is going to target Pumpkin Fest? No, but are there fringe groups that want to make a statement? Yes."[38] Much of the money from UASI grants goes to ramping up police department equipment in ways that seem excessive, even frivolous—tanks, an underwater robot, and an eight-minute video designed to help viewers of "average or above average intelligence" spot potential terrorists[39]—but a good deal of the grants have been used to purchase and install surveillance systems. A hefty investment that ended up failing was Project Shield, a surveillance-camera network in Chicago intended to encompass 180 municipalities in Cook County, Illinois. It failed after nearly $46 million was expended for the program. According to a report by the inspector general of the Department of Homeland Security, faulty equipment, inexperienced first responders, and missing records were among the problems plaguing Project Shield.[40]

In an effort to improve coordination of intelligence, the federal government has spent millions of dollars to connect law enforcement databases at the state and local levels. Coordinating the databases has often been fraught with errors and challenges related to both technology and the protection of citizens' personal information. Many information systems still cannot communicate with one another. Some efforts have failed outright, such as the Matrix system, which employed data-mining technology and was terminated in 2005 due to privacy concerns. The shift toward mega databases raises serious privacy issues, especially given the lack of oversight and regulation regarding what sort of data can be poured into these systems. Compounding the problem is that no accessible mechanisms exist for citizens to know what is in the databases and how to correct inaccurate information. Furthermore, sifting through millions more data points only makes it more difficult to discern real threats to public safety.

The consequences of intensified spying on social networks can have substantial implications when a major demonstration is anticipated, a typical opportunity for exaggerated or misleading information to be disseminated as justification for counterintelligence tactics. In response to internal reports that "violent anarchists" are coming to town to wreak havoc, police departments across the country engage in offensive measures against peaceful crowds. Law enforcement preparation for protests routinely involves spying and the use of agents provocateurs who sometimes instigate violence. Biased after-event reports and flawed intelligence citing the "possibility" of violent protesters continue to form the rationalization for such spying and infiltration, even when news reports and independent review commissions point out their inaccuracies.[41]

National Special Security Events
Surveillance has grown in part because of federal guidelines established in 1998 delineating National Special

Security Events. The NSSE standards govern the roles of federal security agencies in developing local security plans for major events such as political nominating conventions. The secretary of the Department of Homeland Security, in consultation with the Homeland Security counsel, designates NSSEs; the Secret Service takes the lead in creating and implementing the operational security plan for the events.[42] The FBI is the chief agency for intelligence and counterterrorism, but other law enforcement agencies, private security agencies and local police departments are also involved. Private security may play a supporting role or a lead role, depending on the venue.[43] Demand for tighter security at significant political, sporting, or cultural events has emboldened local police departments, as illustrated by a wave of revelations about aggressive spying over the past decade.

Commercial media looking for provocative stories feed into government assertions that critics of corporations and the state pose a threat to national security. In New York, media coverage before the 2004 Republican National Convention reinforced corporate imagery of protesters as deviants. *New York Magazine*'s cover featured teaser headlines such as THE CIRCUS IS COMING TO TOWN: A BUSH-HATING NATION OF FREAKS, FLASH-MOBBERS, AND CIVIL-DISOBEDIENTS IS GATHERING TO SPOIL THE GOP'S PARTY.[44] A front-page headline in the *New York Daily News* boldly exclaimed in a supersize font: ANARCHY THREAT TO CITY: COPS FEAR HARD-CORE LUNATICS PLOTTING CONVENTION CHAOS.[45]

At the Georgia Association of Chiefs of Police conference in Savannah in 2004, a state official revealed that as many as forty undercover narcotics officers had attended classes on how to act and dress like protesters for that year's Group of Eight (G-8) Summit.[46] The officers worked in four teams and held video cameras. A digital database of photographs had been amassed of everyone across the country that was involved in or among the leadership of "anarchist movements," according to Georgia Homeland Security Director Bill Hitchens.[47] An Associated Press article noted that Hitchens boasted that the undercover officers blended in with the actual demonstrators so well that when he brought them into the Multi-Agency Command Center, the Secret Service thought they were protesters.[48]

The tactics are reminiscent of the 1960s and 1970s, when the government used crime and terror to silence critics, organizers, and social visionaries. Many argue that these programs are once again on the rise. With increasingly vague and ill-defined characterizations of what does and does not amount to a threat to national security, government and corporate partners infiltrate and defame organizations in an attempt to restrict and deter the public from freely engaging in activities protected by the U.S. Constitution. When the public reads news stories about unlawful counterintelligence tactics being used against Americans who are exercising their constitutional rights to free speech and assembly, it conjures memories of the criminal state assassination, defamation, and disruption programs of the 1960s. Public indignation shut those programs down then, and should shut them down now. As counterintelligence operations become more frequently deployed to fight social movements and enforce order, people's advocacy, education, and organizing to fight these trends assume greater urgency.

Yet stirring the conscience of Americans, as the next chapter shows, becomes more challenging when corporations attempt to build brand loyalty by focusing their marketing campaigns on younger and younger audiences.

CHAPTER 5

Spying on Children

*The best thing about this product is that it teaches
kids about the realities of living in a high-surveil-
lance society.*

—Online reviewer comment about
Playmobil's Security Checkpoint toy[1]

As soon as children are able to play police-type games,
watch television, or strike a computer key, they are exposed to a wide variety of corporate solicitation. Toys
such as Playmobil's Security Checkpoint help habituate
them to accept daily surveillance. Designed for four- to
seven-year-old children, the toy's characters are a female
traveler and two airport security guards equipped with a
hand scanner and a full-body X-ray screening machine.
Parents' reactions range from dismay that "Security
Checkpoint" normalizes surveillance to praise that it exposes youngsters to the realities of constant monitoring.

McDonald's, the Walt Disney Company, and a host
of other corporations try to access children as early as
possible by routinely engaging in deceptive, inherently

Playmobil's Security Checkpoint toy was recommended by the manufacturer for children four years and up. PHOTO: HEIDI BOGHOSIAN

exploitative marketing practices. Any parent familiar with games like Angry Birds also recognizes the constellation of commercial click-through ads and cartoons that have been designed to create consumer desire in their children. Online ads and websites coax children to befriend fantasy creations of corporate empires and then gather personal information in the process. Data aggregators collect that information to sell to third parties for commercial use.

Children raised on computers develop technical proficiency at an early age. Despite that mechanical aptitude, they do not simultaneously develop the media literacy required to distinguish commercial inducement from other forms of content. They also do not comprehend the consequences of sharing personal information, such as toy preferences, favorite foods, or their names and addresses. Aggressive, all-too-clever techniques enable corporations to capture personal information from millions of children. Legal and regulatory protections have failed to keep pace with ever-changing technology and the methods used to target and expose children to corporate persuasion.

As a result, children are primed to be up-to-date consumers long before they learn what it means to be informed and engaged citizens.

Enticing an Impressionable Audience

A great deal of children's television viewing consists of exposure to commercial advertising often visually indistinguishable from the cartoons or fantasy programs surrounding it. In a conservative calculation of children's exposure to television advertising, the Federal Trade Commission estimated that children ages two through eleven watched nearly 26,000 ads in 2004.[2] A few years earlier, ad agencies had been consulting with psychologists to help them market to children as young as three. In response to a request in 1999 from dozens of psychologists and psychiatrists, the American Psychological Association called for an investigation into the practice of using their profession "to promote and assist the commercial exploitation and manipulation of children."[3]

In addition to television commercials, Internet ads bombard children with a range of virtual worlds populated by fantasy characters that corporations create to increase demand for their products. The lines between substance and commerce are often intentionally blurry, and advertising frequency is high. According to Susan Linn, from the Boston-based Campaign for a Commercial-Free Childhood, the United States lags behind other industrialized democracies in regulating children's exposure to corporate persuasion.[4]

Food industries, including Coca-Cola, Nestlé, McDonald's and Kellogg's, use online engagement-based marketing to get children to associate their brand with enjoyable activities.[5] McWorld, a game featured on McDonald's website, provides an example of the methods corporations use to foster emotional relationships and then capture personal data for targeted selling campaigns. In McWorld users create characters and go on quests. Along the way, McWorld prompts them to enter codes from Happy Meal boxes to unlock special gear for their online characters.

McDonald's was forced to change its Happy Meal website after privacy advocates filed a complaint with the Federal Trade Commission in 2012. The company removed its forward-to-a-friend option, which encouraged children to email e-cards, links, and photos to friends and family. Led by the Center for Digital Democracy (CDD), fourteen groups cited five corporations that used theme websites aimed at the young to engage in commercial exploitation of children by enticing them to play online games or engage in online activities and then encourage them to share their experiences by giving email addresses of their friends.[6] In the complaint five companies and their sites—General Mills, Inc. and its TrixWorld.com and ReesesPuffs.com sites; Turner Broadcasting System's CartoonNetwork.com; Viacom Inc.'s Nick.com site; and Doctor's Associates Inc. and its SubwayKids.com site; in addition to McDonald's Corporation's HappyMeal.com site.option—were charged with circumventing the Children's Online Privacy Protection Act of 1998 (COPPA), which governs the collection of online data from children under the age of thirteen. The watchdog and privacy organizations urged the Federal Trade Commission (FTC) to investigate and end "refer-a-friend" practices because they fail to mandate obtaining consent from the parents of children whose emails were shared.[7]

Disney's Cinderella: New Meaning to Oppression and Reward

To appreciate the extent to which corporations exploit any interaction with a child for monetary gain—and arguably groom future generations of compliant buyers—one need only count how few recreational pastimes are commercial-free or educational. Self-contained worlds erected in theme parks take full advantage of children's attention. In 2002, Stone Mountain Theme Park near Atlanta, Georgia, replicated a 1870s-style barn in which children moved from station to station, earning points by completing farming tasks. Young "farmers" entered personal identifying information on a computer. The information was then embedded into radio-frequency identification (RFID) tags in bracelets. Waving a bracelet over a "magic spot" (an RFID reader) stored each child's points and posted them on an electronic scoreboard.[8] The RFID transponders were made by Texas Instruments and supplied by Precision Dynamics Corporation, the world's largest maker of wristbands.[9] Precision Dynamics began manufacturing RFID-embedded bands in 2000 and has watched demand grow steadily, especially for crowd control, healthcare-related functions, and theme park management.

Visitors at Walt Disney World in Orlando, Florida, can skip long lines at entrance turnstiles and eliminate the need for cash and credit cards when buying food and merchandise, also by waving banded wrists. To avail themselves of this convenience they must turn over, as Stone Mountain visitors do, identifying information and consumer habits to Disney. Sharing a date of birth can result in Cinderella greeting a child by name on his or her birthday. It is not without irony that the figurehead for this particular aspect of corporate profit generation is the beloved fairy tale character who represents the oppressed woman and exploited laborer who ultimately obtains her reward.

Disney World attracts up to 30 million visitors annually. The estimated investment of nearly $1 billion in RFID technology is worth it given that it helps to groom

The Walt Disney Parks and Resorts blog describes the MagicBand as an innovative piece of technology that links the entire MyMagic+ experience together. PHOTO: HEIDI BOGHOSIAN

children—who may someday bring their own children to Disneyland—to become repeat consumers of whatever products Disney may sell. Although other theme parks, such as Great Wolf Resorts, have used RFID chips for years, the sheer size of Disney's global parks operation, exceeding 120 million admissions annually, and generating nearly $13 billion in revenue, is so enormous that it is a standard-bearer for influencing young behavior.

Apps Capture Kids' Data

Parents find corporate methods for collecting information from their children even more troubling than potential interactions with strangers online. When 802 parents were asked to list concerns about their teenagers' use of social networks and online habits, 81 percent were worried about exposing children's personal information to advertisers, whereas 72 percent were concerned about interactions with online strangers. The Pew Internet Project and the Berkman Center for Internet & Society at Harvard University collaborated in the study, which also revealed that parents are increasingly monitoring their children's behavior on social networking sites and are conducting Internet searches to determine what information is displayed publicly about them.[10] While social networking sites such as Facebook are required to gain parental consent before gathering data on children under thirteen years of age or affording them access to interactive features that let them share personal information with others, many children lie about their ages in order to gain fuller access, clicking through to wherever ads may lead.

Apps are adding to parents' collective headache. Apps are software applications, usually for mobile devices, that perform a variety of functions, including information retrieval. Their enormous popularity has spawned a virtual explosion in the development of a wide range of functions. Although many apps are fun, they are also insidious trackers able to pinpoint and store a child's physical location, the telephone numbers of their friends, and more.

Third parties can then create detailed profiles of minors without parental knowledge or consent. Not surprisingly, the FTC found in a survey of four hundred popular children's apps that only 20 percent disclose their practices on data collection.[11]

The FTC report, "Mobile Apps for Kids: Disclosures Still Not Making the Grade," noted that nearly 60 percent of the apps reviewed sent information from the personal device to the app developer or to third parties, such as advertising networks or analytics companies. Noting that nearly 80 percent of consumers believe that data on their personal devices is private, the FTC staff authors wrote that, in fact, information from children's apps being shared with third parties (without disclosure to parents) included geolocation, telephone numbers, and the device identification.[12] Even when applications such as the top-selling Angry Birds disclose their data-collection practices in Web-posted policies, they don't offer an opt-out choice. Angry Birds' maker, Rovio Entertainment, directs customers who do not want their data gathered or who don't want targeted ads to two other websites—youradchoices.com and networkadvertising.org—to opt out. (Each site displays a list of participating companies that have enabled customized ads for the user's browser. Visitors are then given the option to check a box next to the ones they want to opt out of.) Rovio acknowledges that some companies disregard the opt-out lists.[13] One trade group representing app developers said the industry's growth is fueled largely by small businesses, first-time developers, and even high school students without access to either legal counsel or privacy experts.[14]

W3 Innovations, a designer of games for mobile telephones, in 2011 settled a lawsuit brought by the FTC alleging that the company violated the Children's Online Privacy Protection Act by unlawfully collecting and disclosing personal data from tens of thousands of children under age thirteen without parental consent.[15] Marc Rotenberg of the Electronic Privacy Information Center (EPIC) testified in 2010 before the Senate Commerce Committee that COPPA needed to be updated to clarify its application to mobile-devised and social networking services.[16]

The social game site RockYou was ordered to put in place a data security program and pay a quarter of a million dollars in penalties after inadequate security resulted in hackers gaining access to the personal data of 32 million users. RockYou agreed to pay $250,000 in civil penalty for violations alleged in *United States v. RockYou Inc.* that it violated COPPA by knowingly gathering the email addresses and passwords of approximately 179,000 children without first obtaining their parents' consent.[17]

Is Spying on Children Ever Acceptable?
More and more, parents watch their children's online activities to make sure they stay out of trouble. AVG Technologies found that 44 percent of parents monitored children in the fourteen-to-seventeen age group.[18] To accommodate this growing practice, a wide range of digital

monitoring systems has been developed to watch iPhone, cell phone, and Internet activities. Such software, dubbed spyware, allows for surreptitious watching, recording, and filtering of online activities including sites visited, files transferred, keystrokes, chats, and more.

While safety issues may occasionally justify secret surveillance policies by parents, cases such as an instance in Pennsylvania involving nonparental parties, reveal potential abuses. Harriton High School students had no idea what was hidden in the computer laptops that their school had given them. A "one-to-one" laptop computer initiative, partially funded by state and federal grants for technology, was supposed to implement what the school called "an authentic mobile 21st Century learning environment."[19] However, in a remarkable display of audacity, school district administrators were remotely activating built-in laptop cameras to watch students' behavior in the privacy of their own homes.

School officials notified Blake Robbins's parents that he was engaging in improper behavior at home. When Blake's parents went to school, administrators showed them a photo of Blake taken by the remote camera. Only then did the Robbins family learn that the school had spied on Blake. In response to a 2010 class action suit on behalf of all students who were issued laptops, *Robbins v. Lower Merion School District*, school officials reached a $610,000 settlement and admitted that the computers included webcam software that could be remotely activated to view minors surreptitiously, but denied any wrongdoing.

Other pervasive practices of collecting data from children's online activities may not appear as patently objectionable as the Harriton High incident, but the consequences may last a lifetime. As they grow, children become habituated to a corporate infrastructure that entices them to unknowingly barter away their privacy.

Laws Protecting Children's Privacy

Advocacy groups provide a modicum of balance to the ways in which corporations—and sometimes government agencies—harvest students' private information. Such groups have urged Congress to enact greater privacy protections for children, but their task is daunting in scope. In 1996 EPIC's Marc Rotenberg told members of Congress, "government agencies, private organizations, universities, associations, businesses, and clubs all gather information on kids of all ages. Records on our children are collected literally at the time of birth, segmented, compiled, and in some cases resold to anyone who wishes to buy them."[20] Nearly two decades later, the gathering and reselling of children's information continues.

The absence of legal standards makes it virtually impossible to regulate data aggregation. EPIC noted the difficulty of determining the extent to which personal information has been misused, but emphasized that existing practices lack privacy procedures followed in other industries and "pose a substantial threat to the privacy and safety of young people."[21]

Twelve years after COPPA was enacted, in 2012 the

FTC issued final amendments to the Children's Online Privacy Protection Rule, which implements the act. They include prohibitions on using geolocation information and software installed on a computer to gather information, and forbid corporations from covertly gathering personal information about children for advertising purposes without parental consent. Updates to the COPPA Rule expand the types of companies that must obtain permission from parents prior to gathering personal data from children. They list additional types of data as "personal information" that cannot be gathered without notice and consent from parents, including photographs, video and audio files containing a child's voice or image, and screen or user names that are similar to email addresses such that they might lead to direct contact with a child.[22]

These updates to the law are small and late in coming. In general COPPA and its regulations have been slow to keep pace with technology, which becomes more sophisticated and invasive each day. In response to pressure from public interest groups, the FTC is considering changing COPPA to impose more rigorous standards for children under age thirteen.[23]

In addition to lagging in enacting effective regulatory protections, some government agencies entrusted with the power to protect children's information have violated that trust. In 2011, the U.S. Department of Education (DOE) proposed amendments to the Family and Educational Rights and Privacy Act of 1974 (FERPA), which prohibits educational institutions and agencies from disclosing personally identifiable student information without consent from either the student or their parents. The amendments would permit schools to publicly disclose to third parties student identification numbers or other unique personal identifiers used by students to access electronic systems.

In response, EPIC filed public comments saying that by designating nongovernmental actors as "authorized representatives" of state educational institutions, the DOE would improperly delegate its own authority. EPIC noted that by expanding the definition of educational programs, the DOE would expose vast amounts of students' nonacademic, sensitive data.[24] Doing so could potentially expose students' education records as well as special education, job training, career and technical information, and early intervention programs under the Individuals with Disabilities Education Act (which could open up records related to "catheterization, tube feeding and a range of other data").[25] Third parties would be able to use information to identify and target groups of students with similar characteristics.

Later that year, however, the Department of Education implemented the changes. EPIC and others sued in 2012. They asked the court to review some factors, including that at the time the agency issued the final regulations, it had not offered guidelines on student data and cloud computing. After issuing the regulations, for example, the DOE created a document that provided cloud-computing guidance. The document explained that even though "outsourcing information technology (IT) functions" would not "traditionally be considered an audit or evaluation,"[26] the Education Department will consider outsourcing IT functions as "auditing" or "evaluating" under FERPA regulations. FERPA permits nonconsensual disclosure of education records to parties under its direct control, such as contractors who have been designated "authorized representative[s]"[27] for audits and evaluation of federal and state education programs.

Despite advocacy efforts on behalf of children's privacy issues, continued marketing to young individuals and collection of their data by corporations is troubling. Monitoring minors' play habits and reselling information with an eye toward shaping their consumer habits is directly related to the normalization of a security state. Rather than sparking curiosity in children about social issues, corporations prefer that children—and adults—center their worlds around acquiring the latest toys, clothes, and junk food.

Corporations use clandestine methods on the Internet and elsewhere to extract children's private information, to condition them to accept surveillance, and to mold them into unquestioning consumers. As the next chapter shows, when children grow up and publicly resist wasteful or inhumane company practices, they may be subject to different forms of insidious government and corporate spying and infiltration.

CHAPTER 6

Green Squads

Secret police behavior and surveillance go to the heart of the kind of society we are or might become. By studying the changes in covert tactics, a window on something much broader can be gained.
—Gary T. Marx[1]

Ten female environmental protection advocates in Great Britain sued Scotland Yard in 2011 on grounds that they were deceptively lured into long-term intimate relationships with undercover police from 1987 to 2010. The agents were part of a four-decade deep-cover operation targeting people who organized on behalf of environmental sustainability. During this time, two undercover officers fathered children with women they were spying on.[2] According to the *Guardian*, "eight of the nine undercover officers identified over the past 21 months are believed to have had intimate sexual relationships with protesters they were spying on."[3]

The scandal broke not long after the identity of one of the agents became public. An activist known for seven years as Mark Stone (nickname Flash, real name Mark Kennedy) was an intelligence officer who climbed trees, broke into power stations, and participated in many actions designed to draw attention to environmental issues. He was having sex with activists and providing them with money and transportation.[4]

Kennedy reported to a domestic unit run by the Association of Chief Police Officers (ACPO), which was formed to assist businesses scrutinized by citizen advocacy groups. It shares information with clients, including the airline industry and power plants, and even sells data from the Police National Computer. Just as police in Great Britain work directly to serve the interests of businesses, so does the United States partner with corporate clients in spying on, infiltrating, and often entrapping social justice advocates.

Agents Go Under

While Kennedy was still undercover in the United Kingdom in 2006, news broke that the U.S. government had engaged in a similar infiltration of citizen advocacy groups. (Kennedy's activity was not confined to Great Britain; he worked undercover in more than twenty other countries and as of 2012 is employed by the U.S.-based Densus Group, a security consulting firm.)[5]

Working with the FBI, a paid informant known as "Anna" encouraged and, defense lawyers asserted, entrapped three environmental sustainability advocates in planning acts of arson in several Northern California locations. (FBI Special Agent Nasson Walker from Sacramento testified that Anna received at least $75,000 for her work.)[6] In 2005, Anna began discussing plans for a "direct action" with Eric McDavid, Zachary Jenson, and Lauren Weiner, urging that the action include making an explosive device.[7] Defense attorneys contend that Anna not only encouraged building the device, but that she also provided the resources to do so: funds to initiate the plan, airfare for McDavid to fly to another state to attend a "planning session," room and board, literature on how to make explosive devices, and money to purchase necessary supplies.[8] Mark Reichel, McDavid's attorney, referred to her as the "glue," saying: "Take away Anna, and they would have scattered in the wind like so many tumbleweeds."[9]

Anna was closest to McDavid, who was twenty-eight years old. Romantic tension, it was noted, existed between the two for a year and a half after they met. Reichel said they argued like a couple.[10] As a result of Anna's testimony, in 2007 McDavid was convicted of conspiring to use fire or explosives to damage corporate and government property. McDavid's codefendants, Jenson and Weiner, pled guilty and later testified against him at trial. In exchange for their cooperation a judge sentenced the two to time served. McDavid, on the other hand, was sentenced to nearly twenty years in prison for purchasing "bomb making materials," namely household cleaning supplies and Pyrex-brand cookware.[11]

The McDavid case illustrates how informants working for the U.S. government may take advantage of intimate relationships, just as in the UK infiltration cases. As a result, impressionable young adults often find themselves being urged to engage in activities they are disinclined to do or would not have even thought of on their own. At least one juror in the McDavid case was aware of this dynamic.

After the trial, one of the jurors, Carol Runge, submitted a court declaration. Among her many points, Runge's declaration said that she felt the defense attorney Mark Reichel had made "a very strong case of entrapment," that "the FBI agents were "out of control," that the FBI agents' lack of knowledge of FBI procedures was an "embarrassment," and that the main witness, Anna, "was not a credible witness."[12] Runge said she felt that Anna had no oversight from the FBI, that she used McDavid's attraction to her to "keep him on the hook" until the three could be arrested, and that McDavid had only stayed with the group because of his romantic attraction to her. In addition, Runge said that if she had been permitted to consider McDavid's financial, mental, and physical ability to commit criminal acts absent Anna's help, she would have found entrapment. She explained that the jurors were confused about what evidence they were permitted to consider to find entrapment and were confused about other legal instructions.

Stories about FBI entrapment of activists are surfacing with increasing regularity.[13] Surveillance of people conducting education and advocacy related to animal rights and environmental sustainability is a priority of federal law enforcement. Using paid informants, as in the McDavid case, is common practice. Just as police units monitoring actual or alleged communists decades ago came to be known as "red squads," today, intelligence initiatives spying on people engaged in efforts to halt climate change and increase sustainability have grown in scope and intensity to the point that we might well refer to them as "green squads."

Grassroots Activities Stir the Conscience of a Nation

Once dismissed by many as the work of fanatics who threw paint at women wearing fur, animal rights activism has evolved into a formidable social justice movement. In the United States, half a century of activism has resulted in steady and measurable changes in attitudes concerning the way corporations and research facilities treat animals. In 1966, Congress enacted the Animal Welfare Act regulating the treatment of animals in federally funded research. Congress charged the Department of Agriculture with overseeing the inspection of laboratories for compliance. After it was shown that inhumane conditions persisted in laboratories around the country, in 1985 the Act was amended to strengthen standards for the humane handling, treatment, and transportation of animals by dealers, research facilities, and exhibitors. A few years later, in 1991, the Secretary of Agriculture issued regulations implementing the amended act. Laboratory testing of animals dropped 50 percent in the 1990s. An increas-

A 2009 protest by Friends of Animals, a nonprofit, international animal advocacy organization founded in 1957.
PUBLIC DOMAIN PHOTO BY ALEJANDRO HERNANDEZ

ing segment of society is choosing not to financially support industries that use animal products or engage in animal testing, exercising that option by dietary changes, and clothing and cosmetics choices. In response, a new industry has grown to supply humanely produced items for this market.

The environmental movement has also yielded noteworthy and visible policy changes: improving vehicle efficiency and emissions control, repurposing waste into reusable materials, staving off new nuclear power plants, creating hybrid energy centers in many cities, opposing hydraulic fracturing, saving forests, removing acid from rain, and removing lead from gasoline have all contributed to educating the public and protecting the planet's precious environmental resources.

"Not a Serious Threat—but We Need to Watch Them"

Michael Sheehan, former New York City deputy commissioner for counterterrorism, acknowledges that most of the individuals who have actually perpetrated attacks in the United States are "lone wolves," independent agents not aligned with a particular organization. He also recognizes that animal rights and environmental groups are not a danger to the country: "These groups don't really constitute a serious terrorist threat, but we need to watch them. In particular, we should monitor whether they or any radical spin-offs try something more dramatic. Their radical and violent leanings deserve close scrutiny, even if their goals do have some political support."[14]

If Michael Sheehan doesn't really see animal rights and environmental activists as a credible threat, why are so many resources being funneled into conducting surveillance on them? Most likely it is because, like New York bicycle enthusiasts, they make an impact by advancing noncommercial goals like free transportation, compassion for animal life, and ecological balance and sustainability. They have changed the way American consumers think about animal testing, forcing multinational corporations to change their practices. And this has affected corporations where they feel it the most—in their net profits and reputations. Part of the effectiveness of these civic-minded efforts is related to the creative, individualistic, and bold methods used to network their messages and to challenge corporate campaigns that are not in the public's best interest.

As described below, corporate representatives work hand in hand with legislators to craft laws that protect institutional profits, usually without the public's knowledge.

Manufacturing Terrorism

Will Potter is an independent journalist devoted to documenting the government's full-frontal assault on people engaged in supporting animal rights and environmental sustainability. In that world, Potter enjoys nothing short of a cult-hero following. His website, Green Is the New Red,[15] and book by the same name deal with the government's denigration of environmental and animal rights advocacy. Armed with a dry wit and a punchy Power-Point demonstration, in just a few arresting frames Potter shows how the D.C.-based public relations firm Dezenhall Resources manufactured the term "eco-terrorism" and launched a damning campaign to portray animal rights and environmental activists as domestic terrorists. During his talks about FBI infiltration of vegan potluck dinners he shows examples of slick government-commissioned propaganda that depict young people wearing gas masks (and sometimes with hairy legs, to emphasize grassroots inclinations). The images never fail to prompt laughter from Potter's audiences.

Through a Freedom of Information Act request, Potter received a 2005 FBI file that dealt with several people who had become informants and whose identities were later made public. Patterns of infiltration have made many people afraid of possible FBI spying, and that fear alone is enough to sabotage legitimate, legal public interest organizing and advocacy. In one of the files Potter obtained, an FBI agent pointed out that the structure of animal rights groups in particular makes it relatively easy to discredit members, and that modern FBI tactics take advantage of this structure:

> The Animal Rights Movement does little research on newcomers into the movement and basically goes with its gut instinct as to whether a person is an informant or not. Organizers of the Animal Rights Movement can be discredited and removed from the scene by planting rumors that they are plants and/or informants.[16]

Claims of criminal acts have been fabricated by authorities, sometimes planned as propaganda to counteract educational campaigns.[17] In 1990, *San Francisco Examiner* writer Rob Morse discovered that fliers and press releases distributed to the media from the environmental group Earth First! calling for violence during Redwood Summer had actually been written and distributed by the public relations firm Hill & Knowlton.[18] Firm staff members were copied on an internal Pacific Lumber memo indicating that the flier was likely forged. The memo was shared during the discovery phase in a lawsuit for trespass brought by Pacific Lumber against Darryl Cherney and two others for tree sitting to protest logging in the Northern California redwood forests in 1989. On April 29, 1990, Morse described a press kit from the public relations firm on behalf of "Earth First!'s nemesis, Pacific Lumber Co." He wrote:

> The kit included a press release on the Earth First! letterhead, but not written in the usual careful, sweet style of Earth First! It read like a bad Hollywood version of what radicals talk like. . . . At the bottom of this ridiculous flyer was the name of Earth First! leader Darryl Cherney, with his first name misspelled. . . . Not only are trees being clear-cut, but dirty tricksters are turning them into fake press releases.[19]

Hill & Knowlton also represented Louisiana Pacific Corporation, Georgia Pacific Corporation and other redwood logging corporations in a campaign to defeat a November 1990 logging reform voter initiative in California. Had the reform passed, the industries could have lost billions of dollars, so they expended millions of dollars working to defeat it. Although the initiative had significant public support, it failed by a narrow margin.[20]

An Irritant to Corporations

A U.S. senator and an FBI official joined forces to exploit public fears of terrorism by branding socially conscious individuals as a national security threat. Architects of what many call today's "Green Scare" included Senator James Inhofe (R-OK), chair of the Environment and Public Works Committee, and John E. Lewis, the FBI's deputy assistant director for counterterrorism. On May 18, 2005, Inhofe implored fellow senators to "take a look at the culture and climate of support for criminally based activism like ELF [Environmental Liberation Front], and ALF [Animal Liberation Front], and do something about it."[21] The FBI responded with an intensive campaign, issuing subpoenas to activists, conducting large-scale arrests, levying unprecedented penalties for property crimes, and using threats of severe punishment to force people to testify against their former allies in exchange for reduced or waived prison sentences.

The Department of Homeland Security (DHS) helps create and sustain a level of alarm among intelligence agencies, partly by circulating reports that highlight the purported "eco-terrorist" threat. One such report asserted that such mainstream groups as the Humane Society and the Sierra Club have links to terrorism.[22] The intelligence report prepared by a private contractor for DHS included the fact that environmental activists have never hurt any individuals, but it nonetheless alluded to vague "indications" that some might be more militant. The report stated that "the activities of the ecoterrorist movement are significant for several reasons and should be of interest to domestic security and law enforcement officials. [W]hile ecoterrorists thus far have generally refrained from harming individuals, there are indications that some within the movement are advocating more drastic measures to further their sociopolitical agendas."[23] But the report contained contradictory assertions, including the conclusion that "ecoterrorist movement activities do not represent a serious threat to U.S. national security."[24] The report listed twenty-seven "personalities" who were "profiled according to their involvement in organizations and/or activities associated with ecoterrorism."[25] A few sentences later it indicated that "the nature and frequency of ecoterrorist attacks poses a public safety threat to specific segments of American society. . . . Ecomilitants have demonstrated both the willingness and ability to strike a vast array of targets across the United States with virtual impunity."[26]

In trying to make sense of the quest to round up law-abiding social change activists, it is helpful to consider the government's lackluster record of post-9/11 intelligence gathering and the dearth of arrests that have resulted in convictions. Noteworthy arrests of violent terrorists are few. At the same time, acts of disobedience that were once deemed petty crimes have been recast as acts of terrorism. Lowering the bar for what constitutes "terrorism" makes it easier to show concrete counterterrorism results by prosecuting domestic activists. Sociologist Tony Silvaggio noted, "The government's guilt-by-association and divide-and conquer approach has really succeeded. . . . They've targeted this movement because it's an easy target; Al Qaeda is . . . hard. They need to show results. They need to show the American people that 'There are terrorists out there, and we caught them.'" [27]

An Industry with a Beef

A case involving one of the world's most influential women demonstrates the power that animal enterprises have to intimidate critics, even unwitting ones. In 1998 cattle producers sued Oprah Winfrey under the Texas version of a food libel law, the False Disparagement of Perishable Food Products Act of 1995.[28] After an outbreak of mad cow disease in Europe, Winfrey in 1996 aired a show on the disease in which she and a guest made comments critical of the beef industry.

Cattle producers claimed that Winfrey and her guest's remarks caused cattle prices to plummet by $12 million, even though, as Winfrey's attorney explained in his opening remarks at trial, one of the cattle producers actually made $140,000 in the aftermath of the show by betting in the cattle futures market that prices would go down.[29]

In *Texas Beef v. Oprah Winfrey*, the jury in the case found that the Texas statute did not apply to live cattle and that the comments did not constitute libel, determinations which were upheld by the United States Court of Appeals for the Fifth Circuit.[30] But Winfrey never again spoke publicly about the issue, demonstrating the chilling effect that food industries often have on critics.

Corporations Craft Legislation to Protect Profits

The FBI listed animal and environmental rights organizations as top domestic terrorist threats in 2005. Efforts to criminalize environmental activists resulted in passage of a harsh federal law in 2006, the Animal Enterprise Terrorism Act (AETA),[31] which amended the Animal Enterprise Protection Act of 1992.[32] The well-funded conservative American Legislative Exchange Council (ALEC), which drafted AETA in association with the U.S. Sportsmen's Alliance in 2002, is a highly organized lobbying group with a clearinghouse of model bills and legislative strategies to promote its pro-business agenda.[33] In 2012, ALEC's reputation suffered after it received publicity as a major engineer of Florida's Stand Your Ground laws, which were implicated in the high-profile killing of Trayvon Martin.[34]

ALEC's structure and influence give corporate interests significant power over legislation produced at the state level. ALEC has several task forces, each of which is run by a public-sector chair (a state legislator) and a private-sector chair. The latter have included employees of the National Rifle Association and AT&T. As equal partners in the creation of model legislation, unelected private-sector representatives have an unusual opportunity to draft bills furthering their own interests. Once completed, the bills are provided to ALEC's public-sector members with the hope that they will be introduced in as many states as possible.[35]

ALEC's system differs from traditional forms of lobbying and advocacy because although corporations are given extraordinary power to shape bills, there is often no mention of the corporate influence when model bills are introduced. ALEC has been highly successful in pushing its legislation through state legislatures. According to its Legislative Scorecard for the 2007–2008 legislative session, 118 bills were enacted based on ALEC model legislation.[36]

AETA's definition of "terrorism" is so broad that it could be read to encompass peaceful civil disobedience, acts that have been defining moments in U.S. history since the American Revolution. The civil rights movement is rife with now proud examples of civil disobedience and civil resistance. AETA spells out penalties for such offenses as nonviolent physical obstruction of an animal enterprise or a business with a relationship to an animal enterprise that may result in loss of profits, and it's not too much of a stretch to imagine such a definition including the food service business of the Greensboro, South Carolina, Woolworth's lunch counter, circa 1960. The law makes it a crime to cause any business classified as an "animal enterprise," such as factory farms, fur farms, rodeos, and circuses to suffer a profit loss even if caused by acts of peaceful free speech and assembly.

With laws such as AETA, the government protects corporations at the expense of political dissent, meting out disproportionately harsh punishment for expressing views that could harm profits. AETA and related legislation attempt to criminalize and censor free speech activities by associating them with the wanton violence that defines terrorism. This association is often a precursor to more repressive tactics, such as misusing grand juries to browbeat individuals into informing on others. If convicted, the "terrorist" label triggers long sentences with extreme security measures that may include prolonged solitary confinement and restricted communications with loved ones.

The first AETA prosecutions were brought in 2009 when four people were indicted and arrested in California by the Joint Terrorism Task Force for writing on sidewalks with chalk, chanting, leafleting, and conducting Internet research on animal researchers. Each person faced ten years in prison. A federal judge dismissed that case in 2010.

In March 2013, a federal judge dismissed, for lack of standing, a lawsuit that challenged AETA's constitutionality. The Center for Constitutional Rights, along with Boston attorneys David Milton and Howard Friedman and New York attorney Alexander Reinert, mounted the lawsuit *Blum v. Holder* on behalf of animal rights activists alleging that the law violates their right to free speech. Lead counsel Rachel Meeropol noted that, as the judge in the case recognized, "[e]ach of our clients has refrained from engaging in constitutionally protected speech out of fear that she or he will be prosecuted as a terrorist under the AETA. They will continue to be chilled from speaking out on important issues of public concern until this law is struck down."[37]

Whatever motivates these law enforcement actions, a dynamic is at play that inevitably leads to increased surveillance of lawful activism. When powerful private interests are threatened—whether by movements for animal rights or by activities to protect forests—corporations will use their influence to mobilize and even manipulate the government to rally to their defense. By exploiting the official fears of the day, red or green, private interests join with legislators and law enforcement to keep people from expressing criticism of corporate practices and state policies. Once the "terrorist" label has been applied, pressure to wage a war on terror exists at all levels of government and the general population. This creates a culture of distrust, intolerance, and authority that robs us, bit by bit, of our rights, democracy, and freedom.

This milieu of mistrust leads inexorably to even greater government militancy and surveillance.

Listening in on Lawyers

The FBI has used well over 1,000 informants to report on [National Lawyers Guild] activities, and to disrupt Guild meetings. . . . FBI agents repeatedly broke into the NLG national office and into private law offices of key NLG members.

—National Lawyers Guild:
From Roosevelt to Reagan[1]

Government programs and regulations put into place in the recent past have opened the door to violations of attorney-client privilege, but government surveillance of lawyers is not new. From the ascendance of the New Deal through the height of the Cold War, clandestine monitoring of the National Lawyers Guild (NLG) evinced government disregard for the role that lawyers play in safeguarding a democratic society. Years later, other legal organizations would find themselves subjected to surveillance.

Interception of communications, including those between attorneys and their clients, has been permitted since 1968 under Title III of the Omnibus Crime Control and Safe Streets Act. After 9/11, however, two developments afforded additional ways to listen in on lawyers. As part of the Bush administration's "war on terror," the NSA began conducting warrantless monitoring of telephone and electronic communications of persons in the United States if they involved individuals believed to be outside of the country. Also after 9/11, the Foreign Intelligence Surveillance Act (FISA) was amended to include terrorism by entities not related to foreign governments. Although the warrantless monitoring program was discontinued in 2007, a year later Congress passed the FISA Amendments Act of 2008,[2] loosening some of the original FISA court requirements and making it easier to obtain warrantless wiretaps.

In addition to the NSA program and the loosened FISA requirements, less than two months after 9/11 the Federal Bureau of Prisons issued guidelines permitting the Department of Justice to covertly monitor communications between federal inmates and their attorneys. The existence of such a wiretapping program is ultimately harmful to the overall justice system, which should be free of the exercise of arbitrary power. It serves to dissuade lawyers from taking controversial cases and diminishes their ability to effectively represent people who may be subject to monitoring.

Spying on the National Lawyers Guild

A progressive bar association, the National Lawyers Guild was founded in 1937, a year after Franklin Delano Roosevelt won his second term with a record-breaking victory. The coming four-year period was seen as an opportunity to implement the New Deal's progressive plans. But despite Roosevelt's sweeping victory, resistance was mounting to the New Deal. The country was experiencing deep national uncertainty.[3]

The political Right was on the upswing. Many corporate and financial leaders had formed the Liberty League, dedicated to defeating the New Deal. Along with powerful organizations such as the National Association of Manufacturers they engaged in a broad campaign against the most important New Deal legislation and agencies. As in the past, among the corporate Right's most important weapons were organized, mainstream bar associations. In particular, the American Bar Association supported efforts to resist legislative initiatives of the Roosevelt administration.[4]

Against this backdrop, in 1936 twenty-five lawyers met in New York City to plan a new national bar association that would oppose many of the American Bar Association positions and use the law in the service of the people. The next year the National Lawyers Guild was founded as the first racially integrated bar association.[5] Over the years, NLG members would come to be called "people's lawyers," notably by Arthur Kinoy,[6] who successfully argued *United States v. United States District Court*, the U.S.

Atlanta NLG member Brian Spears (right) marching with the United League in anti-Klan demonstration, Tupelo, Mississippi, 1978. PHOTO: NATIONAL LAWYERS GUILD

Supreme Court case that held that Richard Nixon could not engage in warrantless electronic surveillance.

For over three decades, from 1940 to 1975, the FBI conducted a campaign of surveillance, investigation, and disruption against the Guild and its members.[7] (Given some of the modern activities against the Guild—representing and advocating on behalf of clients ranging from animal rights and environmental advocates to the loose confederation of computer hacktivists known as Anonymous—it would not be surprising if surveillance and disruption is still under way.) In 1977 the Guild filed *National Lawyers Guild v. Attorney General of the United States*; the lawsuit yielded more than 300,000 pages of FBI files on the NLG.

No alleged or suspected criminal wrongdoing existed as grounds for the government's intrusion, and the Department of Justice (DOJ) never authorized or brought criminal prosecutions of the Guild or its members. The FBI placed Guild members on its Security Indexes, personnel databases on paper index cards used to track individuals deemed threats to national security. The category included members who were either in leadership positions within the Guild or held actual or suspected membership in other organizations.[8]

The FBI secretly broke into and entered the organization's national office and the offices of Guild members.[9] Some of the information obtained included drafts of a report criticizing FBI surveillance practices and a planned campaign calling for the investigation of the FBI. Without a warrant, the FBI tapped the Guild's national office telephone from 1947 to 1951. Information taken from the unlawful entries was used as a basis for the U.S. attorney general to initiate proceedings in 1953 to designate the Guild a subversive organization under the Federal Employment Loyalty Security Program.

A government informant sat on the organization's board of directors in 1953 and 1954 and reported on its discussions with legal counsel about the Guild's defense against the designation proceedings and its conduct of

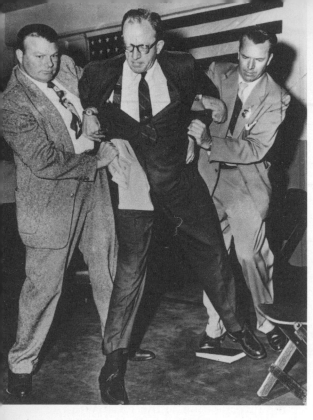

San Diego NLG member John W. Porter being forcibly ejected from the hearing room of the House Un-American Activities Committee on December 8, 1956.
PHOTO: NATIONAL LAWYERS GUILD

litigation against the government. In 1958 and again in 1974, the DOJ determined that it could not go forward with the designation proceedings and the attorney general withdrew the proposal to classify the NLG as subversive.

The FBI continued spying on the Guild. The bureau used informants and confidential sources to glean information about the Guild's work, including its members, staff, and third parties in contact with the organization. The FBI obtained Guild records from banks where the

Guild had accounts and it obtained information from the National Conference of Bar Examiners and some of its character committees, which screen and evaluate lawyers' fitness to practice law. It wiretapped Guild offices and ran "trash covers"—an FBI term for rummaging through garbage cans. To obtain information on the group, the FBI listened in on conversations held at the private law offices of Guild members, directly threatening the attorney-client privilege that is at the heart of our legal system.

In settling the eleven-year-old civil lawsuit on October 12, 1989, the FBI acknowledged investigating and disrupting the NLG even though officials had known for over three decades that they could not prove charges that the organization was subversive.[10] The bureau also acknowledged its spying, noting that many of its activities, if judged by current standards, would be illegal. The settlement provided that data collected by the bureau would be turned over to the National Security Archive under seal until 2025.[11]

A Law Office for the People

The People's Law Office (PLO) was founded in Chicago by several young attorneys who committed their lives to representing individuals and movements victimized by government surveillance, harassment, and disruption. Among the PLO's early clients were members of the Black Panther Party, the Young Lords Organization, the Puerto Rican independence movement, and Students for a Democratic Society. During the 1980s and 1990s, PLO lawyers worked with other members of the National Lawyers Guild to provide monitors at mass assemblies and to represent in criminal court activists arrested for acts of civil disobedience and direct action.

PLO lawyers knew firsthand what it was like to be the targets of police and intelligence surveillance: they themselves underwent daily, often aggressive, monitoring and taunts by the Chicago Police Department's red squad. They later learned that the FBI had rented a room across the street from them, and had regularly filmed them and read their mail. Although PLO attorneys documented the red squad surveillance and drafted a lawsuit challenging it, the press of political defense work never afforded them time to file it. Surveillance of the office, however, was noted by the U.S. Supreme Court. Justice Douglas referred to it in an opinion, writing that attorneys for a petitioner whose telephone conversations with her attorneys were illegally tapped "include an organization in Chicago known as the 'Peoples Law Office.' Peoples is a firm almost exclusively devoted to the criminal defense of 'militants' and 'radicals,' including Chairman Fred Hampton of the Black Panther Party and Bernadine Dohrn and Marc Rudd of the Weatherman faction of the SDS."[12]

Several People's Law Office members were named plaintiffs in a lawsuit filed by others in 1974 to stop police spying and disruption. Later the FBI, the CIA, and Military Intelligence were added as defendants. In 1981 many of the named plaintiffs agreed to enter into consent decrees providing the relief they requested—forbidding political spying and harassment. Lawyers at the PLO asserted that the decrees did not go far enough and that many of the most frequent targets were not sufficiently protected. In 1985, a court decision ended the surveillance of political activists and organizations by the Chicago Police Department's Subversive Activities Unit.

The Attorney-Client Privilege

It is well known that government agencies spy on citizens, particularly critics of domestic and foreign policies. The monitoring of social networks, advocacy groups, and movements seems relatively transparent, as clashes between government authorities and civilians are covered daily in the media—heavily armed and costumed law enforcement shows up at free events, gatherings, and protests and engages in a show of excessive force that suppresses free speech and dissent. But less visible surveillance can have even more corrosive consequences to the constitutional landscape. Such is the case when the government spies on attorneys and the people they represent, corrupting the chance for individual justice and ultimately the judicial system as a whole. Prosecutorial access to attorney-client communications and legal strategy discussions afford the government an unfair legal advantage in pursuing cases in court.

The attorney-client privilege is contained in the Federal Rules of Evidence, and covers communication between a lawyer and the client.[13] Its purpose is to foster full and open communication between them so that larger public interests may be served.[14] A lawyer has an ethical obligation to claim the privilege on behalf of a client.[15]

Regulations enacted by the Bureau of Prisons after 9/11 opened the door to codifying the act of spying on lawyers—and in doing so violating the attorney-client privilege—when those lawyers represent controversial people and cases. In a democratic society that guarantees citizens the dignity of being treated as innocent until proven guilty, access to an unconstrained legal defense for every single man, woman, and minor is essential. Attorneys have discovered or had reason to suspect that their private conversations with the people they were defending in controversial cases were subject to covert government monitoring. Those who represent incarcerated clients may come to feel like pariahs for the work they do; one attorney was even monitored and prosecuted in a high-profile case under terrorism statutes while performing her legal duties. In such a context, discovering that you are being tracked can be devastating.

Public response to modifying the guidelines for prisoners was scant, likely due to the fact that few realize the implications that regulations governing inmates have on the wider American population.

As we've seen, the model that corporations and the state use to stifle dissent is to cry public safety and national security. That's exactly how the spying on lawyers began.

Eavesdropping on Lawyers and Clients

In the wake of the 1993 World Trade Center bombing in New York City and the 1995 bombing of the Alfred P. Murrah Federal Building in Oklahoma City, procedures were initiated in 1997 for imposing special confinement conditions on federal inmates deemed especially dangerous to national security.[16] The head of a U.S. intelligence agency could impose harsh conditions upon finding that the inmate, if permitted to communicate, might reveal classified information that could endanger national security, and when the attorney general determined that there existed "a substantial risk that a prisoner's communications or contacts with persons could result in death or serious bodily injury to persons, or substantial damage to property that would entail the risk of death or serious bodily injury to persons."[17] Such restrictive confinement conditions, or special administrative measures (SAMs), can include imposing solitary confinement, intercepting mail, and restricting telephone calls and visitors.

While the 1997 regulations restricted communication from designated federal inmates to anyone except to their attorneys, a 2001 prison eavesdropping regulation provided for the monitoring of that one final connection.[18] Communications between attorneys and their clients in federal detention may now be monitored. The attorney general needs to determine that there is "reasonable suspicion"—a legal standard that leaves great discretion to the person approving the monitoring—that the verbal and written communications between the lawyer and client are being used to facilitate acts of terrorism.[19] When the DOJ obtains a court order to eavesdrop on an incarcerated person who is talking to his or her attorney, there exists no requirement that notice be given to either one of them.[20]

In 2002 criminal defense attorney Lynne Stewart was indicted on charges that she provided material support to a terrorist organization, the Islamic Group. Although the government had been secretly monitoring Stewart's telephone calls, electronic communications, and in-person meetings with one of her clients for three years, Attorney General John Ashcroft announced that her case represented the first exercise of his authority to monitor attorney-client communications following the enactment of the USA PATRIOT Act.[21] The charges were brought after Stewart violated the special administrative measures imposed on her client, Sheikh Abdel Rahman, by issuing a press release about the sheikh. Stewart was found guilty and was sentenced to ten years in prison. Although Stewart had issued the press release in 2000, when Janet Reno was attorney general under Bill Clinton, it wasn't until the post-9/11 Bush administration that she was charged. It turned out that her meetings, telephone calls, and electronic communications with the sheikh had been monitored for years.

How Spying Chills Lawyering
How does a little-known regulation on prison eavesdropping affect free speech more generally?

Lawyers may now think twice about representing clients with unpopular views. Already subject to criticism for defending the more vilified of society's members, defense attorneys who take on cases with political significance know their communications may be monitored. Representing individuals charged with terrorism-related offenses exposes attorneys to heightened scrutiny. Some, especially those with less experience in the profession, may find this daunting and decide not to take on such politically charged cases. And public confidence in the privacy of communications with lawyers is eroded. People cannot be defended effectively when they are hesitant to share vital information with their attorneys.

The Center for Constitutional Rights (CCR), like the National Lawyers Guild, is a legal and educational organization committed to using the law as a positive force for social change. Founded by attorneys who represented civil rights movements in the South, CCR has been exposing government misconduct and bringing abusive practices to light since 1966.

In 2006 CCR filed *CCR. v Bush* (later *CCR v. Obama*) against President George W. Bush, the head of the National Security Agency, and the heads of the other major security agencies, challenging the NSA's warrantless surveillance of people within the United States as a violation of the Foreign Intelligence Surveillance Act. FISA explicitly authorizes physical and electronic surveillance in the United States against foreign powers or their agents for the purpose of collecting foreign intelligence only upon orders issued by federal judges who sit on a special court. It expressly authorizes warrantless wiretapping only for the first fifteen days of a war and makes it a crime to engage in wiretapping without specific statutory authority. Rather than seeking to amend the statute, President Bush simply violated it.

The NSA and the DOJ refused to turn over the relevant records or to confirm or deny whether the lawyers were subject to surveillance, saying that disclosure would compromise the methods of U.S. intelligence communities.[22] In early 2011, a federal district court dismissed *CCR v. Obama*, finding that CCR had no standing to sue because it had no evidence that its staff and attorneys had actually been monitored (and, of course, they could not obtain or use such evidence in the court proceedings, because such evidence would be a "state secret"). The court acknowledged that even though they could not prove the surveillance, the plaintiffs appeared to have established that their litigation activities have become more costly because of concern related to monitoring.

Shayana Kadidal, managing attorney for CCR's Guantánamo Project and counsel in the case, explained that their clients are "exactly the sort of people the government has said they're listening in on," adding that they believe a harm exists by the very fact that the program poses a risk to their communications.[23]

As a result, CCR cautioned clients and prospective witnesses that there was a possibility their telephone calls and emails were being monitored. Staff attorneys began using expensive and less effective substitutes for telephone and electronic communications, such as traveling overseas to meet witnesses in person or using less reliable foreign mail systems. Given the possibility of wiretapping, it wasn't just Guantánamo detainees who suffered under these constraints—all of CCR's clients experienced the chilling effects.

Kadidal noted the overall harm to society in monitoring privileged communications. The conversations CCR is really worried about, he says, are those between lawyers and their clients, and journalists with their sources. "If the administration can chill those sorts of conversations, they can really cut off a huge avenue for criticism of their policies."[24]

In *Amnesty v. Clapper*, another case filed on behalf of attorneys and other organizations (including members of the press) who engage in privileged telephone and electronic communications with individuals outside the United States, the ACLU challenged the 2008 FISA amendments. As with the warrantless wiretapping program cases, in February 2013 the Supreme Court held that the plaintiffs lacked standing to challenge the program, given that they could not establish that their communications were, or would be, monitored.

How Monitoring Lawyers Imperils Democracy

When people need the services of an attorney, they rightfully expect that their interactions will be held in confidence, and in particular, that information conveyed will not be shared with the state or with opposing counsel. Confidentiality between a lawyer and client, in conversations and in writings, has been a venerated cornerstone of the common law justice system for hundreds of years.[25] Related entitlements, equally honored, are the right of an accused to a zealous legal defense and the right of an attorney to decide whom to represent. These are perhaps most precious to individuals who have been accused of crimes against the United States or who hold viewpoints disfavored by the government.

Although the DOJ claims the monitoring will affect only a small number of people in prison, those who will be monitored are often those who harbor specific views about this country's policies and politics, a class of individuals uniquely vulnerable to state surveillance and repression. Intolerance for dissent is on the uptick as an increasingly militarized domestic intelligence infrastructure is emboldened to carry out operations against anyone critical of its policies. With the advent of the concept of "enemy combatants," American citizens may unwittingly find themselves in temporary detention and subject to eavesdropping merely for being outspoken.

Because they represented people with unpopular, even despised, viewpoints, Lynne Stewart, the People's Law Office, the National Lawyers Guild, and most likely the Center for Constitutional Rights and other progressive attorneys were spied on.

Lawyers are understandably concerned about the extent to which they can provide zealous representation to a person when they must also worry about avoiding prosecution themselves.[26] As the Lynne Stewart conviction shows, an attorney may be charged and convicted with aiding and abetting terrorism in the course of conducting routine counseling-related activities. And in the ultimate possible conflict of interest, a lawyer may be forced to provide testimony against the person he or she is defending and be required to disclose the content of their communications or face prosecution for contempt of court.

In the surveillance of attorneys, core principles of privacy, legal representation, due process, and assumption of innocence—once cornerstones that set the United States apart from totalitarian societies—are imperiled by the very institutions mandated to protect them.

CHAPTER 8

Spying on the Press

We're not going to subpoena reporters in the future.
We don't need to. We know who you're talking to.
—National Security Representative to Lucy
Dalglish, Executive Director, Reporters
Committee for Freedom of the Press[1]

The vaunted freedoms of the news media, the so-called "Fourth Estate," are not nearly as robust as most of the public would like to think. The Department of Justice reported that it issued media-related subpoenas in "approximately 143 matters" from 1991 to 2006.[2] While the DOJ said that only about twenty of the subpoenas were related to confidential sources, lawsuits brought in recent years by individuals or litigated by special prosecutors have involved subpoenaing more than twenty news outlets or journalists. In the case of Wen Ho Lee, for example, six reporters received subpoenas. In the Valerie Plame investigation at least five reporters received them.[3] Reflecting "the attitudes and intentions of governments towards media freedom in the medium or long term," the

United States ranked thirty-second in the 2013 Reporters Without Borders Press Freedom Index, a fall from its former rank of 20 on the 2010 list.[4]

Aggressive efforts to discover reporters' sources date back at least to the beginning of the CIA. The Commission on CIA Activities within the United States, in its 1975 Report to the President, noted, "Presidential concern was continually voiced, during every administration since the establishment of the CIA, that the sources of news leaks be determined and the leaks themselves stopped—by whatever means."[5] The commission identified two instances in which the telephones of "three newsmen were tapped in an effort to identify their source of sensitive intelligence information."[6] In three other cases, reporters were followed in a similar effort to uncover their sources. The investigations spanned the period of 1962 to 1972.

During the 1960s and 1970s, the FBI would only handle leak cases if issued a directive to do so by the attorney general. For this reason, the CIA engaged in leak case investigations by physically and electronically monitouring reporters.[7] More recently, federal prosecutor Patrick Fitzgerald sought the telephone records of *New York Times* reporters Judith Miller and Philip Shenon to find out who leaked information that tipped off two Islamic charities about planned federal raids on their offices in late 2001. From 2004 to 2006, the *Times* fought the request in court. A district judge ruled in the newspaper's favor, but a federal appellate court overturned that decision. Fitzgerald ultimately obtained the records when the Supreme Court declined to step in. No one was ever charged for the leak.

Modern-Day Tapping of Journalists

A two-time Pulitzer Prize winner and member of the American Academy of Arts and Sciences, James Risen is one of the nation's most respected journalists. He began writing for the *New York Times* in 1998, and his 2006 book, *State of War: The Secret History of the CIA and the Bush Administration*, was a national bestseller.[8] As U.S. print, electronic, and Internet outlets have come to be owned by a few large media conglomerates that have slashed budgets in order to maintain profits, Risen stands out as one of a vanishing breed: the investigative journalist.

He was also spied on by federal authorities.

Risen's reporting, among other things, exposed President George W. Bush's domestic wiretapping program and earned the journalist the 2006 Pulitzer Prize. The series sparked vigorous public discourse about the legality of the wiretapping program and led to a judicial inquiry. Arthur O. Sulzberger Jr., publisher of the *Times*, wrote to Risen personally, calling his reporting "an extraordinary asset to the paper" and "a central reason that our Washington report is admired by our readers—not to mention leaders around the nation and the world."[9]

State of War details the Bush administration's pressure on the CIA to torture detainees in secret prisons around the globe, and reveals the ways the administration ignored Saudi involvement in terrorism. The book lays bare the dysfunction of CIA intelligence operations on weapons of mass destruction in Iran, Iraq, and other counties.

Chapter 9 in particular drew the government's ire. It covers Operation Merlin, a 2000 intelligence program that Risen called "deeply flawed and mismanaged,"created for the purpose of destroying Iran's ability to develop a nuclear weapons program.[10]

Relentless Pressure to Divulge Sources

Just after *State of War* was published, the Department of Justice (DOJ) announced that it was investigating disclosures contained in the book. Attorney General Alberto Gonzales announced at a press conference that the DOJ was considering prosecuting members of the press under the Espionage Act, something that had never been done. Officials leaked information that journalists' telephone calls were being covertly monitored, fostering an atmosphere of fear among reporters writing about government misdeeds.

In January 2008, after conservative outcry and a statement from the president that called reporting of the wiretapping program "a shameful act,"[11] Risen received the first of three subpoenas calling on him to testify about his sources before a grand jury. Conservative protesters and bloggers called for the DOJ to prosecute Risen for espionage. The first grand jury dissolved before a judge acted on his motion to quash the subpoena; a judge quashed the second one; the third was served on May 24, 2011.[12] Later that year, a judge quashed the third subpoena.[13]

In capping the leak investigation and grand jury subpoenas of Risen, in 2011 the DOJ indicted former CIA clandestine officer Jeffrey Alexander Sterling for sharing classified information with Risen about the covert attempt to disrupt Iran's nuclear program. The indictment alleged that in April 2003, Risen contacted the CIA's public affairs director to say he was planning to write about the classified program. On April 30, Risen and Jill Abramson (Washington bureau chief for the *Times*) met with national security advisor Condoleezza Rice and CIA director George Tenet, who urged Risen and Abramson not to publish the article about Merlin, which the paper never did.[14]

"Back-Tracking" Calls, Monitoring Personal Records

Sterling's indictment was based on information that did not come from monitoring the former CIA agent: it came from spying on the journalist.

ABC News reported in 2006 that the FBI had confirmed it was tracking incoming and outgoing phone calls of journalists in leak investigations, without their knowledge, to determine the identities of confidential sources. *ABC News* reporters, according to the network's blotter, learned from a federal source that the government was examining the records of their calls.[15] The source noted that reporters were not being tracked in real time, suggesting "back-tracking" of old phone records. In addition to *ABC News*, the FBI sought telephone records from the

New York Times and the *Washington Post*, all pertaining to the Risen-related investigation of CIA leaks.

While Risen was researching *State of War*, the government obtained his credit reports and bank statements and monitored his email and telephone communications with Sterling.

DOJ regulations require that the attorney general sign off on subpoenas and requests for telephone records directed at members of the press, a restriction that does not seem to apply to travel, bank, or credit card records.[16]

The DOJ's covert acquisition of business records could expose a wide array of Risen's sources and confidential contacts—information that might fall beyond the initial investigation leading to Sterling's indictment. The aggressive pursuit of Risen reflects a growing constriction of freedom of the press, the kind that so often accompanies crises of national security.

The Hewlett-Packard Scandal: "Pretexting" to Spy on Journalists

Corporations, like government agencies, invade people's privacy and spy on reporters to determine their confidential sources.

Hewlett-Packard (HP), the world's largest vendor of personal computers, contracted with independent security experts from 2005 to 2006 to investigate journalists in order to find the source of an information leak. In a practice known as "pretexting," the investigators impersonated nine journalists, purportedly from the *New York Times*, the *Wall Street Journal, Business Week*, and *CNET*, to obtain their telephone records, Social Security numbers, call logs, billing records, dates of birth, and subscriber information. This data was used to gather clues on reporters' sources of negative coverage of HP and related matters.

In September 2006, *Newsweek* broke the spying story; that same month the House Committee on Energy and Commerce's Subcommittee on Oversight and Investigation conducted a hearing on HP's use of pretexting. Hewlett-Packard immediately retained the public relations firm Sitrick and Company to handle media relations during the scandal. Although Hewlett-Packard chairwoman Patricia Dunn said that she was unaware of the methods that investigators had used, she resigned the same month. Ann Baskins, HP's general counsel, quit a few days later, just hours before she appeared before the subcommittee. During the hearing, she pled the Fifth Amendment and refused to answer questions.

The committee chair, Representative Ed Whitfield (R-KY), began the proceedings by noting, "For over a year, the most senior levels of management at the company were designing and directing the investigation. This isn't a case of some out of control and overzealous contractor who was hired to conduct a search for a leaker."[17] He added that he found unconvincing HP's argument that it was unaware its consultants were unlawfully accessing confidential telephone records.[18]

The Florida-based private investigative company Action Research Group (ARG) deceived telephone carriers by misrepresenting their identities, claiming to be board members of HP, employees of HP, family members of HP board members, employees, and others affiliated with HP, as well as reporters and family members of reporters—all subjects of HP's internal investigation. ARG employees fooled the telephone carriers by giving part or all of the real subscriber's Social Security number. Grossing between $20,000 and $30,000 for its services, the company passed the information along to a third party that contracted directly with HP.[19] In 2012, Bryan Wagner, a private investigator with the firm engaged by HP, Eye in the Sky Investigations, was sentenced to three months in prison after pleading guilty in 2007 to conspiracy to commit identity theft, wire fraud, false representation of a Social Security number, and accessing a computer without authorization.

In addition to Wagner, Matthew and Joseph DePante of Action Research Group were charged with conspiracy to commit Social Security fraud in the Hewlett-Packard spy scandal. In 2012 the DePantes were sentenced to three years' probation for conspiring to falsely represent a Social Security number. They had obtained personal information for at least fourteen persons later identified as targets of HP's investigation, as well as nineteen other individuals.[20] In a settlement, Action Research Group was permanently barred from obtaining, marketing, or selling customer information derived from records obtained through pretexting. The group was also barred from using others to pretext.[21]

Before the Hewlett-Packard case, impersonation occupied a legal gray area. California had some laws loosely applicable to pretexting, but none existed on a federal level. In 2006, however, Congress passed, and the president signed, the Telephone Records and Privacy Protection Act, which made it a felony to use pretexting to obtain confidential telephone records.[22]

Reporters' Rights and Privileges

In the United States, most jurisdictions protect journalists' right to keep the identities of their sources confidential by means of statutes referred to as shield laws. Thirty-nine states and the District of Columbia have shield laws affording journalists some form of privilege against being compelled to produce confidential or unpublished information.[23] The laws generally establish greater protection to journalists than do the state or federal constitutions.

Similar to the attorney-client privilege, reporters' privilege suppresses evidence to preserve a confidential journalistic relationship. It stems from recognition that certain interests are of such value to society, and are so fragile when it comes to the effects of public exposure, that they should be shielded even in the course of criminal investigations. Members of the press cannot be effective as impartial chroniclers of events if their sources cannot trust that reporters will keep their identities confidential. Forced disclosure of confidential or unpublished sources and information will mean that fewer people will be willing to talk to reporters, ultimately reducing the flow of accurate and complete information to the public. The result is a less informed society. People who serve as sources are often particularly fearful of retaliation if the information they provide concerns issues of social consequence.

DOJ guidelines regulate the use of subpoenas against the press, stating that all reasonable attempts should be made to obtain information from alternative sources. Such subpoenas require approval from the attorney general. While the guidelines include language limiting the scope of the subpoena in reference to subject matter, time frame, and volume of unpublished material, they fall short of establishing a legally enforceable right. If prosecutors do not obtain approval from the attorney general, they are punished only by reprimand or other administrative disciplinary action.

In criminal cases, prosecutors argue that reporters, like other citizens, are obligated to provide relevant evidence concerning the commission of a crime. People who are defending themselves against criminal charges argue that a journalist has information that is essential to their case, and that the Sixth Amendment right to a fair trial outweighs any First Amendment right the reporter may have. Civil litigants may have no constitutional interest to assert, but will argue that nevertheless they are entitled to all evidence relevant to their case.

When asked to turn over notes, documents, or other unpublished material, journalists claim that subpoenas violate their First Amendment right to practice journalism without fear of state or private-sector interference. When journalists' efforts to quash subpoenas fail, they must decide between turning over a source and risking being held in contempt of court, facing penalties or imprisonment.

Most journalists feel an obligation to protect their confidential sources even if threatened with jail time. In 2006, twenty-four-year-old freelance journalist Josh Wolf was charged with contempt of court and jailed for refusing to testify before a federal grand jury or turn over unpublished videotapes and testimony that he recorded at a 2005 demonstration in San Francisco. He had sold some footage to a local news station, and the broadcast drew the attention of local and federal law enforcement agents. He served 226 days, longer than any journalist in U.S. history, for refusing to divulge source materials. Ultimately, he released the video outtakes to the public. In 2006 the Society of Professional Journalists named Wolf Northern California's 2006 Journalist of the Year. In 2011 he graduated from the University of California Berkeley School of Journalism.

When appeals have been exhausted, the decision to reveal a source is a difficult question of journalistic ethics, complicated by the possibility that a confidential source whose identity is revealed may try to sue the reporter and his or her news organization under a theory of promissory estoppel, similar to breach of contract. The U.S. Supreme Court has held that such suits do not violate the First Amendment rights of the media.[24]

Independent journalist Josh Wolf served 226 days in jail, from July 2006 to April 2007, for refusing to turn over video outtakes from a 2005 demonstration. PHOTO: MEL CAMPAGNA

Although the Supreme Court held in the 1972 case *Branzburg v. Hayes* that the First Amendment does not protect a journalist who has witnessed criminal activity from revealing his or her information to a grand jury, the court did recognize a qualified privilege for reporters balancing their First Amendment rights against the subpoenaing party's need for disclosure.[25] Courts should consider whether the information is relevant and material to the case, whether there exists a compelling and overriding interest in obtaining the information, and whether the information could be obtained from any source other than the media. In some cases, courts require a journalist to demonstrate that a promise was made to protect a source's confidentiality.

The DHS Media Monitoring Initiative

With the creation of the Department of Homeland Security came increased ways for the government to collect and retain personal information about members of the press. The DHS Office of Operations Coordination and Planning (OPS) and the Media Monitoring Initiative of the DHS National Operations Center (NOC) are authorized to gather and retain personal information from journalists, news anchors, and others who use traditional or social media in real time—in other words, anyone who uses social media and online networking platforms.

Under Homeland Security's definition of "personal identifiable information," such data may consist of "any information that permits the identity of an individual to be directly or indirectly inferred, including any information that is linked or linkable to that individual."[26] Previous guidelines provided that identifying data could only be collected under authorization set forth by written code, but new provisions mean that any reporter, whether well established, new, or independent, may be subject to information collection. Government officials who issue public statements and any private-sector personnel may be subject to this spying as well.

Intelligence gathering by Homeland Security's NOC Media Monitoring Initiative began in 2010, and the data is being shared with private-sector businesses and international third parties. According to the DHS: "OPS/NOC will share Media Monitoring Reports (MMRs) with Departmental and component leadership, private-sector and international partners where necessary, appropriate, and authorized by law to ensure that critical disaster-related information reaches government decision makers."[27]

Another effort is under way to constrict the media in its sharing of information to the public. In 2012, Senator Ron Wyden (D-OR) distinguished himself as the only Senate Select Committee on Intelligence member to vote against the Intelligence Authorization Act for Fiscal Year 2013, and in doing so prevented it from passing. The bill would greatly restrict news coverage of national security issues and would prevent former government employees who held top-secret, compartmented security clearances to wait one year before agreeing to provide commentary or analysis to media outlets.[28] It would afford intelligence agencies the ability to remove pension benefits from current or past employees whom the agency head determined were responsible for unauthorized disclosure of classified information. Wyden had expressed objection to this provision in the past because he felt it could be used as retaliation against whistle-blowers.[29]

Government and corporate surveillance of journalists, no matter what their medium, is an affront to the U.S. Constitution. Attempts to uncover the identity of confidential informants jeopardize the time-honored principle that whistle-blowers and other sources should be shielded when they share information with reporters. In order to keep the public informed, journalists must feel confident that their communications are free from government intrusion.

Even the *possibility* that the government may be listening in has a chilling effect on the conditions needed for a democratic society, particularly the capacity to keep government in check. State surveillance of journalists directly and aggressively undermines this capacity. Trusting relationships between citizens and journalists are crucial to delivering reliable information to the public and providing the essential information required to sustain a balance of power in which the armed state apparatus is the accountable, compliant servant of society, rather than the other way around.

The Constitutional Cost of Contracting

The U.S. government does not carry out all of its own intelligence operations. It hires private companies to do much of the work. In outsourcing, the disparate missions of government and capitalist corporations converge. One is mandated to serve and protect the entire U.S. population; the other is committed to producing profits for an exclusive group.

Government and corporate collaboration on intelligence work creates an immediate danger that public and private interests will be at odds, and that surveillance operations and the investigations they serve will privilege money and power over the rights of ordinary people. There is a strong possibility that influence and support from corporations will interfere with the integrity and impartiality of law enforcement undertakings. Equally disquieting is the potential for public policy to be influenced by contractors' desire to continue to fuel profits, as when, for example, corporations managing penal institutions lobby for longer prison sentences.

Contracting Intelligence Functions

Government use of private contractors reflects a shift from reactive to preemptive intelligence gathering and policing. Cyber-operations, data mining, and analysis comprise a good deal of the new intelligence frontier. The resulting explosion of data accessible for preemptively neutralizing emerging threats presents a daunting task for federal, state, and municipal police agencies. The definition of what constitutes a threat is constantly changing as well.

To compile and analyze massive amounts of surveillance, government law enforcement agencies depend on partnerships with private security firms, including multimillion-dollar contracts with private corporations. Since 9/11, the number of contractor facilities receiving National Security Agency clearance expanded from 41 in 2002 to 1,256 in 2006, revealing the extent to which non-government employees have access to classified information.[1] Military manufacturing companies such as Boeing, Booz Allen Hamilton, Northrop Grumman, and Lockheed Martin have created their own intelligence divisions.[2]

Private industry supplies a broad range of technologies and integrated systems for surveillance, intrusion detection, access control, personal identification numbers, smart cards, and video comparator systems (which enable the comparison of two or more video images). Since such equipment requires trained and qualified personnel to run it, corporations also provide personnel to run provided systems and technologies. One area in which the commercial sector has developed special expertise is cybersecurity.

The American Federation of Government Employees (AFGE) has raised objections to the government practice of regularly contracting out intelligence and surveillance operations to the private sector. From 2000 to 2012, Department of Defense (DoD) contract spending—much of which was supposed to be short term—more than doubled to over $150 billion. AFGE noted that the size of the department's civilian workforce has not changed during that time. In a statement on the Fiscal Year 2013 National Defense Authorization Act, AFGE wrote:

> The Pentagon has imposed a cap on the size of the civilian workforce—which prevents it from growing in excess of its complement in 2010. As DoD officials have acknowledged, this cap is forcing managers to use contractors instead of civilians because spending on contractors is uncapped. Declared one Army official in Congressional testimony from March 2012: "Cost-effective workforce management decisions ought to be based on allowing for the hiring of civilians to perform missions, rather than contractors, if the civilians will be cheaper. The lifting of the civilian workforce cap would restore this flexibility."[3]

What's Wrong with Outsourcing Military Contractors?

Reliance on contracting with corporations raises concerns about the effectiveness and legitimacy of U.S. intelligence gathering. Yet thorough analyses have not been conducted to identify and address weaknesses in the outsourcing of intelligence.

The country's leadership does not have a complete grasp of the contracting workforce and the issues germane to outsourcing, according to the Senate Select Committee on Intelligence in its 2008 Senate Intelligence Authorization bill. Legislation calling for more oversight passed both the Senate and the House but was vetoed by President Obama, and the attempt to override the veto in the House failed.[4] Oversight is basic to holding government accountable in any operation. When national security and civil liberties interests are involved, however, oversight is critical to keeping the country safe. The government's reliance on outsourcing and lack of accountability should be of profound concern to Americans. If the agencies tasked with protecting us are not aware of weakness, bias, or self-interest in contractor performance, how are we to trust and improve outsourced security?

To address the lack of information related to outsourcing, U.S. Representative Jan Schakowsky reintroduced the Stop Outsourcing Our Security Act to eliminate the use of private companies. The Act would prohibit the use of private contractors for intelligence, military, and several other functions. It would also call for greater transparency over existing contracts by increasing reporting requirements and congressional oversight.[5]

Another problem stems from the fact that the rapid growth of contracting has left a dent in federal intelligence staffing that may bring new vulnerabilities to the staffs of intelligence agencies.[6] As fundamental functions are taken over by contractors, certain operations may be compromised. This is especially so if contracts are awarded based on factors other than expertise.

Conflict of interest and waste of financial resources are also more likely when contractors are used. According to former intelligence officer Frank Naif, major intelligence contractors regularly assign managers to proposals based on their personal relationships with government contracting officials or decision-makers—even though such managers might be otherwise poorly qualified. Naif elaborates: "In numerous instances that I recall, CIA contracting personnel maintained various levels of close, continuing personal relationships with contractor personnel, ranging from friendship to marriage. Add to that the CIA's practice of awarding contracts in secret, with minimal opportunity for outside review or disclosure, and the result is an environment ripe for corruption, fraud, and waste."[7]

A 2009 Government Accountability Office (GAO) study found the ability of the DHS Federal Protective Service (FPS) to safeguard the nation's federal facilities to be hampered by weaknesses in its contract security guard program.[8] FPS employs 1,200 full-time staff and oversees approximately 14,000 private guards at roughly 9,000 federal facilities. The annual cost of the guard program is roughly $1 billion and represents the largest line item in the organization's budget. The GAO reported that FPS does not fully ensure that guards receive necessary training and certifications. It also found that FPS has limited assurance that guards comply with post orders (the rules security officers must follow at a given post) once they have been deployed to a federal facility. A host of serious infractions was discovered, including one armed guard falling asleep at his nighttime post after having taken a painkiller. Another guard failed to identify, or did not X-ray, a box of semi-automatic handguns.[9] Investigators found "substantial security vulnerabilities" in the guard program and were able to pass undetected through access points at ten federal facilities in four major cities they tested.[10]

Local Private-Public Partnerships

Over the past quarter century, efforts have been made to increase coordination between police and private security and to more effectively enlist private actors in supporting police work. For example, the New York Police Department established NYPD SHIELD, a program that trains private industry to defend against terrorism and allows private security managers to access and share information with the police department. Its Operation Nexus is a nationwide business network that reports "suspicious business encounters."[11]

The NYPD's Area Police/Private Security Liaison

(APPL) is the largest cooperative program in the country. Founded in 1986 by the NYPD commissioner and four former NYPD chief security directors, it has grown from thirty security organizations to more than one thousand at present. APPL's goals are to increase private-public co-operation, exchange information, and diminish the mutual distrust that existed between sworn police officers and private security officers. Toward that end, the NYPD training curriculum was revised to cover private security awareness, and police were invited to visit private security organizations. The police academy also instituted a course on police science for private security first-line supervisors. Private security and police meet regularly to discuss crime trends and to share information. APPL holds monthly and annual meetings, keeps an inventory of private-sector closed-circuit TV installations, monitors security-related legislation, conducts training sessions for security personnel, and brings private security representatives into the NYPD command and control center during some emergencies.[12]

Such partnerships are mutually beneficial to state and business, and both are quick to tout the benefits of such collaboration—and to downplay the dangers.

Corporations Fund Local Policing Initiatives

Government relies heavily on private industry to conduct both civilian and military intelligence gathering. According to the Office of the Director of National Intelligence, in 2007 contractor personnel comprised over 25 percent of overall intelligence personnel. Of approximately 100,000 civilian and military personnel, up to 37,000 are private contractors.[13] Payments to private security contracts are likely in the tens of billions of dollars. In the first disclosure of funding being sought for civilian intelligence, in 2012 the Obama administration asked for $55 billion for the CIA and other civilian intelligence agencies (as opposed to military intelligence, funding for which was $27 billion in 2010).[14]

A few examples shed light on the close relationship between corporations, local police departments, and other authorities—and raise obvious questions. Will police put the interests of their Wall Street patrons above those who might criticize or protest those patrons? Is it possible to be impartial toward someone who tenders massive amounts of cash, goods, and services? Whatever the answers, corporate-police relationships risk undermining public trust in law enforcement, trust that is necessary for effective police operations and for the legitimacy of government agencies in a democratic society.

The New York Police Department partnered with Microsoft to design and develop the Domain Awareness System, announced in 2012. It aggregates and analyzes existing public safety data streams in real time from camera feeds, 911 calls, and mapped crime patterns, providing NYPD investigators and analysts with a comprehensive view of potential threats and criminal activity. Analysts are notified of suspicious packages and vehicles, and NYPD personnel can search for suspects using technologies such as smart cameras and license plate readers. The city will receive 30 percent of gross revenues on Microsoft's future sales of the system to other governments.[15]

Bank of America pledged in 2011 to donate ten houses to the City of Detroit's Project 14 (police code for "return to normal operation") program, which sells houses to police officers with as little as a $1,000 down payment.[16]

Beginning in 2010, JPMorgan Chase & Co. contributed $4.6 million in cash, goods, and services to the New York Police Foundation. They explained, "We are helping to strengthen security in the Big Apple through a partnership with the New York City Police Department — the world's largest police department. Valued at over $4.6 million, our donation of technology, time and skills to improve the NYPD's technology infrastructure was the largest in the history of the New York City Police Foundation. Through our Technology for Social Good program, we donated 1,000 personal computers across the police department, 2,000 new patrol car laptops, and provided funding to ensure that all of the equipment was properly installed and functioning. We also donated funding for critical programming of in-car Cisco mobile access routers and the implementation of structured network cabling across seventy-six locations and 29 police precincts."[17] Other donors to the New York Police Foundation included Goldman Sachs, NewsCorp, and Barclays PLC.

Motorola Solutions Foundation has provided support for more than two decades to the Police Executive Research Forum in Washington, D.C. PERF's executive director Chuck Wexler wrote in one report, "It is no exaggeration to say that Motorola's support over the last 20 years through the Critical Issues series has helped produce real advances in the field of policing, in areas ranging from crime reduction and prevention of gang- and gun-related violence to hot-button issues such as immigration enforcement and management of special events."[18]

IBM, along with business partners Firetide and Genetec, helped the City of Chicago Office of Emergency Management and Communications establish a citywide video security system. Launched in 2008 as part of Chicago's Operation Virtual Shield, the surveillance system is designed to "capture, monitor, and fully index video from surveillance cameras. The software used to run the system will be able to recognize not only specific license plates, but also vehicle descriptions, and even patterns of behavior."[19] Hundreds of new surveillance cameras were installed, linked with 150,000 pre-existing cameras. The cameras can zoom in to monitor small objects from afar and use facial-recognition capabilities enabling computers to search for individual faces. The cameras have automatic tracking capabilities allowing them to continuously monitor an individual or vehicle in motion by jumping from one camera to another.

Financial institutions are especially invested in coordinating security with local law enforcement agencies. At a 2009 U.S. Senate hearing, Police Commissioner

Ray Kelly testified that the NYPD's "vast public private partnership" with corporations in the financial district afforded the department access to hundreds of private surveillance cameras, and that footage from these cameras is monitored in a center in downtown Manhattan.[20]

Working in cooperation with the Secret Service, the FBI, and Interpol, Microsoft announced in 2003 an Anti-Virus Reward Program, initially providing $5 million to assist law enforcement in the arrest and conviction of individuals unleashing worms and viruses on the Internet.[21]

General Electric provided funding in 2003 to purchase closed-circuit TV cameras for MacArthur Park that linked to the Los Angeles Police Department through the Internet. Motorola contributed $1.2 million in identical funding.[22]

The goals of maximizing profits and of stifling public scrutiny, criticism, and dissent often go hand in hand, creating a corporate interest in facilitating crackdowns on free speech, advocacy, and organizing. The lawsuit *Rodriguez et al. v. Winski et al.*, brought on behalf of individuals involved in the Occupy movement, alleged that private corporations played a significant role in curtailing free speech. It asserted that an agreement was formed between the City of New York, the New York City Metropolitan Transportation Authority, Mayor Michael Bloomberg, Police Commissioner Kelly, and several private corporations to deprive protesters of their constitutional right to access public spaces. The complaint alleged that Mitsui and Brookfield Properties Management, the custodian of Zuccotti Park where Occupiers were encamped, colluded with authorities to remove ongoing free events and gatherings from public space, and that JPMorgan and the NYPD worked together to deny Occupy participants access to public space at One Chase Manhattan Plaza.

A snug alignment between the capitalist economy and all levels of the aggressive domestic security grid should be of concern to Americans. When individual rights compete with corporate interests, will the police enforce the Constitution as they are sworn to do? Or will corporate gifts of cash, goods, and services buy the power to determine what acts of free speech and assembly are considered threats, and what might be done, both pre-emptively and reactively, to eliminate them? Increased reliance by local police departments on corporate contributions of equipment and technology would seem to sway allegiance from ensuring the public welfare to protecting the interests of a few.

Computers Can't Commit Crimes

It sounds like scene direction for a film: "Maria wakes up, grabs the remote control, and tunes in to an alternative-rock radio station. She gets up, goes to the kitchen, grabs a bottle of water, and goes to the third bedroom, which doubles as the workout room. She runs on the treadmill for thirty minutes."[1] Maria's morning is actually part of a short narrative that some corporations use to help develop consumer marketing strategies. At a glance, retailers view information about prospective patrons categorized according to stages in their lives, such as getting married, having a child, or preparing for retirement.[2] Descriptive summaries include such specifics as the amount of time people spend online shopping for flat-screen televisions to the kind of beer they drink.

Maria is in the group of financially comfortable young adults who spend money on items for themselves, their children, or their friends' children. They grew up in the wake of 9/11, after the debut of the television show *American Idol*. They go to bed around 11:30 p.m. after a half hour of Pilates and watching *Scrubs* reruns on television.

This so-called "Life Stage" segmentation system, PersonicX Classic Cluster Perspectives, is the brainchild of Acxiom. Known as a data aggregator, Acxiom is one of many corporations comprising a multibillion-dollar industry that collects and sells personal data to third parties for targeted advertising and other purposes. Clients of data aggregators include financial service, direct marketing, technology, telecommunications, insurance, media, retail, health care, and travel companies. As *New York Times* reporter Natasha Singer has written of Acxiom, "It peers deeper into American life than the F.B.I. or the I.R.S. . . . If you are an American adult, the odds are that it knows things like your age, race, sex, weight, height, marital status, education level, politics, buying habits, household health worries, vacation dreams—and so on."[3]

The U.S. government is also a client.

Why does our government contract with a firm that supports market research?

For the immense amount of data it can provide and the capacity to sort and analyze this data. Since the advent of the Total Information Awareness program, conceived shortly after 9/11, and the creation of fusion centers (established between 2003 and 2007 under the Department of Homeland Security to increase information sharing between federal and local agencies),[4] data mining has been the gold standard for spying on democracy. In contracting with government agencies, the private sector enables the Department of Justice (DOJ) and the FBI to access a treasure trove of personal information on U.S. citizens. This allows them to sidestep the restrictions of the Privacy Act of 1974, enacted to safeguard privacy by protecting records that can be retrieved by personal identifiers such as name or Social Security number. The Act also prohibits the government from gathering information for one purpose and using it for another.[5]

Consumers are largely in the dark about the extent to which their personal data is being shared among different industries and government agencies and for what purpose. What is known, however, is that businesses and other organizations in the United States expend more than $2 billion annually to purchase personal information on individuals.[6]

Computer Matching: From Government Fraud Detection to Corporate Data Aggregation

Computer matching is the integration and comparing of electronic data records from two or more sources. Software enables computer searches and record linking based on a configuration of common elements such as names, addresses, and Social Security numbers.

The U.S. government first used computer matching in the 1970s to compare recipients of Aid to Families with Dependent Children with state wage information to find out if government employees were inappropriately receiving benefits. Project Match, as it was called, identified thousands of employees who appeared to be ineligible for welfare. It yielded such a huge volume of information,

Works Progress Administration: "Aid to dependent children keeps families together." NATIONAL ARCHIVES AND RECORDS ADMINISTRATION, COLLECTION FDR-PHOCO: FRANKLIN D. ROOSEVELT LIBRARY PUBLIC DOMAIN PHOTOGRAPHS, 1882–1962

however, that officials were unable to conduct follow-up to determine the accuracy of the data.[7]

At the time Project Match was under way, the Carter administration was conducting a privacy initiative and grappling with how to balance the competing interests of privacy and law enforcement. As computer matching grew, guidelines were created in 1982 to protect the privacy rights of individuals. The federal Office of Management and Budget mandated that once matches were completed, files would either be destroyed or be returned to the originating agency.[8]

The official sanctioning of data sharing between federal government agencies became codified in the Computer Matching and Privacy Protection Act of 1988.[9] The act amended, and essentially undermined, the 1974 Privacy act by laying out procedures for federal agencies to perform computer matching. The 1988 act created some protections for applicants and recipients of federal benefits and sought to ensure a level of data integrity. It called for reports about matching programs to be submitted to Congress and the Office of Management and Budget and for the verification of match findings prior to any reductions or denials of benefits. But while the act provides that applicants and those receiving benefits are to be notified that their records are subject to matching, the institutionalization of federal computer matching seems antithetical to the privacy protection part of the act's title. Two years later, Congress enacted the Computer Matching and Privacy Protection Amendments of 1990, to further explain the law's due process provisions.[10]

Surveillance of the general public is accomplished in large part by computer matching. One form of matching entails checking individuals and property against watch lists such as the Treasury Enforcement Communication System, which tracks people leaving or entering the country. Another is the National Crime Information Center collection of criminal records.[11]

Disclosure of data from one entity to another is called cross-checking and may be done informally or formally, often without the knowledge or permission of the individual involved. Cross-checking may occur, for example, during the application process for a loan or employment, or during "front-end verification" (verifying information before a particular service or benefit is provided) takes place. A wide range of database services are available to prospective landlords, employers, and others for this sort of activity. But the technology may be used in ways that cross the line from legitimate purposes to invading privacy for political reasons. After 9/11, many librarians were asked to share Internet sign-in lists and names of books borrowed. In response to FBI requests, the IRS and Social Security Administration searched thousands of their files.

Corporate data aggregators aggressively gather personal data from hundreds of sources for the purpose of selling this information to third parties. They take source information from a range of public records and databases, including voter registration lists, court records, and merchant records, and assemble them into reports that can be sold to businesses and government agencies.

Experian's Data Select is one good example. It is an online marketing list-rental system that touts a marketing analytics team comprised of PhDs, statisticians, and corporate marketers who "take data and create intelligence" enabling corporate customers to develop and execute marketing strategies.[12] Experian notes on its website that because consumers have more and more options for what they purchase and from whom, savvy marketers have "adjusted their communication strategies to become nothing short of customer obsessed" and rely on Experian Marketing for tools to connect with customers. For example, Experian describes partnering with megastore BestBuy to build a larger database for direct-mail marketing. Experian "enhanced" upward of 50 million customer records, using data culled from more than 3,500 public and private data sources, including the individual's age, work information, and data describing specific purchases.[13]

In recent years, Experian has acquired several other businesses to amass a wide array of information-gathering tools, including Hitwise, an Internet monitor providing daily, online consumer behavior reports; Tallyman, a collection-and-recovery software management system; RentBureau, which allows Experian to collect updated rent histories from property management companies nationwide every twenty-four hours, and makes them available to property managers; and SearchAmerica and Medical Present Value, Inc., healthcare payments data and software providers. Experian then markets products such as "Experian Healthcare," which provides a "suite of patient access, claims and contract management and collections products and consultative services" (or "financial intelligence") to healthcare providers.[14]

Over time, the transfer of large amounts of account data from the account provider to the aggregator's server could transition into a comprehensive profile of a user, detailing his or her financial transactions and balances, as well as travel history. As concerns about data protection increase, data aggregators are under scrutiny for using such data for their own purposes and for sharing it with website operators and other third parties, including the government. In addition, a high rate of error exists in many of aggregator companies' reports. A study of Axciom and ChoicePoint found at least one error in 100 percent of their reports. Errors in biographical information were very high; Acxiom's error rate was 67 percent and ChoicePoint's was 73 percent.[15]

Government Contracts with Private Data Aggregators

The aggregator ChoicePoint has said that it has contracts with at least thirty-five government agencies. In a 2006 hearing, Senator Patrick Leahy (D-VT) criticized the Department of Justice and its FBI division for entering into a five-year, $12 million contract with ChoicePoint, which contracted to provide investigation analysis software to the bureau. Alluding to a data breach of the company in 2005, Leahy said, "I consider them the poster child for lax security protection."[16] A day before Leahy's comments, the Government Accountability Office issued a report revealing that some of the data resellers contracting with the DOJ and other federal agencies (at a cost of approximately $30 million in 2005) were not in compliance with federal rules governing data collection.[17]

At the same hearing, the FBI's management expertise was called into question. Senator Richard Shelby (R-AL), chairman of the Justice Subcommittee of the Senate Appropriations Committee, noted that in March 2005 the FBI abandoned a costly case-management project, "Triology Virtual Case File System," in which it invested $170 million over a four-year period. One year after giving up on Trilogy, the FBI entered into a contract with Lockheed Martin Corporation to design a replacement case-management and information-sharing system for $425 million. Robert Mueller, director of the FBI, explained that Lockheed Martin would be subjected to audits.[18]

Under the USA PATRIOT Act, Americans' medical, banking, educational, business, travel, credit card, and magazine subscription records are available to the FBI if an agent claims that the records are required for an "authorized investigation" related to international terrorism. Previously, an agent needed to show reason to deem the subject a foreign agent before gaining such broad access to their information. Citizens also face increased scrutiny in conducting financial transactions. The private sector has been required to file currency transactions and reports since 1992, as well as "suspicious activity reports" whenever transactions are not the sort that a particular customer would "normally be expected to engage in," or when a transaction would be relevant to the possible violation of a law or regulation.[19]

Attempts at data aggregation regulation are imperfect shields against privacy invasion and intelligence operations. With the government's increasingly wide latitude to spy on citizens absent any evidence of criminal activity, the contractual relationships between data brokers and government agencies raise the specter of a minimally regulated mass surveillance apparatus.

Regulation of Data Resellers

Data aggregation raises several liability and security issues.

"By combining data from numerous offline and online sources, data brokers have developed hidden dossiers on almost every U.S. consumer," according to a letter from the Congressional Privacy Caucus sent in July 2012 to nine of the country's largest resellers of consumer information (also known as data brokers).[20] The Federal Trade Commission's March 2012 report on consumer privacy indicated that the commission planned to focus attention on data resellers, companies that to date have skirted regulation. In December 2012 the FTC announced that it was opening an inquiry into nine data brokers, and issued administrative subpoenas to eBureau, Intelius, Peek-You, Acxiom, and others.

Two years earlier, the FTC launched an investigation into the practices of more than a dozen data brokers. One of them, Spokeo, later entered into a settlement for violating federal law by selling consumers' personal information for employment screening. Enforcement actions against several other data resellers are pending.

Data brokers may skirt the letter of the law in many cases. The Fair Credit Reporting Act regulates enterprises defined as consumer-reporting agencies, which bundle personal data and create consumer reports to sell to employers, credit agencies, and other businesses. But many data brokers are not subject to regulation under this law, either because they are not primarily engaged in credit reporting or because they conduct data aggregation separately from the credit-reporting business.

Responsibilities to protect aggregated data were established by the Financial Modernization Act of 1999, also known as the Gramm-Leach-Bliley Act, which requires companies defined as financial institutions—a broad category under the law—to guarantee the security and confidentiality of personal data for customers. In implementing Gramm-Leach-Bliley, the FTC issued a Safeguards Rule, mandating that financial institutions have written measures in place to keep customer information secure.

The Health Insurance Portability and Accountability Act of 1996 (HIPAA), among other things, protects personally identifiable health information held by certain entities. Likewise, the Sarbanes-Oxley Act of 2002, which mandates expanded financial control audits of public companies, also addresses information security.

Mandatory Data-Retention Policies and Backdoor Access

The George W. Bush administration asked the European Union (EU) to require mandatory, routine data-retention regimes among communication service providers. Yet there are no mandatory data-retention laws in the United

States or even in the Convention on Cybercrime. In 2006, the European Union enacted a Directive on Mandatory Retention of Communications Traffic Data, mandating that member states require ISPs and telecommunications providers operating in Europe to keep subscribers' telephone numbers, location information, IP addresses, and other Internet traffic data for a minimum of six months and up to two years.[21] The directive requires operators to make the information available to law enforcement authorities, if requested, for the purposes of investigating, detecting, and prosecuting crime and terrorism.

In 2006, FBI Director Robert Mueller III and Attorney General Alberto Gonzales held a private meeting at the Department of Justice with telecommunications industry representatives to urge them to keep subscriber and network data for two years, claiming that retention was needed for child pornography and terrorism cases. Service providers are increasingly being mandated to restructure systems to allow state agents to monitor electronic communications. Since 1994, landline phone companies have been required to design their equipment according to the FBI's specifications, to enable law enforcement to better wiretap customer communications. The Federal Communications Commission, succumbing to pressure from the DOJ, the FBI, and the Drug Enforcement Administration, in 2006 issued an order requiring providers of Voice over Internet Protocol (VoIP) service to comply with the Communications Assistance for Law Enforcement Act.

The United States currently has no mandatory data-retention law. Nevertheless, if providers of public electronic communications or remote computing services do store electronic communications or communications records by their own policies, the government can obtain access to that stored information under the Stored Communications Act. The SCA was enacted as part of the Electronic Communications Privacy Act in 1986.[22] It provides for mandatory preservation of stored data for up to 180 days if the provider is asked to do so by the government.[23]

There is inconsistency about data-retention policies even among government agencies. In early 2011, a hearing convened by the House Committee on the Judiciary's Subcommittee on Crime, Terrorism, and Homeland Security considered issues related to data-retention policies of Internet service providers and Web-hosting companies. Testimony from a Department of Justice representative indicated that gaps or insufficiencies in data-retention policies can impede criminal investigations. While no legislation was proposed during the hearing, the DOJ has recommended that Congress enact mandatory data-retention requirements to assist law enforcement and prosecutors. In response, advocates for the public cite the dangers to privacy in businesses' storing of confidential consumer information.[24] While previous data-retention legislation would have required some Internet companies to keep Internet protocol addresses for a period of two years, advocates point out that such proposals conflict with other government bodies' suggestions calling for storage of less consumer information. The Federal Trade Commission's proposed privacy framework, for example, recommends that industry keep data "for only as long as they have a specific and legitimate business need to do so." These dynamics provide a glimpse into the degree of influence, if not control, that government intelligence and law enforcement agencies wish to exercise in the gathering and retention of personal data by private corporations.

Risks Associated with Aggregated Data

Storing and managing aggregated electronic data poses many privacy and security risks. It heightens the potential to compromise the identity and privacy of individuals if the security for storing aggregated data is inadequate. With the use of technology comes a high rate of inaccurate information entry, something that even the government has acknowledged with respect to profiles in the National Crime Information Center (NCIC) database; the errors pose significant risks to innocent people in cases of mistaken identity.[25]

In 2012 Experian notified the New Hampshire Department of Justice of a data breach in which unauthorized third parties may have gained access to consumer credit reports over a sixteen-month period. The information compromised in the Experian case included partial Social Security numbers, bank account numbers, and sensitive personal information and financial information from consumer credit reports.

In 2003, the FBI published a Federal Register notice and final rule exempting the NCIC database from the Privacy Act of 1974 requirement that agencies "maintain all records which are used by the agency in making any determination about any individual with such accuracy, relevance, timeliness, and completeness as is reasonably necessary to assure fairness to the individual in the determination,"[26] even though an earlier Bureau of Justice Statistics study of NCIC determined that search by name lacks reliability and that "criminal records files may be inaccurate or incomplete, especially in case disposition information."[27] The Electronic Privacy Information Center wrote a letter on behalf of nearly ninety organizations urging the Office of Management and Budget to evaluate the effect the decision would have on records integrity and require the bureau to reverse the rule.[28]

The NCIC system provides more than 80,000 law enforcement agencies with access to data. The Privacy Act established a Code of Fair Information Practice for the gathering, maintenance, use, and sharing of personally identifiable information about individuals, maintained and controlled by federal agencies. The act prohibits the disclosure of information absent the written consent of the individual involved unless the disclosure falls under one of twelve statutory exceptions.[29]

The DOJ's discharge of the FBI's duty to ensure the accuracy and completeness of the more than 39 million records maintained in the NCIC database poses danger to both privacy and law enforcement. Acknowledgment of the rate of error in personal data was echoed by the Office of the Inspector General in its June 2005 Audit Report, which stated that the Terrorist Screening Center could not ensure the completeness or accuracy of its information, finding instances in which the database both omitted names that should have been included and included inaccurate data on those who were listed.[30]

Technological advances enable the public and private sectors to cast a broad spy net on Americans, making possible with a few keystrokes the scanning of vast amounts of data in violation of the privacy of millions of people. Passage of the USA PATRIOT Act paved the way for increased, highly invasive spying power by government agencies and corporations. At the heart of this trend is the ability to access thousands of databases and to conduct searches on the immense amount of private information amassed through daily interactions with corporations and government agencies.

Long before computers were widely available or had the power to process voluminous quantities of data with extreme speed, the public at large was apprehensive that technology might violate privacy and leave the citizenry vulnerable to spying and crime. In 1981, to allay such concerns, IBM ran an advertisement for computers that read as follows:

> The computer didn't do it.
> Computers can't commit crimes.
> But they can be misused . . .

True, there's probably no such thing as total security. But with proper precautions, computers can be more than just safe places to keep information.
They may well be the safest.

Three decades later, no proper precautions exist to protect the public against computer-related spying or crime. As computers have changed the daily life of Americans, they have also subtly altered our notions of privacy and security. Reliance on computers has enabled retailers, hospitals, insurance providers, and others to amass personal information on every detail of our lives. A shift in policing strategies and government policy makes this data increasingly available to law enforcement. Combined with weakening protections against domestic spying, this shift in the use of technology makes the very notion of privacy seem naïve. As expectations of privacy wane, the foundation of political liberty is weakened. Citizens and democracy suffer the consequences.

CHAPTER 11

Celestial Eyes

Nerds, engineers, and readers of *Model Airplane News* may have been tempted by the cash prizes offered in a 2011 U.S. Department of Defense–sponsored competition to design small, unmanned aerial vehicles (UAV):

> Put on your mad scientist thinking cap! If you can come up with a design for a quiet UAV that can fit in a backpack and operate for 3 hours, you could win $100,000 in a competition sponsored by the Defense Advanced Research Projects Agency (DARPA) and Naval Warfare Systems Center Atlantic. . . . The winning team gets that big check and a chance to showcase its design in an overseas military exercise! Additionally, the winning team will work with a government-selected UAV manufacturer to produce a small quantity for warfare experimentation.[1]

Unmanned aerial vehicles, or drones, increasingly dominate military strategy. Remote-controlled, they come in all shapes and sizes and can be equipped with a wide range of features, such as heat sensors, motion detectors, and license plate readers. Although developed for military applications, drones are being adapted for civilian security purposes and in settings deemed too dangerous for piloted aircraft.

Drones are yet another piece of equipment used to spy on Americans. The rush is on to develop sophisticated, miniature stealth drones—some shaped like birds or mosquitoes—with advanced spying capabilities, in an environment where extensive domestic spying is accepted by law enforcement. Drone manufacturers and drone lobbyists have successfully pushed to open the U.S. airspace to drones, all but ensuring that whatever positive uses drones may have are matched, and likely exceeded, by insidious ones.

It All Began with a Kite

The progression of aerial surveillance traces back to kite flying. Since its invention in China over two thousand years ago, the kite has been a tool of war as much as a plaything. In roughly 200 B.C., General Han Hsin ingeniously used a kite to measure the distance necessary to tunnel under the walls of an opposing fortress. Kites were used to send instructions to the Korean fleet that repelled a Japanese invasion in the sixteenth century. And, according to legend, large kites in ancient China and Japan carried soldiers aloft for surveillance and sniping.

For peacetime use, Frenchman Arthur Batut, using

a camera affixed with string, adapted the kite for aerial photographs in 1889, followed by Englishman Douglas Archibald who used kites to measure wind velocity in 1893. An American, Corporal William A. Eddy, realized the potential of the camera kite for warfare surveillance, writing, "The mid-air kite camera would be useful in time of war."[2] During the Spanish-American War, he took hundreds of surveillance photographs from a kite outfitted with a shutter release attached to its string. These first aerial wartime surveillance photographs afforded invaluable intelligence to the United States about the adversaries' positions and battlements.

In the 1930s British movie star Reginald Denny, a lifelong aviation enthusiast who had served in the Royal Flying Corps during World War I, founded Reginald Denny Industries. With business partners, he opened a model-plane shop in 1934 that would evolve into the Radioplane Company and, later, into the multibillion-dollar military manufacturer Northrop Grumman. Denny recruited a team of radio engineers from Lockheed Corporation to develop large, remote-controlled airplanes. They produced highly successful, fast UAVs known as OQ Targets, which the U.S. Air Force ordered by thousands. The radio-controlled OQ drones, which took off via a large slingshot and landed with help from a long parachute, were used to train anti-aircraft gunners.[3]

The Development of Surveillance Drones

The Department of Defense refers to unmanned aerial vehicles as an essential element in "information dominance," citing their use historically for surveillance and reconnaissance.[4] The first covert surveillance drone was an AQM-34 Ryan Firebee, created in 1960 by the U.S. Air Force. Engineers were able to reduce the jet-powered Q-2C Firebee's radar footprint by fitting a screen over the engine's air intake, placing radar-absorbing blankets on the fuselage sides, and painting it with specially designed antiradar paint. More than a thousand of the AQM-34 Ryan Firebees, also called Lightning Bugs, were deployed during the Vietnam War. The Lightning Bugs were used to activate North Vietnamese antiaircraft missiles and send signals to manned aircraft before being destroyed.[5] Firebee drones carrying conventional cameras were used for reconnaissance; later they were deployed for night photography missions and surface-to-air missile radar detection.[6]

At the height of the Cold War, reliable reconnaissance images were in great demand. The CIA commissioned Lockheed to create a high-speed, ultra-stealth UAV, impervious to attack. The D-21 was the fastest UAV yet and rode on the back of a piloted Lockheed M-12 mother aircraft. When released, it could reach Mach 4 and had an impressive range of three thousand miles. Covered in Lockheed's signature plastic antiradar coating (a precursor to that used on the Stealth Fighter and Stealth Bomber), it operated at eighty thousand feet.

In the 1960s and 1970s the Pentagon acquired nearly one thousand UAVs but their inadequate command, control, and communications capacities limited the kinds of missions they could handle. After the Israeli Air Force used UAVs in Lebanon in 1982, the U.S. Navy added UAV capabilities, and in 1987 the Reagan administration asked for increased funding.[7] The United States acquired the Pioneer from Israel for use against Iraq in Operation Desert Storm.[8] During the Balkans conflict the air force conducted surveillance missions with Predator drones.[9] In the 1990s, global positioning system navigation, computerized mission planning, and satellite communications improved significantly, making it feasible to operate drones remotely. During the Clinton administration, interest in UAVs like the Predator offered an attractive way to conduct reconnaissance.[10]

The Predator continues to be a mainstay of the U.S. Air Force. It can remain airborne for up to forty hours and can transmit video and radar images to stations on the ground. Although originally intended as a surveillance vehicle, the Predator is a lethal-weapon delivery system. Laser designators allowed the Predator to guide weapons from other aircraft before it was equipped with its own missiles.[11] The Predator and missile combination was first tested in 2001.[12] It is believed that armed Predators were used to conduct strikes in Afghanistan in 2002, so that if granted permission to release weapons, drone operators could shoot at suddenly emerging targets.

Members of the USAF 11th Reconnaissance Squadron in Indian Springs, Nevada, perform pre-flight maintenance checks on a Predator drone before a November 2001 Afghanistan mission.
PHOTO: U.S. AIR FORCE, BY TECH. SGT. SCOTT REED

Opening Public Airways to Drones and to Domestic Spying

Although we largely associate them with faraway theaters of war, drones are becoming a fixture in U.S. airspace. In 2012, the Federal Aviation Administration (FAA) gave clearance for more drones to fill civilian skies in years to come.

Adding impetus to this trend, Congress provided the drone industry and law enforcement with $64 billion to expedite drone deployment, tasking the FAA with determining how to use drones commercially before 2015. Rumors are flying about an FAA prediction that somewhere in the vicinity of thirty thousand MQ-9 Reaper drones will be in operation in U.S. skies by 2020, although a spokesperson for the agency says she does not know where that number originated. She suggested it came from an aerospace industry forecast that as many as thirty thousand drones could fly worldwide by 2018.[13]

The Electronic Frontier Foundation filed a Freedom of Information request with the FAA in April 2011 asking for copies of the certificates of authorization (COAs) and the special air-worthiness certificates that the FAA issues to any agency that wants to fly a drone in the United States. The COAs apply to public entities including state and local law enforcement, universities, and the government. At that time, the FAA indicated that eighty-one entities had applied for COAs, seventeen of which were local police and sheriffs' offices.[14] (A total of 327 COAs were active as of February 15, 2013.)[15] In fact, the FAA has indicated that, "one of the most promising potential uses for SUAs [small unmanned aircraft systems] is in law enforcement."[16] It continued: "The FAA is working with urban police departments in major metropolitan areas as well as national public safety organizations on test programs involving unmanned aircraft."[17]

Law enforcement agencies in a dozen jurisdictions have used or are using surveillance drones. In 2011, the City of Miami Police Department announced that they were the first force in the country to use drones with cameras to keep a watchful eye on the city. Orange County,

Florida, experimented with two surveillance drones over Orlando in 2012. The Montgomery County Police Department in Texas was the first in that state to obtain an FAA certificate of authorization to deploy surveillance drones; it applied in 2010, was approved, and renewed the certificate in 2012.[18]

In Little Rock, Arkansas, the police department has a Rotomotion SR30 with the ability to carry zoom and infrared cameras. Designed to track objects, it can fly autonomously. The FAA authorized the department to fly the drone between 2009 and 2012 at altitudes of up to four hundred feet. As of 2012 it has largely been flying over unpopulated areas and high-crime neighborhoods while waiting for use elsewhere.[19]

The fact that local police departments may use drones for surveillance of civilians is cause enough for concern, but possible use of drones for deploying less-lethal munitions at mass assemblies could dramatically change the nature of public gatherings. Law enforcement agencies have announced that they will equip drones with less-lethal munitions such as Tasers, rubber bullets, and tear gas. Despite their names, these potentially lethal weapons are already routinely used against civilians at public assemblies around the country, drawing complaints from civil liberties groups, the United Nations Commission on Human Rights, and independent review commissions investigating uses of excessive police force.[20] Deploying these munitions from the skies is sure to result in even more abuses, injuries, and fatalities than already occur on the ground.

Corporations Lobby for Drones

Congress's push for opening the airspace to drones continues the trend of repurposing military technology for civilian use and, equally troubling, signals concessions to aggressive lobbying by drone manufacturers.[21]

Government and business are expected to spend up to $90 billion on drones in the decade following the FAA's approval for their use in domestic skies.[22] Many private companies and industries are already making plans to manufacture drones for a range of purposes. The Schiebel Corporation, an Austrian company, is working with two U.S. companies, Brain Farm and Snaproll Media, to develop its Camcopter news-gathering device, an alternative to piloted news helicopters. In addition to cutting back on staffing costs, the agile drones don't require runways or launch systems as helicopters do.[23]

The FAA Modernization and Reform Act of 2012 greatly increases the ability of the FAA to issue drone certificates and authorization to fly.[24] The act was passed with great stealth. As Trevor Timm from the Electronic Frontier Foundation says: "It wasn't until after it passed that it started getting attention in the media. There is a reason that nobody knew about it; because they didn't really want us to know about it. Even the Privacy Caucus in Congress knew nothing about this until it passed. There was virtually no lobbying by privacy groups, or anybody, to stop this from happening."[25]

Timm points out that the drone lobby spent millions of dollars just in the first quarter of 2012 to get the bill passed. He notes that the website RepublicReport.org obtained a PowerPoint presentation in which the Association for Unmanned Vehicle Systems International (AUVSI) bragged about the fact that nobody had changed anything in the FAA bill except at AUVSI's suggestion; the drone clause in the bill is taken "word for word" from its proposal. In addition, the PowerPoint presentation lists obstacles to more drone use in this country; at the top of the roster is civil liberties. "They take civil liberties as a business obstacle not something they have to work with. They're trying to route around it. As far as the FAA bill goes, it kind of worked because no one was paying attention."[26]

The leading global organization representing unmanned systems and robotics community, AUVSI, is trying to recast itself as an "academic and philanthropic organization," according to the Republic Report website. AUVSI has purchased Twitter ads boasting that drones can monitor endangered species, and on its website it proclaims that it "sponsors science fairs and competitions aimed at getting young engineers to create UAVs."[27] As Republic Report points out, AUVSI's major donors include the world's largest military contractors and makers of weapon-carrying drones, including General Dynamics, Honeywell, Lockheed Martin, Boeing, Raytheon, and DRS Defense Solutions.

The FAA has issued to corporations special permits to test new drones, with permit holders Raytheon, General Atomics, Telford Aviation, and Honeywell. In 2012, ManTech International, a provider of technology services to the government, landed a three-year, $46 million contract. ManTech will provide flight-test support for unmanned drones and manned aircraft for the Naval Air Systems Command.[28]

Drones and Privacy

As drones begin to play a variety of domestic law enforcement roles, concerns about privacy are acute, especially since the FAA has failed to establish safeguards for the explosion in drone use and lawmakers are not holding the agency accountable. The 2012 National Defense Authorization Act mandates that the FAA work with the air force and the Department of Defense in creating Unmanned Aerial System test ranges in the national airspace.

Many of the anticipated functions of drones, such as the ability to take photographs from a great distance or to record license plate numbers, are already used by law enforcement. A key difference is the drones' ability to track subjects over an extended period, including sophisticated technology such as laser radar that can detect images through walls, which severely challenges traditional expectations of privacy and protections against unreasonable search and seizure.

Specific design advances strongly suggest that drones are being developed with an eye to domestic spying. En-

The CIA Office of Research and Development developed this Insectothopter micro UAV in the 1970s as part of an initiative to explore intelligence collection by miniaturized platforms. CIA PUBLIC DOMAIN PHOTO

gineers at Johns Hopkins University, funded by the U.S. Air Force Office for Scientific Research and the National Science Foundation, are studying butterflies in an attempt to create micro aerial vehicles (MAVs) for reconnaissance.[29] MAVs are ideal for infiltrating areas such as densely populated urban centers where larger drones cannot safely navigate.

"Drones in Domestic Surveillance Operations," a 2012 report commissioned by Congress, raises questions about how drones relate to the Fourth Amendment's pro-

This Tethered Aerostat Radar System (TARS) near Marfa, Texas, provides drug interdiction radar surveillance. Balloons filled with helium tethered to a single cable serve as radar platforms.
PHOTO: JOHNMC-BRIDEPHOTOGRA-PHY.COM

tection against unreasonable search and seizure.[30] While individuals can expect substantial protections against warrantless government intrusion into their homes, the Fourth Amendment offers fewer restrictions on government surveillance occurring in public places. The report's author notes that drone technology differs significantly from that employed in manned aerial surveillance cases ruled on by the Supreme Court, and suggests that existing Fourth Amendment case law may not be relevant in settling drone-related privacy questions.[31]

Public Relations Challenge

Outcry over drones has been universal from across the political spectrum. Even the conservative Heritage Foundation cautioned in 2012 that the surveillance capabilities of drones render them a potential threat to privacy and civil liberties.[32] The group called for Congress to establish guidelines for drone use and oversight, urging that armed military drones be used only in situations of invasion or insurrection. Further, the foundation stated that drones should not be used for long-term surveillance of a specific area or to amass data that could be used to "form the basis for sophisticated tracking and behavioral analytics."[33]

By their very nature, drones conjure images of war. In fact, in early 2013 Defense Secretary Leon Panetta announced the creation of a new warfare medal (described by Pentagon officials as higher in rank than the Bronze Star but below the Silver Star) to honor drone pilots and computer experts. The medal was to be conferred on individuals who pilot Predator or Reaper drones in combat situations from remote control posts.[34] Given public trepidation about the use of drones over civilian populations, governments and corporations urging their proliferation face a public relations challenge. The British trade group Unmanned Aerial Vehicle Systems Association embarked on a public relations initiative to reinvent the image of drones, and hopes to rename and repaint them to make them more palatable for commercial use within the United Kingdom. [35]

Incidents involving drones already negatively influence public perceptions about them. For instance, an object flying in controlled Denver airspace in 2012 nearly collided with a commercial jet.[36] A year earlier, in North Dakota, a Predator drone was used to spy on a family who refused to return some cows that had ventured onto their farm.[37] Given the planned increase in UAVs in future years, stories like these will inevitably surface. As happened in the United Kingdom, Americans may soon see a highly orchestrated public relations campaign to broadcast positive messages about drones in an attempt to counter the reality that they pose a major threat to privacy and possibly safety.

The speed with which Congress has moved to open the airspace over the United States to drones, along with its failure to enact sufficient safeguards against privacy and civil liberties violations, indicates a brazen attitude toward domestic spying. While some uses of unmanned aerial vehicle systems can be justified for safety or other benign practical reasons, the predicted number of aircraft and the huge contracts between government and big business hint at a highly coordinated plan to institute routine surveillance throughout the country. It may be that DARPA is engaging in a plan to further develop critical technologies before their national security significance becomes entirely clear. At any rate, DARPA's billions of dollars of funding toward the development of drones for domestic use is disquieting on a number of fronts, from the normalization of spying to the blurring of lines between military and civilian applications.

Given that notions of privacy have changed so rapidly and that under current laws no expectation of privacy exists when surveillance is conducted in public places, the proliferation of drones over U.S. airspace could mean that omnipresent surveillance of the general public becomes routine.

CHAPTER 12

Location, Location, Location

Manal Al-Sharif was among the first in Saudi Arabia to tweet about the fact that Saudi women, children, and foreign workers were monitored electronically by their male guardians when they left the country.[1] In a notification system established in 2010, guardians of women, underage children, and some workers can register with the Interior Ministry to receive the notifications when their dependents' passports are scanned.

While news of the monitoring system was received with international outrage, Americans are routinely tracked by monitoring systems without their knowledge. Each day U.S. authorities have the capacity to use global positioning system units in mobile phones and other devices to track the movements of millions of individuals. Days after the Boston Marathon attack, the carjacking of a Mercedes-Benz enabled authorities to track the location of Tamerlan and Dzhokhar Tsarnaev. After the car owner provided his personal identification number to the car manufacturer, Mercedes activated the factory-installed global positioning system (marketed as the Stolen Vehicle Location Assistance function) to pinpoint the car's precise location. Because the fleeing owner left his iPhone in the car, authorities could also have tracked the Tsarnaevs through its GPS.

Government authorities made 1.3 million requests for subscriber data from mobile phone providers in 2011.[2] Officials also bypass carriers and use "International Mobile Subscriber Identity" locators that pull data as they track cell signals.

Global positioning is a government-maintained, space-based satellite navigation system that provides information about location and time from any place on earth where an unobstructed line of sight exists to at least four satellites. Anyone with a GPS receiver can access the navigation system. Initially conceived in 1973 by the Department of Defense, it became operational in 1994.

In addition to being able to track location by GPS-enabled cellular phones, the system can determine the location of non-enabled cell phones by triangulation. Every seven seconds mobile phones ping to towers and microsites, registering locations within a 150-foot radius.[3] Each phone is assigned a unique numerical identifier. By law, wireless companies must retain records of unique data exchanged by phones with cellular networks and must keep numbers to which calls are placed, making locational tracking simple.[4] Telephones are served by several towers at any given time, so investigators can triangulate the location of a device. Even in dense urban areas, tracking is accurate to within several yards. Unless the power is turned off, a mobile phone stays in constant communication with the nearest cell towers even when not being used for a call.

Some employers use GPS-enabled phones to monitor employees' locations. Other "locator" phones provide GPS coordinates and can even dial emergency numbers; third parties such as family members or caregivers are able to track a phone's location and receive alerts when the phone leaves a specified area.[5]

The Federal Communication Commission will require that cell phone location information be able to pinpoint locations within fifty feet by 2018. New GPS technology enables satellites to pinpoint the location of cell phones even more precisely. Federal magistrate judges issue more than thirty thousand covert search orders annually under the Electronic Communications Privacy Act.[6]

Geographic location-based services such as radio-frequency identification chips, GPS, and location-enabled WiFi have several beneficial uses. They also have tremendous potential to serve as surveillance tools, with their ability to track human beings from great distances and without the knowledge of the person being tracked. As with other conveniences, their dangers must be balanced with the positive gains they bring to society. As familiar as most people are with location-tracking technologies, many are unaware of the full capabilities and the potential for abuse.

Search Warrants Needed for Police GPS Tracking

In 2012 the U.S. Supreme Court ruled on a GPS-related case with far-reaching privacy implications, addressing the question of whether law enforcement can use GPS devices without obtaining a warrant to track individuals suspected of crimes. At the time the court considered the case, the FBI was tracking approximately three thousand GPS devices. The court in *United States v. Jones* held that police exceeded their legal authority by putting a GPS tracker on the car of a suspected narcotics dealer, monitoring the individual for twenty-eight days, without first obtaining judicial approval and a search warrant. In a much awaited decision, the court voted unanimously that police agencies must obtain search warrants before they can install GPS tracking devices on suspects' vehicles.

One potentially important protection for users of location-based services and cell phones, the Location Privacy Act of 2011, was introduced in late 2012 by the Senate Judiciary Committee, but was not passed.[7] The bill would have required affirmative consent for the collection and disclosure of location information to nongovernmental third parties. The Electronic Privacy Information Center had recommended similar privacy protections in comments filed with the Federal Communications Commission. It would require app developers to obtain consent from users before recording their locations on mobile devices. It would also ban the creation of stalking apps (apps that enable the installation of software to monitor telephone calls, text messages, and the location of a mobile device) and would mandate mobile services to disclose the names of advertising networks or third parties with which they share users' location information. The bill aims to prevent corporations from compiling a detailed dossier of an individual's most personal associations, consumer habits, and even health status. Many civil liberties experts consider mobile surveillance and storing movement data as a form of trespass, without warrant, by corporations.

RFID Detection: From Friendly Fire to Lipstick Colors

As with drones, radio-frequency identification (RFID) applications began with the military and were later adapted for civilian use. During World War II, radio-frequency codings helped to distinguish enemies from allies.[8] In the 1950s, RFID tags were developed to track radioactive material.

Four decades later, a store manager in charge of Procter & Gamble's Oil of Olay lipstick needed to keep track of a popular shade that kept selling out. He asked two MIT researchers to devise technology to monitor inventory. They came up with the idea of putting a computer chip with a unique ID number in each tube of lipstick.[9] It would make tracking more accurate than bar codes, which only identified categories of products. After securing funding from Procter & Gamble, Gillette, and the Uniform Code Council, in 1999 the researchers founded the MIT Auto-ID Center, a network of academic research labs in the networked RFID field.[10] Its focus was on simple and inexpensive RFID tags for the consumer-goods industry.[11] In 2003 it licensed its research results to EPC (Electronic Product Code) Global. There were no limits to what they could track. By eliminating human error, companies could reduce theft, cut costs, and increase customer convenience. In addition to having to put RFID chips in everything, however, the industry realized it would need to install RFID tag readers in many locations, from factories to retail space and even to garbage trucks. It would also need to create a way for RFID readers to communicate tag information in real time to those in charge of the supply chain.

Each chip would have a unique EPC number, similar to issuing a Social Security number. VeriSign, the company that manages web-page addressing for the Internet, agreed to create what the clients conceived as the "Internet of Things," built on top of the existing Internet, by which inanimate objects are able to communicate with manufacturers, retailers, and each other, allowing for uninterrupted tracking of physical items. Because the applications of RFIDs far exceed inventory tracking and the monitoring of spending habits, authors of the book *Spychips: How Major Corporations and Government Plan to Track Your Every Purchase and Watch Your Every Move*, Katherine Albrecht and Liz McIntyre, have dubbed them "spy chips."[12]

Lifesaving, Inexpensive, and Potentially Invasive

Radio-frequency ID technology has transformed Americans' lives, making everyday transactions more efficient and cost-effective. Libraries, for example, use chips to replace bar codes in books and DVDs. Because RFID tags can be read through most materials, librarians don't even need to open the book or DVD case, giving staff more time to assist library visitors.

Approximately seventy thousand lost pets are reunited annually with their owners thanks to RFID chips implanted painlessly under the skin. Most shelters and veterinarians have scanners that can read the codes containing the owners' information. The tags can also be used to track livestock or capture years of information on wild animals, giving scientists and biologists useful data about the habitat and migratory patterns of other species, or even the histories of individual animals. RFIDs keep track of vehicle fleets, inventory, and cargo being shipped around the world. The Federal Highway Administration hopes to embed RFIDs into all U.S.-manufactured cars, installing a global positioning transmitter that can track every vehicle by satellite and a wireless device that uploads locations as cars pass certain hot spots.

A preschool in Richmond, California, began embedding RFID chips in children's clothing in 2010.[13] Students in Texas carry identification cards embedded with RFID chips to track their movements on campus.[14] Reasons for issuing the cards are budgetary in part—state-financed schools may not receive funding for students not

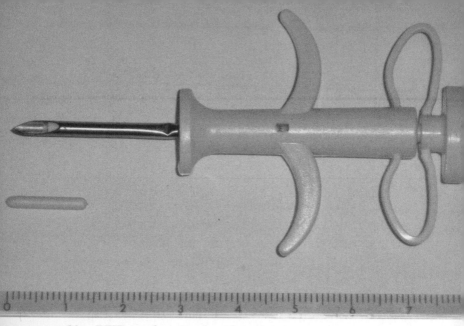

Glass RFID tag for animals with syringe. PHOTO: UWE GILLE

in attendance. While many parents oppose the chips on privacy grounds, others claim the technology reassures them, because they know their child is safe. Corporations, notably AT&T, are eager to offer RFID chips for monitoring students. AT&T's advertising materials say that homeroom teachers no longer need to use class time calling attendance, but can just read the tags embedded in each student's ID card.[15]

A $700,000 grant from the Centers for Disease Control and Prevention funded a 2012 study of Pennsylvania students wearing RFID devices around their necks.[16] The University of Pittsburgh began a program called Social Mixing and Respiratory Transmission in Schools

(SMART) in which 450 students in selected Pennsylvania school districts will be monitored via RFID chips around their necks. [17] The chips can track how many people each individual child comes into contact with to determine how a pandemic could be transmitted.

The Problem with Storage

The retention and potential reuses of scanned records raise another set of privacy concerns. Information gathered in nightclubs shows how this can happen. Many bars and clubs use ID scanners to ensure that patrons are of legal drinking age. Scanner software clips onto a bouncer's iPhone or iPod and reads information from a driver's license barcode or magnetic strip to extract gender, age, ZIP code, and time of entry.[18] The information goes to the company's database for aggregation and analysis and is available to other bars and marketers.

Authorities in San Francisco are urging that establishments be required to store such information for a certain period so that it can be turned over upon request to aid in crime investigation.[19] In New York City one nightclub contracted with the police department to allow police access to patrons' personal information in exchange for permitting the club—which had faced the possibility of being closed down due to a rash of problems, including violence—to remain open.[20] In Barcelona and other European locations, nightclubs have gone a step further, offering to implant chips in human beings to facilitate entry and payment.[21]

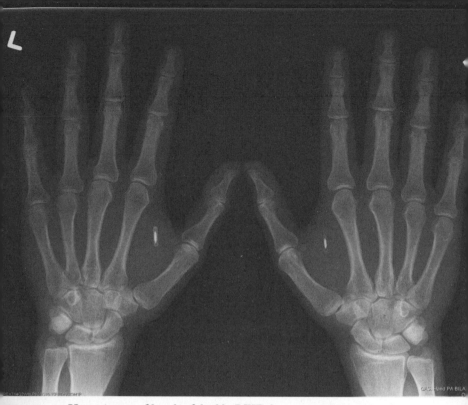

X-ray image of hands of double-RFID human implantee Amal Graastra. PHOTO: AMAL GRAAFSTRA, WWW.AMAL.NET

From Animals to Humans

In 1998, a professor in the United Kingdom injected himself with an RFID tag. When Kevin Warwick implanted the chip, as part of an experiment known as Project Cyborg, it heralded a new era of privacy-related concerns ranging from tracking individual movements to remote control of the human body. Warwick, a cybernetics expert, earned the name Captain Cyborg when he implanted an

RFID transmitter in his arm. He used the chip to interact with his environment, turning on lights, opening doors, and adjusting thermostats and other computer-controlled devices just by waving his hand.[22] Others followed suit. Mikey Sklar embedded a chip to eliminate the need to carry keys or type in computer passwords.[23] Amal Graafstra has chips implanted in both hands; he uses them to turn on his motorcycle, access his home, and open a safe in his house. He documents his experiences on a website and in his book, *RFID Toys*.[24]

In 2004 the U.S. Food and Drug Administration approved VeriChip, an RFID implant, to be used subdermally in humans for medical purposes.[25] Some of the plans for subdermal chips include enabling hospitals to retrieve medical information from embedded individuals by passing a scanner over them in the event of a medical emergency. Information stored on VeriChip Corporation's website, provided by the patient, would be accessible by the hospital. Other possible uses include injecting the chips into elderly Alzheimer's patients in Florida.[26] Chip producers say implantation should always be voluntary, but many question the ethics of conducting research on medically impaired persons.

The VeriChip Corporation, which in 2009 changed its name to PositiveID Corporation, obtained approval from the FDA in 2004 to market VeriChip (also known as VeriMed) implants.[27] News broke in 2008 that similar implants caused cancer in laboratory animals, and PositiveID Corporation stopped marketing implantable human microchips two years later.[28] In 2012, the VeriTeQ Acquisition Corporation (owned by Scott Silverman, former chair and CEO of both PositiveID and VeriChip Corporation) acquired the VeriChip implantable chip and related technologies, including the web-based personal health record system Health Link from PositiveID Corporation.[29]

Social Costs and Benefits of Location-Based Tracking

Anyone who has cruised through the E-ZPass lane at a toll booth, used a subway swipe card, or searched for nearby locations on a cell phone should know that all movements have the potential to be recorded for possible use at a later date. Such tracking violates what is known as location privacy, or the ability to move in public free of monitoring. Associational information, such as what restaurant you went to for dinner, what movie theater you visited, and what addresses you dropped by—and potentially, what religious service or political gathering you attended—can be stored to create a portfolio of interactions and personal habits.

Katherine Albrecht describes plans to install RFID readers in public doorways so that even greater information could be scanned. She gives a personal illustration of the implications: "I stopped and made an inventory of all the things I was wearing and carrying in [corporations' and the governments'] vision of the future that would have an RFID tag. It was my shoes, my underwear, my stockings, my skirt, my purse, my briefcase, my notebook, my Chapstick. If I did have a can of Coke from someone else it would be more useful; because as I walk through the doorway it would tell who I was associating with."[30]

While the tracking of individuals is relatively straightforward in urban areas and other places with vast surveillance infrastructures, tracking of associations and groups is more difficult. Albrecht explains how doorway scanners, coupled with ubiquitous RFID-implanted products, facilitates relationship tracking through products we wear or hold: "It creates the potential to not only know all about me but to know the people I hang out with." One day, for instance, "I was [carrying] a cheap 50-cent ball point Bic pen that I'd actually accidentally taken from a reporter I'd met with earlier that week. If they'd scanned that, they'd know interviews. That's the kind of connection that you can make once the individual items are tracked."[31]

The Electronic Frontier Foundation contends that modern cryptography makes it possible to design data-processing systems that accommodate a host of privacy policies, including the capacity to prevent monitoring that violates user privacy. To avoid being tracked at tollbooths, for example, electronic cash, a way someone can pay for something with a special digital signature that provides anonymity but also allows the holder to redeem it for money, provides a way to avoid creating a record. As the E-ZPass holder drives over bridges and through tunnels, the tolling transponder anonymously pays the tolls.

Location-based service providers' websites give instructions on loading GPS tracking software into cell phones and activating it. Services can already show the phone's location on an online map, and may even be able to indicate the speed at which the phone and owner are traveling, and how long the phone remains in one place.

Private entities such as corporations may be subject to legal requests from police to retain logs tracking the locations of civil litigants. Such requests entail difficult legal questions about whether compliance is required, or if whether compliance poses a potential liability risk.[32]

As discussed earlier, the George W. Bush administration pushed to mandate businesses and government agencies to maintain electronic records for years. Should location-based data, especially information that has accumulated over many years, get into the hands of corporate data aggregators, the potential for abuse is vast. For government officials and corporate executives, location tracking provides additional data for inclusion in electronic dossiers of Americans.

CHAPTER 13

"Troublemakers" Bring Us to Our Senses

What a huge debt this nation owes to its "trouble-makers." From Thomas Paine to Martin Luther King Jr., they have forced us to focus on problems we would prefer to downplay or ignore. Yet it is often only with hindsight that we can distinguish those troublemakers who brought us to our senses from those who were simply . . . troublemakers. Prudence, and respect for the constitutional rights to free speech and free association, therefore dictate that the legal system cut all non-violent protesters a fair amount of slack.

—Hon. Jed S. Rakoff, in *Garcia v. Bloomberg*, 2012[1]

Judge Rakoff made his acknowledgment of "troublemakers" in reference to a federal class-action lawsuit filed on behalf of seven hundred Occupy protesters arrested on the Brooklyn Bridge on October 1, 2011. The lawsuit alleges that members of the New York Police Department escorted marchers onto the vehicular roadway of the bridge and then unlawfully entrapped and arrested them.

When the activist magazine *Adbusters* called for an occupation of Wall Street on July 13, 2011, they could not have known how many "troublemakers" would respond globally and how the call of three words, "Occupy Wall Street," would stir a dormant democracy. What came to be known around the world as the Occupy movement brought forth issues related to free speech, public space, civic power, and protest, and mobilized public conscience regarding the degree to which national economic security had been breached by widespread corporate crime and predation. Unprecedented critiques of class disparity, corporate personhood, economic injustice, and political accountability were suddenly thrust into the national discourse. At its height, the Occupy movement claimed space in many hundreds of locations around the world and influenced the 2012 U.S. presidential election season.

In agitating on behalf of a public interest vision of democracy, the Occupy movement directed attention to many other related national issues, including the essential role that public space plays in the exercise of civic power. In public space—parks, plazas, streets, and sidewalks—protest and dissent are protected as free speech by the U.S. Constitution. Despite these liberties and their protections, however, many people are unaware of the extent to which corporations control urban public spaces and the behaviors permitted in them. For example, many public city sidewalks are closely monitored by private security guards and police, especially when the sidewalks pass by high-end stores, big banks, and financial institutions. In areas near government buildings, where laws sometimes permit individuals to engage in camping as political speech, police flagrantly violated those laws to remove people involved with the Occupy movement. Such tactics not only impinge on constitutionally guaranteed rights, making would-be practitioners of free speech more likely to remain silent, they also deny the movement a public face and presence.

Privately Owned Public Spaces

Public spaces, indoor and out, under the control of corporations are known as privately owned public spaces (POPS) or as privately owned public open spaces (PO-POS). In New York, more than five hundred POPS cover 3.5 million square feet of space, as a result of zoning concessions by which the corporations allocate part of their space for public use to obtain the needed variances.[2] In San Francisco, a 1985 downtown plan required that new hotel or office developments incorporate POPOS, resulting in approximately seventy throughout the city. Twenty-five years after the plan, the city updated the ordinance requirements to make the spaces more inviting to the public. Signage or plaques identifying the space must now be easily visible and legible, and a Web tool will chart the location and amenities of each.

When corporations control these quasi-public spaces, they are allowed to establish "reasonable" rules gov-

A portable New York Police Department Skywatch Tower was brought to Manhattan's privately owned public space, Zuccotti Park, in 2011 to watch over Occupy protesters with cameras, a spotlight, and sensors. PHOTO: JOHNMCBRIDEPHOTOGRAPHY.COM

erning their use. Typically prohibited are activities such as camping or lying on the ground or on benches, all of which impact the homeless as well as non-homeless political protesters involved in Occupy and other acts of constitutionally protected speech. Many of these spaces are located directly in front of buildings that house banks, hedge fund brokers, and similar financial institutions.

Police Break the Law

The Occupy movement embodied the largest challenge to authority in this country since the Vietnam War protests, garnered worldwide recognition, and raised public consciousness about the global economic recession, its causes, and its consequences at many levels of society. In response, law enforcement and other local and federal authorities engaged in a wide range of tactics to suppress the movement.

As of 2013, more than 7,700 Occupy-related arrests had been made in 122 U.S. cities. Many of the arrests involved the use of overly aggressive tactics directed at people engaged in peaceful demonstrations. Specific practices reveal the extent to which various authorities violated constitutional protections to deter people from joining and perpetuating the Occupy movement.[3] To diminish the spontaneous civil gatherings that arose in cities and towns across the country, officials took these actions:

- Used excessive force, including chemical weapons, against people participating in assemblies;
- Deployed helicopters to accompany a twenty-person march;
- Conducted mass arrests without probable cause, including over 700 arrested on the Brooklyn Bridge on a single occasion;
- Overcharged individuals arrested just to keep them in detention;

Police used orange netting to encircle and arrest Occupy demonstrators on the Brooklyn Bridge motorway on October 1, 2011. After walking with protesters onto the bridge, police arrested 700 on charges of disorderly conduct. A class action lawsuit asserts that by escorting marchers through traffic lights and onto the bridge, they effectively led protesters into an unlawful trap and arrest. PHOTO: GREG RUGGIERO

- Issued false alerts of threats to officers' safety as justification to arrest people;
- Barricaded Wall Street;
- Conducted midnight raids on the Occupy encampment in New York City during which journalists were kept at a two-block distance and credentialed City Council members were similarly kept from observing;

- Arrested journalists attempting to document instances of police misconduct;
- Diverted law enforcement at times to focus solely on Occupiers;
- Photographed and videotaped people arrested for disorderly conduct and other offenses for which police would not ordinarily take mug shots, to intimidate individuals and amass a bank of photos of politically active persons;
- Subpoenaed Twitter for the GPS locations and other data related to tweets from people arrested at an Occupy protest.

Homeland Security Coordinated Surveillance of the Occupy Movement

As fiercely as NYPD Commissioner Raymond Kelly has worked to resist court oversight and constitutional restraint, civil rights attorney Mara Verheyden-Hilliard works to hold law enforcement accountable for engaging in patterns of constitutional infractions. The Partnership for Civil Justice Fund (PCJF), the organization she founded with Carl Messineo, has successfully litigated many protest-related cases that set national precedents. Their lawsuits have exposed illegal police practices in New York City and in the nation's capital; their settlements have secured long-lasting changes in police policies relating to mass assemblies and First Amendment–protected activities.

FBI documents obtained by the PCJF through several Freedom of Information Act requests reveal that from Occupy's inception, as early as August 2011, the FBI and federal authorities met with the New York Stock Exchange and deployed counterterrorism forces against the movement, even while acknowledging in writing that Occupy organizers explicitly called for peaceful protest and did not condone the use of violence.[4] By September, the FBI alerted businesses that they might be the focus of an Occupy Wall Street (OWS) protest.

Verheyden-Hilliard says the files reveal that protests are portrayed as potential criminal and terrorist activity: "The documents also show a very deep and close partnership that the FBI and the DHS have with Wall Street and with the banks and businesses in the U.S. The documents show the U.S. intelligence agencies and supposedly security agencies really working as the private intelligence arm for private businesses. You have the people of the U.S. rising up in opposition to an economic crisis, an economic devastation caused by the banks and by Wall Street and the U.S. government acting in partnership with the banks and Wall Street against those people."[5]

Extensive coordination took place between the FBI, the DHS, and corporations. The Domestic Security Alliance Council (DSAC), described by the federal government as "a strategic partnership between the FBI, the Department of Homeland Security and the private sector," issued a report that reveals the nature of secret collaboration between intelligence agencies and corporate clients. It contains a "handling notice" stating that the information is "meant for use primarily within the corporate security community. Such messages shall not be released in either written or oral form to the media, the general public or other personnel."[6]

DSAC issued several tips to its corporate clients on "civil unrest," defined as ranging from "small, organized rallies to large-scale demonstrations and rioting." It advised clients to dress conservatively, avoid political discussions, and avoid large gatherings related to civil issues. It noted: "Even seemingly peaceful rallies can spur violent activity or be met with resistance by security forces. Bystanders may be arrested or harmed by security forces using water cannons, tear gas or other measures to control crowds."

On December 7, 2011, the Jackson, Mississippi, office of the FBI attended a meeting of the Bank Security Group in Biloxi, Mississippi, with multiple private banks and the Biloxi Police Department, at which they discussed an announced protest for "National Bad Bank Sit-In-Day."

The Federal Reserve in Richmond, Virginia, appears to have had personnel monitoring OWS planning. The monitors were in contact with the FBI in Richmond to deliver information on the movement. Repeated communications were made between the two "to pass on updates of the events and decisions made during the small rallies and the following information received from the Capital Police Intelligence Unit through JTTF [Joint Terrorism Task Force]."

In addition to coordinating with local financial institutions and corporations, local JTTFs across the nation coordinated with university campus police, who in some cases reported to the FBI on student and faculty involvement with Occupy encampments. "Domestic Terrorism" briefing reports on the spread of the Occupy movement were prepared in some states, as were counterterrorism preparedness alerts and Potential Criminal Activities Alerts. The Memphis, Tennessee, JTTF met to discuss "domestic terrorism" threats. Seemingly to avoid the appearance of bias, they lumped together "Aryan Nations, Occupy Wall Street, and Anonymous."[7]

Verheyden-Hilliard says of the multilevel coordination, "It goes beyond information sharing. We're well aware of the FBI's collecting and constant use of massive data-warehousing systems, the ChoicePoint history of collecting commercial information on the people of the United States and the government's absolute willingness to tap into that and access that information; but beyond that, these documents show, for example, that the FBI was communicating with the New York Stock Exchange a month before the first tent was set up on Zuccotti Park. It shows FBI communicating with businesses."[8]

Austin Police Infiltrate Occupiers
Just as undercover agents infiltrated Critical Mass bicycle rides for years and insinuated themselves among animal rights and environmental advocacy circles, agents made their way into Occupy encampments as well.

On December 12, 2011, activists in Oakland called for a nationwide action to shut down ports in solidarity with the International Longshore and Warehouse Union, which was embroiled in a labor dispute. In an act of civil disobedience, twenty individuals in Houston lay down at the Port of Houston's entrance. Seven of them linked their arms together with lockboxes in a "sleeping dragon," a method of civil disobedience that has been used often in the environmental movement.[9]

As they were arrested and being removed from the sleeping dragon, police covered them with a large red tent. Lawyers contend that police used the tent to hide their actions from the press, contrary to Houston officials' assertions that the tent was erected to contain sparks from cutting the lockboxes. The seven individuals said that officers illegally concealed their names and badge numbers with tape.

The activists were charged with a felony, unlawful use of a "criminal instrument," which carries up to two years in state prison. After a judge dismissed the charges, the Houston district attorney brought the case to a grand jury, which reindicted them on the same charges. In February 2013 the felony charges were dismissed. But it's what happened prior to the dismissal that is significant. The activists received an anonymous email about an Occupy Austin member named "Butch"—who encouraged the use of the lockboxes—saying that he was really an undercover officer named Shannon. One of the protesters, Ronnie Garza, did some research and learned that

Butch was an Austin narcotics detective named Shannon Dowell. Garza recalled that Dowell was present at Occupy Austin prior to the port action.

Garza's attorney, Greg Gladden, noted, "This case uncovered the fact that at least six Occupy Austin members have been undercover police infiltrators, voting members on their committees and provocateurs since the inception of Occupy Austin in the fall of 2011. Over Austin Police Department's and their Fusion Center's objections the identities of three of the undercover, infiltrating, police narcotics officers were disclosed by the Harris County District Attorney's office in December 2012. Termination of the prosecution had the effect of avoiding the other three infiltrators' identities being disclosed, and the question of what role the federal government may have played in this police misconduct will remain unanswered—for now."[10]

In an August 2012 hearing, Dowell admitted he had worked with two other undercover agents and several higher-ranking officers. He admitted deleting emails related to the investigation and claimed that he had not authored any official reports about his undercover work because the department was not conducting an official criminal investigation of police conduct.

According to Gladden, "The police built [the lockboxes], furnished them, paid for them, adapted them and delivered them." Gladden also asserted that police knew from the outset of the case that the seven would be arrested on felony rather than misdemeanor charges, and that the Houston Police Department may have been involved in the covert entrapment scheme.[11]

Entrapment in Cleveland and Chicago—"Billion-dollar Protection Rackets"

Police entrapment also led to felony charges for Occupiers in Cleveland. Five men were arrested on April 30, 2012, in relation to an alleged plot to blow up a bridge before May Day protests. An FBI informant posing as an activist in Occupy Cleveland had infiltrated the group for months and supplied some of its members with alcohol, drugs, and employment before arranging for them to purchase fake explosives.[12]

A few weeks later, two undercover police detectives in Chicago reportedly encouraged activists to engage in a plot against the 2012 NATO Summit.[13] After a midnight raid on the home of Occupy Chicago activists a few days before the summit, NATO protesters charged with terrorism and other felonies were held for nearly forty-eight hours before being officially charged.[14] Among those arrested in the raid were the two undercover officers known as "Mo" and "Glove," both of whom had infiltrated Occupy Chicago months prior to the protests. As of this writing, three Occupy activists have been held nearly one year in Cook County Jail on $1.5 million bond each, as a result of the entrapment. Defense attorneys with the People's Law Office and the National Lawyers Guild were denied access for several months to defense-related items, including content from computers seized in the raid.[15]

Sarah Gelsomino, who along with Michael Deutsch and paralegal Brad Thomson represent one of the "NATO 5," Brian Jacob Church, notes that a pattern of police infiltration followed by terrorism charges in protest-related cases has had the effect of instilling fear in other activists. "People are very afraid, particularly people in the Occupy movement, because they now feel so violated. Someone said to me, 'Occupy is about bringing people together and making movement for social change. We weren't doing anything wrong.' Now they feel that they were being targeted just for trying to make positive social change in the world. People are afraid. They don't know who to trust. They don't know how to move forward."[16]

High-profile terrorism charges seem to surface after significant amounts of money and personnel are invested in monitoring and infiltrating activist groups, such as Occupy. As National Lawyers Guild member Kris Hermes noted in an article about the NATO prosecutions, in addition to needing to justify investigation, infiltration, and prosecution, "there is also a coordinated effort by local and federal officials to perpetuate a billion-dollar 'protection racket,' in which law enforcement uses an aggressive counterterrorism approach to both instill fear in the public and then, after solving the 'crime,' induce the perception of safety."[17]

The Chicago lawyers are challenging the Illinois State terrorism statue, which they claim is so vague in its language that it was applied unconstitutionally to the activists. If they prevail, the most serious felony charges against the accused men could be dismissed.

The Occupy movement's public encampments mostly lasted between one and four months, and the sweeping, multilevel repression of the movement demonstrates the ferocity with which the U.S. financial and political systems will confront society when it mobilizes to criticize authority and demand accountability.

Hundreds of Occupy-related court cases have made their way through the justice system, drawing attention to issues of corporate-controlled public spaces, unlawful police tactics, and corporate and government surveillance. For many Americans, it was the first time they had thought about such issues. For many others, it was a time to see the extent to which the FBI continues to engage in political intelligence gathering and surveillance. No longer under the vigilant eye of J. Edgar Hoover, the modern FBI is equally restrictive and suspicious about people's movements.

"This is Obama's FBI," says Verheyden-Hilliard. "This is Attorney General Holder's FBI. This is an FBI that acts as it has continued to act in its historic role from the fifties, the sixties, the seventies. The role of the FBI in acting as a secret police is an element of police state–ism in its efforts to shut down, disrupt, threaten the black liberation movement, the antiwar movement, the progressive movement in the United States. When they feel the power of the people in the streets the U.S. intelligence agencies and the law enforcement agencies go into high gear, because it is the movement of the people that really does cause change in society."[18]

Surveillance and counterintelligence operations conducted to repress pro-democracy movements like Occupy have implications beyond the rights of those most actively participating. When social networks and mobilizations are hindered by such excessive government actions, it is the free flow of ideas and perspectives vital to democracy that is injured. To be genuine, our democracy must not only protect personal and civil liberties, openness, and dissent, but must also actively encourage them.

Custodians of Democracy

Like a pint-sized brain surrounded by a heavily protected, half-million-square-foot body, a diminutive Dell computer in the basement of the National Counterterrorism Center is at the core of the Bush administration's war on terror.
— James Bamford, *The Shadow Factory*[1]

In describing the National Security Agency's Terrorist Identities Datamart Environment (TIDE), best-selling author James Bamford, whose reporting in the 1980s revealed the existence of the NSA, calls the database used to store names gathered from the federal eavesdropping programs a disaster. The advent of digital communications and mass storage, he says, coupled with a failure of law and policy to keep abreast of technological advancements, and an NSA "where the entire world's knowledge is stored, but not a single word understood,"[2] yields "the capacity to make tyranny total in America."[3]

Much of the information in government databases such as TIDE is collected with the cooperation of corporations. Although the U.S. surveillance state is colossal in scope, Americans need not be complicit in sustaining it. Tethered to electronic gadgets, under watchful corporate and government command, Americans have a choice about the amount of information afforded to authorities. We can embrace the positive aspects of technology while electing to actively resist and dismantle its invasive and anti-democratic aspects.

To do so, it is essential to reject outright the premise on which a domestic surveillance grid has been erected: that it makes us safer. Comprehensive monitoring, and the targeting of certain individuals and social networks for greater observation, is demonstrably ineffective in its purported function of making Americans more secure.

Surveillance Does Not Make Us Safer

As illustrated in this book's examples—FBI targeting of environmentalists, animal rights advocates, lawyers representing politically active clients, and members of the press—a great deal of the bureau's focus is not on investigating specific acts of violence or plans for violent attacks, but rather on monitoring communities and individuals holding particular political and religious ideologies. This approach is ineffective, and likely makes the nation less secure by deflecting attention from legitimate law enforcement.

Aside from the impractical scope of monitoring all religious and ideological adherents for prospective acts of violence, this strategy encourages stereotyping that diverts intelligence agencies from uncovering actual threats that may not fit a particular law enforcement paradigm. In *Terrorism and the Constitution*, David Cole and James X. Dempsey argue that stifling dissent—a basic vehicle by which we question authority and bring about social change—may encourage individuals who don't value peaceful change.[4] And when entire communities are targeted as enemies, stigmatized groups become less likely to cooperate with law enforcement in pursuing real leads.

In addition to possibly making the country more vulnerable to terrorist acts, the fixation of the FBI and other intelligence agencies on fighting terrorism has worsened an already compromised economy. Indeed, a direct correlation can be found between a focus on high-profile counterterrorism initiatives and the quality of life for Americans, civil liberties concerns notwithstanding. Describing an unforeseen consequence of the bureau's antiterrorism agenda, Tim Weiner, winner of the Pulitzer Prize for Investigative Reporting for his work on national security and intelligence issues, wrote, "The investigation and prosecution of white-collar crime plummeted, a boon to the Wall Street plunderings that helped create the greatest economic crisis in America since the 1930s."[5]

With resources diverted to the so-called war on terror, staffing for such white-collar crimes as predatory lending and mortgage fraud investigations was slashed to 26 percent of 2001 levels, a loss of 625 agents as of 2008.[6] Prosecutions against financial institution fraud dropped 48 percent from 2000 to 2007, insurance fraud cases dropped 75 percent, and securities fraud cases declined 117 percent.[7] Syracuse University estimates that the number of FBI white-collar crimes fell by 50 percent.[8] While thousands of Americans have gone to jail for protesting that banks must be held accountable for causing massive national economic damage and loss, not a single banker has been arrested for defrauding, evicting, and repossessing the homes of millions of American families.[9] In light of the devastation brought on by the plunder, it's only reasonable to ask what has posed the greater material threat to our national security, freedom, and liberties: predatory bankers or the protesters who have camped out to insist that these predatory bankers be held accountable? That the U.S. government and its corporate partners have overwhelmingly chosen to act as if the latter, and not the former, have harmed the nation speaks volumes about the real priorities and alliances of those in power today.

In addition to diverting resources from prosecuting white-collar crime, huge sums spent on surveillance gadgets contribute little, if anything, to public safety. As cities invest hundreds of millions of dollars in surveillance cameras, no evidence exists that they deter crime. A New York University study analyzing data from 2002 to 2005 of two large housing complexes in Manhattan concluded that no persuasive evidence existed that cameras reduced crime in the two complexes.[10] A 2008 San Francisco study concluded that public surveillance cameras served no deterrent function whatsoever.[11] In addition to

New York City Police Department wireless video cameras on a lamp post on the corner of West 111th Street and Frederick Douglass Boulevard in Harlem. PHOTO: JOHNMCBRIDEPHO-TOGRAPHY.COM

the NYU study, as of 2009, four additional studies had been conducted to determine if closed-circuit televisions were effective in deterring crime. Only one case showed success, a study of East Orange, New Jersey, where a multipronged approach involving cameras, instant police reports, and electronic listening devices saw a crime reduction of 50 percent from 2003 to 2006.[12] Despite this, New York City has devoted millions of dollars to installing a "Ring of Steel," modeled after London's system by the same name, in midtown and lower Manhattan with cameras, license plate readers, explosive-trace detection systems, and armed officers.

Four Minutes to Redefine Values

Much of the modern surveillance state can be traced back to World War I propaganda, when the Committee on Public Information (created by President Woodrow Wilson to influence public opinion about U.S. participation in the war), deployed volunteer "Four Minute Men" to deliver short pro-war propaganda to captive audiences in movies, churches, labor union halls, and other venues. Pointers on how to frame the short speeches advised sparseness of words, with fifteen-second openings and final appeals. Speakers were encouraged to look for new slogans and ideas to continuously perfect their speeches.

Later, Edward L. Bernays would further refine techniques of propaganda. Acknowledging the deceptive nature of public relations campaigns, Bernays himself said, "The conscious and intelligent manipulation of the organized habits and opinions of the masses is an important element in democratic society."[13] Political and social strategies that helped define the course of history have relied on many of Bernays's techniques. One of the best-known public relations firms, Hill & Knowlton, was instrumental in molding public opinion through its representations of several influential industries, including tobacco, steel, and aviation.

It would be refreshing if Americans could offer their own four-minute versions on how individuals can reclaim free speech, community, personal autonomy, liberty, and happiness. Some modern-day equivalents already exist, as described below: the pupils who resisted carrying RFID-embedded student identification cards, or those who refused to have their biometrics gathered in palm scans at the school cafeteria. They are the modern-day equivalents of "Four Minute Men." Each time these women, children, and families take a principled stand against intrusive surveillance, they make it easier for others to do so.

Just as public relations firms and corporate marketing departments know the power of online advertisements and thirty-second television spots, so should Americans become independent and outspoken experts in redefining—rebranding—our core values. We can shift from state and corporate propaganda to publicly created narratives. Articulating social realities and delivering the message with care and creativity helps counter the coercion and control we are subjected to daily and builds a diverse culture of resistance.

Instead of the "conscious and intelligent manipulation" of the public by state authorities and corporations, nonprofit efforts to improve society can work with the powerful real-life stories of people overcoming adversity, of confronting corporate and government authority, and of mobilizing vibrant communities. Doing so would counter the numbing daily barrage of commercial messages. The act of sharing of facts, art, creative interpretations, dramatizations, and stories of community and humanity is a far more interesting reflection of society than are the profit-obsessed messages of corporate America. Community narratives that are spontaneous, emotional, and unvarnished should be readily available for others to hear and emulate.

When armed with the facts, and when unafraid to speak out against governmental and corporate authorities, people in the United States have been able to organize to resist and reverse policies and practices that infringe on civil liberties, freedom, and democracy.

Americans interested in staving off a cyber-surveillance state should familiarize themselves with the initiatives of organizations and individuals actively working to protect civil liberties across the country. Many have made noteworthy progress in holding government and corporate intelligence agencies accountable for constitutional infractions. Litigation by the American Civil Liberties Union, the Center for Constitutional Rights, the Electronic Frontier Foundation, the National Lawyers Guild, the Partnership for Civil Justice Fund in Washington, D.C., the People's Law Office in Chicago, and other organizations exposes and challenges government policies that infringe on First and Fourth Amendment rights. In the case of surveillance, these organizations go a long way toward holding federal intelligence agencies accountable and reminding the judiciary and legislators that they have not kept pace with technology that changes day to day. The very act of bringing litigation serves an important function in drawing attention to injustices and educating the public about issues that impact their privacy.

Because these individuals and groups defend the most precious elements of our society—our basic rights and liberties—they are literally the custodians of democracy.

Denying Drones

In 2013 Mayor Mike McGinn of Seattle, in response to protests from community members and privacy advocates, ordered the police department to abandon its plan to deploy two Draganflyer X6 drones obtained through a federal grant. The small devices, which are able to fly indoors and outdoors and carry a camera, were returned to the vendor. The department had received approval from the FAA but had not yet used them. It had held public demonstrations to show off the capabilities of the drones, which it planned to use for overhead views of large crime scenes, disasters, accidents, and search and rescue operations. But Seattle residents objected to the program at a city council meeting. Council members were considering an ordinance that would grant police authority to use facial-recognition software in the drones, although it would have prevented police from using them over mass assemblies.

The people of Seattle were not alone in their victory. Also in 2013, the city council of Charlottesville, Virginia, succeeded in passing a resolution that imposes a two-year moratorium on drone use within the city limits. And in response to public pressure, lawmakers in at least eleven states—California, Florida, Maine, Missouri, Montana, Nebraska, North Dakota, Oklahoma, Oregon, Texas, and Virginia—are also considering plans to restrict the use of drones over their airspace in response to concerns that the unmanned aircraft may be used to spy on democracy.[14]

Refusing RFID Chips

High school sophomore Andrea Hernandez refused to wear a new identification card issued by the Northside Independent School District in San Antonio, Texas. The district's "Student Locator Project" tracks students using ID cards embedded with RFID chips, to the purported end of encouraging maximum attendance and thus increasing the district's revenue from the state government. Hernandez was informed that failure to participate in the program would result in denial of access to the school library and cafeteria and that she would not be able to buy tickets for extracurricular events. Previously, students had been threatened with expulsion, fines, or involuntary transfers for refusing to be tracked by the program. When officials told Hernandez that she could wear the new ID without the chip, she refused on grounds that it would give the appearance that she supported the program and sued to stay at Jay High School, a magnet school for science and engineering. In early 2013 a federal judge ruled that Hernandez could be reassigned to another school for refusing to wear the ID, even one without the RFID chip.[15]

The Rutherford Institute, a civil liberties organization representing Hernandez, said it would appeal the decision to the United States Court of Appeals for the Fifth Circuit.

Boycotting Biometrics

Mike Webb objected to his son being forced to participate in a biometric palm-reader program at Carroll County Public Schools in Maryland.[16] More than fifty school systems and 160 hospital systems in fifteen states and Washington, D.C. are using palm vein-scanning identification devices. As part of the Carroll County lunch program, children have to scan their palms, which are matched by unique identifiers to stored information about their lunch accounts, in order to purchase food. As with most technology, the palm scanners are touted for their convenience—in this case to shorten lunch lines and reduce errors in student meal accounts.

In late 2012, the Carroll County superintendent of schools announced that the district would cancel the installation of the biometric equipment in the rest of its forty-three schools. The software and hardware cost would have been $300,000 plus maintenance contracts with PalmSecure, a product of the only company to manufacture the scanners to date, Fujitsu. The superintendent made the announcement after he was asked to review an opt-out program, compared to one in which parents would opt-in to allow their child's palm to be scanned.[17]

Campaign for a Commercial-Free Childhood

It is crucial to roll back the level of access and influence that corporations have over children. In 2002, to address the chronic problem of commercialism aimed at children, Susan Linn founded the Campaign for a Commercial-Free Childhood (CCFC). Two events in particular sparked the activist organization and the movement to reclaim childhood from corporate marketers. A group of parents, academics, educators, and healthcare providers, concerned about corporate influences on children, held a conference at Howard University in 1999. The next year, joined by others, they rallied outside the Grand Hyatt Hotel on 42nd Street in New York City to protest the Golden Marble Awards, the advertising industry's celebration of marketing to children. CCFC continued to protest the Golden Marbles until the industry cancelled them in 2003.[18]

CCFC has grown in numbers and uses a range of education and outreach to stop the practice of child-targeted marketing so that, in their words, "children can grow up—and parents can raise them—without being undermined by greed."[19]

Among its victories, CCFC insisted that the Walt Disney Company stop falsely marketing Baby Einstein videos as educational for babies. Disney complied and offered refunds to parents who had been deceived by the company's false claims.[20] CCFC also organized parents around the country to stop BusRadio, a company that broadcasted student-targeted ads on school buses. After a three-year campaign, BusRadio went out of business.[21] CCFC worked with parents and educators to defeat state legislation allowing advertising on school buses in several states, including Florida, Idaho, Kentucky, New York, Ohio, Oklahoma, Rhode Island, and Washington. The group also stopped McDonald's from advertising on report card envelopes in Florida. The advertisements promised elementary school students free Happy Meals as a reward for good school performance.[22] CCFC's successful efforts, in coordination with concerned families and community groups, demonstrate that corporate behavior can be regulated and controlled through focused public interest organizing and advocacy.

Political Research Associates

The social justice think tank Political Research Associates (PRA) was founded in 1981 to defend human rights and provide support to social justice advocates. The group's investigative research and analysis on the U.S. Right has been useful to educators, journalists, scholars, advocates, and the public, both in understanding right-wing influence domestically and abroad, and in mounting challenges to its practices and policies. Acknowledging the numerous threats to human and civil rights, PRA contends that "the most robust opposition over the past few decades has emerged from the U.S. Right, which routinely employs harmful scapegoating and clever slogans that oversimplify complex policy issues." In response, PRA offers in-depth analysis that reveals the underlying agendas of right-wing leaders, ideologies, and institutions.

In addition to publishing the quarterly magazine *The Public Eye*, PRA produces investigative reports, articles, and activist resource kits. Its staff members provide expert commentary for media outlets and advise policy makers and social justice advocates. Core issue areas are civil liberties, economic justice, reproductive justice, LGBTQ rights, and racial/immigrant justice. PRA's report *Manufacturing the Muslim Menace: Private Firms, Public Servants, and the Threat to Rights and Security* details a systemic failure to regulate content in nationwide counterterrorism training, with the result that Islamophobic messages are spread through law enforcement. Another report, *Platform for Prejudice: How the Nationwide Suspicious Activity Reporting Initiative Invites Racial Profiling, Erodes Civil Liberties, and Undermines Security*, examines the push to enlist law enforcement personnel as intelligence officers by encouraging police to report First Amendment–protected activities such as photography, taking notes, making diagrams, and advocating so-called extremist views.

Electronic Frontier Foundation

John Perry Barlow and Mitch Kapor formed the Electronic Frontier Foundation in 1990 to advocate for Internet civil liberties. The EFF provides education, lobbying, and litigation pertaining to digital speech. Its lawsuits against National Security Agency warrantless surveillance have helped highlight the program's unconstitutionality and have compelled the government to defend the program in the courts for years. The EFF, along with the other groups and individuals fighting for increased transparency, regularly submits requests for documents under the Freedom of Information Act in an effort to determine the extent to which the government uses technologies for spying on democracy. EFF white papers cover a range of issues relevant to technology and civil liberties, from location privacy and biometric data protection to best practices for online service providers.

As described earlier, the EFF's 2008 case *Jewel v. NSA*, suing the NSA and other government agencies on behalf of AT&T customers to stop warrantless surveillance of their communications and communications records, remains one of the few pending legal challenges that has not been dismissed on grounds of standing or sovereign immunity.

Electronic Privacy Information Center
Founded in 1994, the Electronic Privacy Information Center (EPIC) works to focus public attention on emerging civil liberties issues and to protect privacy, the First Amendment, and constitutional values. EPIC publishes reports and an online newsletter on civil liberties in the information age.

In 2012 the group filed a FOIA request and subsequent lawsuit to force the disclosure of FBI documents concerning technical specifications of the Stingray, a device that can triangulate the source of a cellular signal by acting in effect as a fake cell phone tower. It measures signal strengths of a particular device from several locations. With Stingrays, government agents can locate, interfere with, and intercept communications from cell phones and wireless devices. The FBI has used simulator technology of the same kind since at least 1995. Use of the Stingray drew scrutiny in a 2012 lawsuit, *United States v. Rigmaiden*, as the government tried to keep the technology from discovery. The government admitted in the lawsuit that its actions were intrusive enough to rise to a Fourth Amendment violation.

The People's Law Office

The Chicago group known as the People's Law Office (PLO) was founded in 1969 and has a storied history of defending civil rights of individuals and entire communities. Early cases including defending the rights of Black Panther Fred Hampton, murdered by the FBI, to representing members of the Puerto Rican community working for Puerto Rican independence.

Among the cases involving individuals deemed worthy of government monitoring for their political views, many of whom are falsely discredited by with charges of terrorist-related offenses, PLO lawyers defended Scott DeMuth, an animal-rights advocate accused of being a member of the Animal Liberation Front (ALF) and destroying an animal testing lab. DeMuth was subpoenaed by a federal grand jury in Iowa, where he refused to testify and was charged with engaging in "animal enterprise terrorism." After months of pretrial challenges, the Iowa charges were dismissed in return for a six-month sentence for a separate incident in Minnesota.

As mentioned earlier, it was PLO attorneys who represented Brian Jacob Church, one of several activists arrested in a midnight raid days before the 2012 NATO Summit. They were subsequently charged with terrorism and several other felonies, and as of this writing have spent over six months in custody on bonds of $1.5 million.

Attorneys from the office have represented activists targeted by the government for their political activities, including environmentalists, antiwar activists, people raising awareness of police brutality, and individuals active in many other movements.

Katherine Albrecht and Liz McIntyre

Two women care a great deal about mass surveillance and the increasing influence of corporations. Katherine Albrecht and Liz McIntyre coauthored the book *Spy Chips: How Major Corporations and Government Plan to Track Your Every Move*, winner of the November 2005 Lysander Spooner Award for advancing the literature of liberty. They founded Consumers Against Supermarket Privacy Invasion and Numbering (CASPIAN), a national consumer organization created in 1999 to educate consumer-citizens about shopper surveillance.

Albrecht and MacIntyre advocate fighting RFID chips by identifying companies using RFID irresponsibly and encouraging consumers to refuse to shop in their stores or purchase their products. Given that RFID tags are easily hidden, they developed model legislation that would require items containing RFID tags to indicate their presence. They support campaigns such as opposing tags in our passports, and suggest paying cash at toll booths instead of using automatic toll transponders. The two advocates also discourage shopping at places requiring frequent shopper or loyalty cards, and encourage paying cash for purchases. They insist on deactivating or removing RFID chips in products and practicing good privacy hygiene by teaching children about privacy.

Albrecht is also committed to Internet privacy and advises using proxy search options to prevent corporations and others from tracking search habits. She serves on the board of the free search engine Ixquick, touted as the world's most private search engine. Ixquick does not record IP addresses, make a record of users' searches, or record details about proxy usage. The company's data-collection practices are third-party certified with the "European Privacy Seal" and considered by many to be the best in the industry.

Nicholas Merrill

If telecommunications providers willingly turn customer data over to the NSA, why not create a provider guaranteed to protect customers from surveillance? That's what Nicholas Merrill is doing. After receiving a national security letter from the FBI seeking electronic records (which he refused to turn over), Merrill became the first individual to sue the FBI and Department of Justice.

He's raising money to start a nonprofit telecommunications provider with the mission of preserving privacy. The ISP will use ubiquitous encryption, by which customers will own their data and be the only ones who can decrypt it. It will also sell mobile phone service and, for a modest monthly fee, Internet connectivity. The ISP will challenge demands for information from the government if they seem unconstitutional. It will be run by Merrill's nonprofit, the Calyx Institute.

Under the Communications Assistance for Law Enforcement Act, put in place in 1994, telecommunications companies must configure their networks to be easily wiretapped by the FBI. But ISPs are not responsible for decrypting communications if they don't possess the information needed to do so.

Freedom of the Press Foundation
Without a free press to expose and challenge it, surveillance will continue unabated in its many forms. The Freedom of the Press Foundation was founded in 2012 to support journalism that uncovers unlawful and corrupt government practices and that aims for increased transparency and accountability on the part of our leaders. The foundation recognizes that modern media are strongly influenced by corporations and government agencies, resulting in vapid news coverage and outright censorship.

Acknowledging the great competition for funding, the foundation offers funding support for media outlets and individual journalists who have been censored or shut out for their work in these areas. Using "crowd-source" funding, every two months the foundation highlights four deserving news and "transparency" organizations and makes it easy for individuals to allocate funding for each. The board of directors selects two additional projects twice a year and distributes grants to them.

The foundation has provided support for WikiLeaks, Truthout, the Center for Public Integrity, the Bureau of Investigative Journalism, MuckRock News, the National Security Archive, and the UpTake. Board members include Daniel Ellsberg, Glenn Greenwald, John Cusack, John Perry Barlow, and others committed to alternative media, free expression, and government transparency.

Cogent Commentators

A rash of news reports after the Boston Marathon attacks applauded the role of surveillance cameras in apprehending the suspects, some even calling for increased monitoring. With some notable exceptions, few journalists criticized constant electronic observation. In his *Counterpunch* article "Boston Overkill" Andrew Levine wrote that "one of the more disconcerting aspects of the coverage of the events in Boston was what it revealed about how pervasive surveillance has now become in the Land of the Free."[27] Explaining that privacy, "once an American's birthright," has virtually vanished, Levine noted,

"The level of surveillance in Boston was doubtless more intrusive than viewers were shown," suggesting that in addition to cameras, there were likely other ways that individual privacy was intruded upon, such as the information authorities may be getting from drones, about which the public is largely ignorant.

James Warren, in "Surveillance's Dark Downside"[28] for the *New York Daily News*, considered what happens to information gathered and retained by the government without consent—such as license plate numbers photographed to catch speeding drivers—and used for other purposes. He writes that such data "can wind up exploited in ways totally unrelated to the reasons originally appreciated by the individual, maybe subpoenaed in a divorce proceeding or scrutinized by a prospective employer." Warren quotes Lior Strahilevitz from the University of Chicago Law School: "One has to supervise how people use surveillance data, and that might mean surveilling the people charged with surveillance."

Former U.S. representative Ron Paul observed in his blog that the Boston events gave authorities the chance to turn a routine police investigation into a military-type occupation of an entire city. Paul wrote, "This unprecedented move should frighten us as much or more than the attack itself." Criticizing the lockdown as ineffective, he added, "While the media crowed that the apprehension of the suspects was a triumph of the new surveillance state—and, predictably, many talking heads and members of Congress called for even more government cameras pointed at the rest of us—the fact is [that] none of this caught the suspect."

A CNN opinion piece by Washington University law professor Neil M. Richards asserts that installing additional surveillance cameras would be bad policy, and would threaten civil liberties. Richards urges rejecting the premise that additional surveillance of public areas will make us safer; while some may feel more secure, he says, this is but an illusion of safety. "History has shown repeatedly that broad government surveillance powers inevitably get abused," he notes, "whether by the Gestapo, the Stasi, or our own FBI."[30]

Commentaries such as these provide a counterbalance to often alarmist essays and news reports issued in the wake of high-profile events, especially when the specter of terrorism arises.

Divulging Deepnet Data—Institutionalizing the Threat to Democracy

James Bamford alerted the nation to the existence of the National Security Agency in the 1980s. In 2012 he wrote an article for *Wired* detailing the agency's $2 billion Utah Data Center. The colossal center—a million square feet—will store private emails, mobile phone calls, Internet searches, and vast troves of other personal data. It will also break codes, important given that so much of the data it collects will be encrypted, and will be able to access and warehouse "deepnet" data that is out of the public's reach. Government reports, password-protected data, and many sources of information of interest to the Department of Defense, will be captured, stored, and thoroughly searched. If anyone doubts whether a U.S. surveillance state exists and is spying on democracy and all aspects of our personal lives, awareness of the Utah Data Center should make matters clear.

Recruiting More Resolute Resisters

This country's leaders should acknowledge that attempts to improve the national intelligence infrastructure have been an abject failure. As Judge Richard Posner urges in *Uncertain Shield: The U.S. Intelligence System in the Throes of Reform*, domestic intelligence might best be performed by an entity separate from law enforcement. In addition, a level of oversight should be institutionalized, perhaps by designation of a nongovernmental civil liberties auditor and a domestic intelligence oversight board, composed (as Posner suggests) mostly of civil liberties and constitutional attorneys. No matter what form intelligence gathering takes, it is essential to restore the limits on political and religious spying on ordinary Americans enacted to deter the FBI's COINTELPRO misdeeds and CIA spying on our own.

In 1975 President Gerald Ford established the Commission on CIA Activities Within the United States to ascertain whether domestic CIA activities had exceeded the agency's authority. Among other findings, it concluded that the CIA's program of intercepting mail between the United States and the Soviet Union as it came through New York was unlawful. It also found that Operation CHAOS, which amassed voluminous material on domestic dissidents and their activities, exceeded the CIA's authority. Significantly, the commission's report to the president emphasized that "the mere invocation of the 'national security' does not grant unlimited power to the government."[33] Decades later, the Bush and Obama administrations lost sight of these guiding principles.

To reclaim freedom and democracy, we need to remind our leaders of those values.

We need to follow the examples of the schoolgirl in Texas who said no to holding an RFID-embedded identification card, and the schoolboy in Carroll County who refused to have his palm scanned. We need to follow the model of those who speak out against unlawful and objectionable government and corporate practices. We need to defend and encourage those who challenge authority and demand accountability, and not let ourselves become bystanders to repressive tactics used against social movements that champion the use of protest, civil disobedience, and resistance. We should draw inspiration from those who work against the trend of forcing the non-elite citizenry to conform. We should stand up in support of those who volunteer time and effort on behalf of the collective public interest, who launch campaigns, movements, and lawsuits to challenge unconstitutional actions and corporate crimes. We should support all those who speak out to educate the public through new and traditional media, whether it means using a computer, a letter to the editor, a community radio station, or a zine.

In short, if we want to prevent ourselves from becoming silenced, compliant subjects in a corporatized society where everything we do passes through technology connected to a militarized surveillance grid, we should resist by declaring allegiance to all who dare to defend their rights and freedoms by exercising them.

All who resist are the custodians of democracy.

ENDNOTES

INTRODUCTION
1. 389 U.S. 258, 264 (1967).

CHAPTER 1
1. J. David Goodman, "Police Records Detail Large Presence at Critical Mass Rides," *New York Times*, Cityroom blog, October 20, 2010. Accessed April 1, 2013: http://cityroom.blogs.nytimes.com/2010/10/20/police-records-detail-large-presence-at-critical-mass-rides.
2. Jim Dwyer, "Police Infiltrate Protests, Videotapes Show," *New York Times*, December 22, 2005. Accessed March 30, 2013: www.nytimes.com/2005/12/22/nyregion/22police.html.
3. *See* "Bicyclists: Network and Statistics," New York City Department of Transportation. Accessed February 28, 2013: www.nyc.gov/html/dot/html/bicyclists/bikestats.shtml.
4. Chris Carlsson, email message to the author, February 19, 2013.
5. Andrea Bernstein, "Citibank Spins Publicity with NYC BikeShare," American Public Media, *Marketplace Morning Report*, May 14, 2012. Accessed March 30, 2013: www.marketplace.org/topics/sustainability/transportation-nation/citibank-spins-publicity-nyc-bikeshare.
6. Christopher Dickey, *Securing the City: Inside America's Best Counterterror Force—The NYPD* (New York: Simon & Schuster, 2009), 186.
7. Ibid.
8. Ibid.
9. Ibid.
10. Patrice O'Shaughnessy, "Fury at Anarchist Convention Threat," *New York Daily News*, July 12, 2004. Accessed March 30, 2013: www.nydailynews.com/archives/news/fury-anarchist-convention-threat-article-1.594031; and Craig Horowitz, "How to Care for An Angry Mob," *New York Magazine*, May 17, 2004. Accessed March 30, 2013: http://nymag.com/nymetro/news/rnc/n_10370/.
11. Editorial, "Cyclists, the Police and the Rest of Us," *New York Times*, December 29, 2006. Accessed March 30, 2013: www.nytimes.com/2006/12/29/opinion/29fri2.html.
12. New York Police Department, Intelligence Division, Intelligence Collection Coordinator, Deputy Commissioner's Briefing, April 25, 2008. Accessed February 28, 2013: http://hosted.ap.org/specials/in-

teractives/documents/nypd/dci-briefing-04252008.pdf.

13. Bill DiPaola (founder and director, Time's Up), interview with the author, September 15, 2012.

14. *City of New York, et al. v. Time's Up, Inc., et al.*, 11 Misc. 3d 1052(A), 814 NY2d 890, 2006 NY Slip Op 50189(U) (Sup Ct, NY County Feb. 14, 2006) at 2; accessed February 28, 2013: http://law.justia. com/cases/new-york/other-courts/2006/2006-50189.html.

15. Ibid., 9.

16. Bill DiPaola (founder and director, Time's Up), interview with the author, September 15, 2012.

17. New York Police Department, Intelligence Division, Intelligence Collection Coordinator, Deputy Commissioner's Briefing, April 25, 2008. Accessed February 28, 2013: http://hosted.ap.org/specials/interactives/documents/nypd/dci-briefing-04252008.pdf.

18. Brigitt Keller (executive director, National Police Accountability Project), interview with the author, February 10, 2013.

19. Jim Dwyer, "Videos Challenge Accounts of Convention Unrest," *New York Times*, April 12, 2005. Accessed March 29, 2013: www.nytimes.com/2005/04/12/nyregion/12video.html.

20. Jefferson Siegel, "Police May Be Backpedaling from Crackdown on Cyclists," *The Villager*, Vol. 75, No. 41, March 1–7, 2006. Accessed April 1, 2013: http://thevillager.com/villager_148/policemaybebackpedaling.html; Lou Young, "Critical Mass Gets Dangerous: One Woman Claims She Was Thrown from Her Bike by the NYPD," *WCBSTV*, March 7, 2006, originally at http://wcbstv.com/local/local_story_066002543.html, reprinted at http://times-up.org/2006-interest/2006-03-07-cm-gets-dangerous-wcbstv. Accessed March 29, 2013.

21. Thomas J. Lueck, "City Settles with Protester Who Claimed She Was Kicked," *New York Times*, April 18, 2007. Accessed April 1, 2013: www.nytimes.com/2007/04/18/nyregion/18settle.html.

22. Kareem Fahim and Jim Dwyer, "At Least 18 Arrests Made in Tense Night of a Monthly Cycling Protest," *New York Times*, April 30, 2005. Accessed April 1, 2013: www.nytimes.com/2005/04/30/nyregion/30bike.html.

23. "Bicyclists Give Gift to a Chief Who Gave Them Hell," *The Villager*, Vol. 76, No. 40, February 28–March 6, 2007. Accessed April 1, 2013: http://thevillager.com/villager_200/bicyclistsgivegift.html.

24. Cate Doty, "Bike Riders in New York Win Settlement," *New York*

Times, October 28, 2010. Accessed March 29, 2013: www.nytimes.com/2010/10/19/nyregion/19critical.html?ref=criticalmass.

25. Chris Carlsson, email message to the author, February 19, 2013.
26. Bill DiPaola (founder and director, Time's Up), interview with the author, September 15, 2012.

CHAPTER 2

1. Travis Reed, "Growers Want FDA to Clear Fla.'s Whole Tomato Crop," *USA Today*, July 16, 2008. Accessed April 1, 2013: http://usa-today30.usatoday.com/money/economy/2008-07-16-873563645_x.htm.
2. "Ending Abuses and Improving Working Conditions for Tomato Workers," *Before the Committee on Health, Education, Labor and Pensions, United States Senate*, 110th Cong. (April 15, 2008) (statement of Mary Bauer, Director, Immigrant Justice Project, Southern Poverty Law Center), 2. Accessed February 28, 2013: www.help.senate.gov/imo/media/doc/Bauer.pdf.
3. Ibid.,10.
4. Amy Bennett Williams, "Burger King VP Puts Self on Grill: Daughter Says Dad Wrote Anti-Coalition Postings, *Fort Myers News-Press*, April 28, 2008. Reprinted at www.sanders.senate.gov/newsroom/news/?id=2c925b8d-bda6-4288-8b33-6d0839c9a362. Accessed April 1, 2013.
5. Eric Schlosser, "Burger with a Side of Spies," *New York Times*, May 7, 2008. Accessed April 1, 2013: www.nytimes.com/2008/05/07/opinion/07schlosser.html.
6. Amy Bennett Williams, interview by Rachel Martin, *Bryant Park Project*, National Public Radio, May 8, 2008. Accessed April 1, 2013: www.npr.org/templates/transcript/transcript.php?storyId=90268069.
7. Lauren Shepherd, "Burger King Profit Rises 42%, Tops Estimates," *USA Today*, August 21, 2008. Accessed April 1, 2013: http://usato-day30.usatoday.com/money/companies/earnings/2008-08-21-burger-king_N.htm.
8. "AlarmForce Announces Board of Directors Appointment," *Wall Street Journal*, March 12, 2010. Accessed April 1, 2013: http://3gcapital.com/AlarmForce%20Board%20Appt%203G%20Capital%20WSJ%20MAR%202010.pdf.
9. Coca-Cola Human Rights Statement. Accessed April 1, 2013: www.coca-colacompany.com/our-company/human-rights-statement.

10. Wikileaks, The Global Intelligence Files, re: PETA, released on February 27, 2012. Accessed April 1, 2013: http://wikileaks.org/gifiles/docs/5447352_re-peta-.html.

11. Gianluca Mezzofiore, "The WikiLeaks GiFiles: Coca-Cola Hired Stratfor to Monitor Peta Activists at Winter Olympics," *International Business Times*, February 27, 2012. Accessed April 1, 2013: www.ibtimes.co.uk/articles/305295/20120227/wikileaks-gifiles-assange-coca-cola-stratfor-vancouver.htm.

12. Ira Winkler, *Spies among Us: How to Stop the Spies, Terrorists, Hackers, and Criminals You Don't Even Know You Encounter Every Day* (Indianapolis, IN: Wiley, 2005).

13. Frank J. Donner, *The Age of Surveillance* (New York: Alfred A. Knopf, 1980), 460.

14. Ibid., 431–33.

15. *Nader v. General Motors Corporation*, 25 N.Y.2d 560, 255 N.E.2d 765, 307 N.Y.S.2d 647 (1970).

16. Ibid.

17. Eveline Lubbers, *Secret Manoeuvres in the Dark: Corporate and Police Spying on Activists* (London: Pluto Press, 2012), 45.

18. "New York City during the Republican National Convention: A Look behind Police and Security Efforts to Insure Guest Safety," Reprinted from the October 2004 issue of *Hotel/Casino/Resort Security*. *Accessed* February 28, 2013: www.strategicsecuritycorp.com/downloads/gop_conv_security.pdf.

19. "Guidelines for the Establishment of State and Local Private Security Advisory Councils," report prepared by the Private Security Advisory Council to the Law Enforcement Assistance Administration, U.S. Department of Justice, 1977, iii–iv.

20. Edward Connors, "Planning and Managing Security for Major Special Events: Guidelines for Law Enforcement," Institute for Law and Justice (2007), 10. Prepared for the U.S. Department of Justice, Office of Community Oriented Policing Services. Accessed February 28, 2013: www.cops.usdoj.gov/files/ric/Publications/e07071299_web.txt.

21. "New York City during the Republican National Convention: A Look behind Police and Security Efforts to Insure Guest Safety," Reprinted from the October 2004 issue of *Hotel/Casino/Resort Security*. *Accessed* February 28, 2013: www.strategicsecuritycorp.com/downloads/gop_conv_security.pdf.

22. "Threat Analysis and Intelligence Briefing, 47th Annual Meeting of the Society of Toxicology and ToxExpo 2008, March 16-20, 2008, Washington State Convention and Trade Center, Seattle, WA," Report prepared by INA, Inc.. Accessed March 2, 2013: www.greenisthenewred.com/blog/wp-content/Images/ina_toxexpo_threat.pdf.

23. Jeremy Scahill, "Blackwater's Black Ops," *The Nation*, October 4, 2010. Accessed April 1, 2013: www.thenation.com/article/154739/blackwaters-black-ops.

24. Ibid.

25. Ibid.

26. Max Abelson, "Wall Street Tracks 'Wolves' as May 1 Protests Loom," *Bloomberg*, April 26, 2012. Accessed April 1, 2013: www.bloomberg.com/news/2012-04-26/wall-street-tracks-wolves-as-may-1-protests-loom.html.

27. Max Abelson, "Banks Cooperate to Track Occupy Protesters," *San Francisco Chronicle*, April 27, 2012. Accessed March 29, 2013: www.sfgate.com/business/article/Banks-cooperate-to-track-Occupy-protesters-3513838.php.

28. *Greenpeace, Inc, v. The Dow Chemical Company, et al.*, Civil Action No. 0008036-11 (D.C. Super. Ct. 2011). Complaint accessed March 1, 2013: www.greenpeace.org/usa/Global/usa/planet3/PDFs/SpyGate/DC%20Superior%20Court%20Complaint.pdf; *see generally* www.greenpeace.org/usa/en/news-and-blogs/news/spygate/.

29. James Ridgeway and Daniel Schulman, "Greenpeace Sues Chemical and PR Firms for 'Unlawful' Spying," *Mother Jones*, November 29, 2010. Accessed April 1, 2013: www.motherjones.com/environment/2010/11/greenpeace-sues-dow-sasol-dezenhall-ketchum-spying; see also James Ridgeway, "Black Ops, Green Groups," *Mother Jones*, April 10, 2008. Accessed March 29, 2013: www.motherjones.com/environment/2008/04/exclusive-cops-and-former-secret-service-agents-ran-black-ops-green-groups.

   See generally www.greenpeace.org/usa/en/news-and-blogs/news/spygate. Accessed March 1, 2013.

30. Kim Zetter, "Congress Asks to Review DoD and NSA Contracts With HBGary," *Wired*, March 17, 2011. Accessed on April 1, 2013: www.wired.com/threatlevel/2011/03/congress-and-hbgary.

31. Eric Lipton and Charlie Savage, "Hackers Reveal Offers to Spy on Corporate Rivals," *New York Times*, February 11, 2011. Accessed April 1, 2013: www.nytimes.com/2011/02/12/us/politics/12hackers.

html?_r=0; Parmy Olson, "Congress Opens Investigation into HBGary Federal Scandal, *Forbes*, March 17, 2011. Accessed April 1, 2013: www.forbes.com/sites/parmyolson/2011/03/17/congress-opens-investigation-into-hbgary-scandal.

32. Mark Williams, "The Total Information Awareness Project Lives On," *MIT Technology Review*, Massachusetts Institute of Technology, April 26, 2006. Accessed April 1, 2013: www.technologyreview.com/news/405707/the-total-information-awareness-project-lives-on.

33. Bill Quigley and Rachel Meeropol, "Attention Left, Liberal and Radical Groups: Pennsylvania Has Been Monitoring You!", *Counterpunch*, October 6, 2010. Accessed April 1, 2013: www.counterpunch.org/2010/10/06/pennsylvania-has-been-monitoring-you.

34. Ibid.

35. Dana Priest and William A. Arkin,"Top Secret America: A Hidden World, Growing Beyond Control," *Washington Post*, July 19, 2010. Accessed April 1, 2013: http://projects.washingtonpost.com/top-secret-america/articles/a-hidden-world-growing-beyond-control.

36. Casey Newton, "Google Reaches $7 Million Settlement with States over Street View Case," *CNET*, March 12, 2013. Accessed April 1, 2013: http://news.cnet.com/8301-1023_3-57573837-93/google-reaches-$7-million-settlement-with-states-over-street-view-case.

37. Zainab Akande, "Street View Scandal: Google to Pay 38 States $7 Million," PolicyMic, March 15, 2013. Accessed April 1, 2013: www.policymic.com/articles/29947/street-view-scandal-google-to-pay-38-states-7-million/405544.

38. Ibid.

CHAPTER 3

1. Curt Gentry, *J. Edgar Hoover: The Man and the Secrets* (New York: W.W. Norton, 1991), 11.

2. Tim Weiner, *Enemies: A History of the FBI* (New York: Random House, 2012), 11.

3. Federal Bureau of Investigation, "A Brief History of the FBI." Accessed March 3, 2013: www.fbi.gov/about-us/history/brief-history.

4. Raymond J. Batvinis, *The Origins of FBI Counterintelligence* (Lawrence: University Press of Kansas, 2007), 54.

5. Ibid., 57–58.

6. Ibid., 63.

7. Geoffrey Rips, *Unamerican Activities: The Campaign against the Under-*

ground Press (San Francisco: City Lights, 1981), 166.

8. Ibid., 81.

9. Tim Shorrock, *Spies for Hire: The Secret World of Intelligence Outsourcing* (New York: Simon & Schuster, 2008), 13.

10. Sebastian Abbott, "The Outsourcing of U.S. Intelligence Analysis," *News 21*, July 28, 2006. Accessed April 1, 2013: http://newsinitiative. org/story/2006/07/28/the_outsourcing_of_u_s_intelligence.

11. Alice Lipowicz, "CSC Captures NSA Groundbreaker Extension," *Washington Technology*, June 6, 2007. Accessed April 1, 2013: http:// washingtontechnology.com/articles/2007/06/06/csc-captures-nsa-groundbreaker-extension.aspx.

12. "CSC-Led Alliance Receives Three-Year Option for National Security Agency Groundbreaker Contact," *PR Newswire*, June 6, 2007. Accessed April 1, 2013: www.prnewswire.com/news-releases/csc-led-alliance-receives-three-year-option-for-national-security-agency-groundbreaker-contract-57908027.html.

13. Arshad Mohammed and Sara Kehaulani Goo, "Government Increasingly Turning to Data Mining," *Washington Post*, June 15, 2006. Accessed April 1, 2013: www.washingtonpost.com/wp-dyn/content/article/2006/06/14/AR2006061402063.html.

14. *See* "Intelligence Activities and the Rights of Americans, Final Report, Book II," U.S. Senate Select Committee to Study Governmental Operations with Respect to Intelligence Activities, S. Rept. 94-755 (1976), 67.

15. Mireya Navarro, "New Light on Old F.B.I. Fight; Decades of Surveillance of Puerto Rican Groups," *New York Times*, November 28, 2003. Accessed April 1, 2013: www.nytimes.com/2003/11/28/nyregion/new-light-on-old-fbi-fight-decades-of-surveillance-of-puerto-rican-groups.html.

16. Geoffrey Rips, *The Campaign against the Underground Press* (San Francisco: City Lights, 1981), 14.

17. Christopher Pyle, interview by Amy Goodman, "Christopher Pyle, Whistleblower Who Sparked Church Hearings of 1970s, on Military Spying of Olympia Peace Activists," *Democracy Now!*, July 29, 2009. Video and transcript accessed April 1, 2013: www.democracynow. org/2009/7/29/pyle.

18. *See generally* James Kirkpatrick Davis, *Spying on America: The FBI's Domestic Counterintelligence Program* (New York: Praeger, 1992), 1–22.

19. David Cunningham, *There's Something Happening Here: The New Left,*

the Klan, and FBI Counterintelligence (Berkeley: University of California Press, 2004), 36.

20. Curt Gentry, *J. Edgar Hoover: The Man and the Secrets* (New York: W.W. Norton, 1991), 682–83.

21. The Church Committee held hearings on the FBI's role in COINTELPRO in November and December 1975. The body of its publicly released work included 1) an interim report with findings on U.S. involvement in assassination plots against foreign leaders; 2) seven volumes of public hearings; and 3) seven additional "Books" on various topics, including Book II, Intelligence Activities and the Rights of Americans (April 26, 1976), and Book III, Supplementary Detailed Staff Reports on Intelligence Activities and the Rights of Americans (April 23, 1976). These reports are available at www.intelligence.senate.gov/churchcommittee.html. Accessed March 3, 2013.

22. Ibid.

23. U.S. Department of Justice (March 7, 1983), reprinted in *1983 Senate Subcommittee Hearing on Smith Guidelines* at 47. The Smith Guidelines can be found at *FBI Domestic Security Guidelines:* Oversight Hearings Before the Subcommittee on Civil and Constitutional Rights of the House Committee on the Judiciary, 98th Cong. 67–85 (1983). For an overview and history of the Attorney General's Guidelines, *see generally* Emily Berman, "Domestic Intelligence: New Powers, New Risks," Brennan Center for Justice, 2011. Accessed March 29, 2013: www.brennancenter.org/sites/default/files/legacy/AGGReportFINALed.pdf.

24. Antiterrorism and Effective Death Penalty Act of 1996 (AEDPA), Pub. L. No. 104-132, 110 Stat. 1214 (1996).

25. *See* Uniting and Strengthening America by Providing Appropriate Tools Required to Intercept and Obstruct Terrorism Act of 2001 (USA PATRIOT Act), Pub. L. No. 107-56, 115 Stat. 272 (2001).

26. Charlie Savage, "California: Judge Strikes Down Law on National Security Letters," *New York Times*, March 15, 2013. Accessed April 1, 2013: www.nytimes.com/2013/03/16/us/california-judge-strikes-down-law-on-national-security-letters.html.

27. U.S. Department of Justice, *The Attorney General's Guidelines on General Crimes, Racketeering Enterprise and Terrorism Enterprise Investigations*, May 30, 2002. www.justice.gov/ag/readingroom/generalcrimea.htm.

28. ACLU Fact Sheet—New Attorney General Guidelines, October 8,

2008. Accessed March 29, 2013: www.aclu.org/print/national-securi-ty/fact-sheet-new-attorney-general-guidelines.

29. Mike German, interview by Michael Ratner, *Law and Disorder,* WBAI, June 20, 2011. Accessed April 1, 2013: http://lawanddisorder. org/2011/06/law-and-disorder-june-20-2011.

30. Ibid.

31. *See*, e.g., *Alliance to End Repression v. City of Chicago,* 91 F.R.D. 182 (N.D. Ill. 1981) and 561 F. Supp. 537 (N.D. Ill. 1982); in New York, *Handschu v. Special Services Division,* 605 F. Supp. 1384 (S.D.N.Y. 1985).

32. *Handschu v. Special Services Division,* 605 F. Supp. 1384 (S.D.N.Y. 1985).

33. *Alliance to End Repression v. City of Chicago,* 91 FRD 182 (N.D. Ill. 1981) and 561 F. Supp. 537 (N.D. Ill. 1982).

34. *See* Michael Moss and Ford Fessenden, "America under Surveillance: Privacy and Security; New Tools for Domestic Spying, and Qualms," *New York Times,* December 10, 2002. Accessed April 1, 2013: www. nytimes.com/2002/12/10/us/america-under-surveillance-privacy-security-new-tools-for-domestic-spying-qualms.html; Ford Fes-senden with Michael Moss, "Threats and Responses: Privacy; Going Electronic, Denver Reveals Long-Term Surveillance," *New York Times,* December 21, 2002. Accessed March 29, 2013: www.nytimes. com/2002/12/21/world/threats-responses-privacy-going-electronic-denver-reveals-long-term-surveillance.html.

35. Jeremy Gorner, "City Settles in Police Spying Case," *Chicago Tribune,* April 26, 2011. Accessed April 1, 2013: http://articles.chicagobreak-ingnews.com/2011-04-26/news/29476638_1_city-probes-chicago-police-undercover-officer.

36. Chris Hawley and Matt Apuzzo, "Schools Raise Privacy Concerns over NYPD Spying on Muslim Students," *Associated Press,* October 11, 2011. Accessed April 1, 2013: www.pulitzer.org/files/2012/investi-gative_reporting/ap/nypd6.pdf.

37. Ibid.

38. Johanna Fernandez (professor, Baruch College), email to the author, August 13, 2012.

39. Chris Hawley and Matt Apuzzo, "Schools Raise Privacy Concerns over NYPD Spying on Muslim Students," Associated Press, October 11, 2011. Accessed April 1, 2013: www.pulitzer.org/files/2012/investi-gative_reporting/ap/nypd6.pdf.

40. Traci Yoder and Nathan Tempey, "Developments in the Policing of National Special Security Events: An Analysis of the 2012 RNC and DNC," National Lawyers Guild, January 2013, 13. Accessed April 1, 2013: www.nlg.org/developments-policing-national-special-security-events-analysis-2012-rnc-and-dnc.

41. Ibid.,14.

42. Mike Carter, "Activist Spied On? Man Wins Settlement," *Seattle Times*, May 7, 2010. Accessed March 29, 2013: http://seattletimes.com/html/localnews/2011780363_spysettle05m.html.

43. Ibid.

44. Julian Sanchez, "Leasing the Surveillance State: How to Reform Patriot Act Surveillance Authorities," Cato Institute, May 16, 2011. Accessed March 29, 2013: www.cato.org/doc-download/sites/cato.org/files/pubs/pdf/PA675.pdf.

45. Authorization for Use of Military Force Act, Pub. L. No. 107-40, 115 Stat. 224 (2001).

46. Electronic Frontier Foundation, www.eff.org/NSA-spying. Accessed March 3, 2013.

47. David B. Caruso, "Twitter Fights Subpoena in Occupy Arrest Case," *USA Today*, May 9, 2012. Accessed April 1, 2013: http://usatoday30.usatoday.com/tech/news/story/2012-05-08/twitter-occupy-subpoena/54847164/1.

48. Janon Fisher, "Twitter Gives Judge Three Months' Worth of Tweets from Occupy Wall Street Protester Malcolm Harris," *New York Daily News*, September 14, 2012. Accessed April 1, 2013: www.nydailynews.com/new-york/twitter-judge-months-worth-tweet-occupy-wall-street-protester-malcolm-harris-article-1.1160067.

49. *Mount Hope Church v. Bash Back!, et al.*, Case 2:11-CV-00536-RAJ, Document 20, Filed 4/21/11 (9th Cir.), 6.

50. Michael Avery, interview by Heidi Boghosian and Michael Smith, *Law and Disorder*, WBAI, September 18, 2006. Accessed April 1, 2013: www.lawanddisorder.org/2006/09/law-and-disorder-september-18-2006.

51. Ibid.

52. *ACLU v. NSA*, 493 F. 3d 644 (6th Cir. 2007).

53. *Hepting v. AT&T Corp.*, 439 F. Supp. 2d 974 (N.D. Cal. 2006).

54. *See* In re Nat. Sec. Agency Telecommunications Records Litigation, 669 F.3d 928 (9th Cir. 2011).

55. *See Jewel v. Nat'l. Security Agency, et al.*, 673 F.3d 902 (2011).

56. *See* "Jewel v. NSA: Electronic Frontier Foundation." Accessed March 8, 2013: www.eff.org/cases/jewel.

CHAPTER 4

1. James Kirkpatrick Davis, *Spying on America: The FBI's Domestic Counterintelligence Program* (New York: Praeger, 1992), 120–21.
2. Ibid., 120, citing FBI Memorandum, Headquarters to Los Angeles Field Office, May 1970; Joyce Harber, "Miss A Rates as Expectant Mother," *Los Angeles Times*, May 19, 1970, 11.
3. Curt Gentry, *J. Edgar Hoover: The Man and the Secrets* (New York: W.W. Norton, 1991), 648.
4. James Kirkpatrick Davis, *Spying on America: The FBI's Domestic Counterintelligence Program* (New York: Praeger, 1992), 121.
5. For a detailed account of the killing of Fred Hampton, *see* Jeffrey Haas, *The Assassination of Fred Hampton: How the FBI and the Chicago Police Murdered a Black Panther* (Chicago: Chicago Review Press, 2009).
6. Alexandra Natapoff, *Snitching: Criminal Informants and the Erosion of American Justice* (New York University Press, 2009), 149.
7. Kevin Wilson, interview by Richard Gonzales, "Oakland Police Spy on Anti-War Group," *Morning Edition*, National Public Radio, August 8, 2006. Accessed April 1, 2013: www.npr.org/templates/story/story.php?storyId=5626076.
8. Thomas Cincotta, email to author, February 2, 2013.
9. Ibid.
10. Ibid.
11. *See* "Federal Support for and Involvement in State and Local Fusion Centers," United States Senate Permanent Subcommittee on investigations, Committee on Homeland Security and Governmental Affairs, October 3, 2012, 27. www.hsgac.senate.gov/download/?id=49139e81-1dd7-4788-a3bb-d6e7d97dde04. Accessed March 4, 2013.
12. Ibid., 61.
13. Colin Moynihan and Scott Shane, "For Anarchist, Details of Life as F.B.I. Target," *New York Times*, May 28, 2011. Accessed April 1, 2013: www.nytimes.com/2011/05/29/us/29surveillance.html.
14. Ibid.
15. *See*, e.g., *Riggs v. City of Albuquerque*, 916 F.2d 582 (10th Cir. 1990); *Ghandi v. Police Department of City of Detroit*, 747 F.2d 338 (6th

Cir. 1984); *Handschu v. Special Services Division*, 349 F. Supp. 766 (S.D.N.Y. 1982).

16. Council of the District of Columbia, Committee on the Judiciary, "Report on Investigation of the Metropolitan Police Department's Policy and Practice in Handling Demonstrations in the District of Columbia," March 11, 2004. Accessed April 1, 2013: www.dcwatch. com/police/040311.htm.

17. Ibid.

18. *Julianne Panagacos et al., v. John J. Towery et al.*, Case No. 11-35538 (9th Cir. 2011).

19. National Lawyers Guild, "Court Rules Peace Activists Can Sue the U.S. Military for Infiltration," news release, December 18, 2012. Accessed April 1, 2013: www.nlg.org/news/court-rules-peace-activists-can-sue-us-military-infiltration.

20. Larry Hildes, email to author, January 18, 2013.

21. Ibid.

22. National Lawyers Guild, "Court Rules Peace Activists Can Sue the U.S. Military for Infiltration," news release, December 18, 2012. Accessed April 1, 2013: www.nlg.org/news/court-rules-peace-activists-can-sue-us-military-infiltration.

23. Larry Hildes, email to author, January 18, 2013.

24. Ibid.

25. Ibid.

26. Letter to Attorney General Bill Lockyer from Mark Schlosberg, ACLU of Northern California, April 21, 2004. Accessed March 29, 2013: www.aclu.org/free-speech/letter-attorney-general-bill-lockyer.

27. American Civil Liberties Union of Northern California, "Attorney General Bill Lockyer Finds Sheriff's Department Infiltrated Peace Fresno; ACLU Calls for Enforcement of Stricter Guidelines," news release, February 10, 2006. Accessed March 29, 2013: www.aclunc. org/news/press_releases/attorney_general_bill_lockyer_finds_sheriffs_department_infiltrated_peace_fresno.shtml.

28. Associated Press, "Handschu Guidelines Govern How NYPD Can Monitor Groups," *New York Daily News*, February 23, 2012. Accessed April 1, 2013: www.nydailynews.com/news/handschu-guidelines-govern-nypd-monitor-groups-article-1.1027761.

29. Chris Hawley and Matt Apuzzo, "Infiltration of Colleges Raises Privacy Fears," *Associated Press*, October 11, 2011. Accessed April 1, 2013: www.ap.org/Content/AP-In-The-News/2011/NYPD-infil-

tration-of-colleges-raises-privacy-fears. On April 16, 2012, Associated Press reporters Matt Apuzzo, Adam Goldman, Chris Hawley, and Eileen Sullivan were named winners of the 2012 Pulitzer Prize for Investigative Reporting for their series detailing NYPD covert surveillance of Muslim and other minority communities since 9/11.

30. "Court Filing Seeks to End NYPD Surveillance of Muslim Community," New York Civil Liberties Union, February 4, 2013. Accessed April 1, 2013: www.nyclu.org/news/court-filing-seeks-end-nypd-surveillance-of-muslim-community.

31. David E. Kaplan, "Spies among Us," *U.S. News & World Report*, April 30, 2006. Accessed April 1, 2013: www.usnews.com/usnews/news/articles/060508/8homeland.htm.

32. Ibid.

33. Ibid., 10-11.

34. Senator Tom Coburn, "Safety at Any Price: Assessing the Impact of Homeland Security Spending in U.S. Cities," December 2012, 3. Accessed April 1, 2013: www.coburn.senate.gov/public/index.cfm/pressreleases?ContentRecord_id=bcd61d71-5454-4a81-9695-e949e0253faa.

35. Ibid., 15.

36. Ibid., 18.

37. Ibid., 17.

38. Ibid., 42.

39. Ibid., 5.

40. Ibid.

41. *See* Report of the [2008, St. Paul, Minnesota] Republican National Convention Public Safety Planning and Implementation Review Commission, January 14, 2009. Accessed April 1, 2013: www.stpaul.gov/DocumentCenter/Home/View/7405; and Report of the WTO Accountability Review Committee, Seattle City Council, September 14, 2000. Accessed April 1, 2013: http://depts.washington.edu/wto-hist/documents/arcfinal.pdf.

42. Edward Connors, "Planning and Managing Security for Major Special Events: Guidelines for Law Enforcement," Institute for Law and Justice (2007), vi. Prepared for the U.S. Department of Justice, Office of Community Oriented Policing Services. Accessed February 28, 2013: www.cops.usdoj.gov/files/ric/Publications/e07071299_web.txt.

43. Ibid., ix.

44. Craig Horowitz, "How to Care for an Angry Mob," *New York Magazine*, May 17, 2004. Accessed April 1, 2013: http://nymag.com/nymetro/news/rnc/n_10370.

45. Patrice O'Shaughnessy, "Fury at Anarchist Convention Threat," *New York Daily News*, July 12, 2004. Accessed April 1, 2013: www.nydailynews.com/archives/news/fury-anarchist-convention-threat-article-1.594031.

46. "Many G-8 Protesters Were Undercover Cops," *Atlanta Journal-Constitution*, July 27, 2004.

47. "One in Nine of the G8 Protesters Were Actually Police," Associated Press, July 27, 2004.

48. "'Protesters' at G-8 Summit Were Undercover Cops," *Orlando Sentinel*, July 27, 2004. Accessed April 1, 2013: http://articles.orlandosentinel.com/2004-07-27/news/0407270167_1_undercover-cops-summit-group-of-eight.

CHAPTER 5

1. *See* "Amazon.com: Loosenut's Review of Playmobil Security Check Point," September 9, 2005. Accessed March 8, 2013: www.amazon.com/review/RGJ8WVRL6MWBD/ref=cm_cr_rdp_perm.

2. Debra J. Holt, Pauline M. Ippolito, Debra M. Desrochers, Christopher R. Kelley, "Children's Exposures to TV Advertising in 1977 and 2004: Information for the Obesity Debate," Federal Trade Commission, Bureau of Economics Staff Report, June 1, 2007. Accessed April 1, 2013: www.ftc.gov/os/2007/06/cabecolor.pdf.

3. Public Citizen's Commercial Alert, "Psychologists, Psychiatrists Call for Limits on the Use of Psychology to Influence or Exploit Children for Commercial Purposes," news release, September 20, 1999. Accessed March 29, 2013: www.commercialalert.org/issues/culture/psychology/commercial-alert-psychologists-psychiatrists-call-for-limits-on-the-use-of-psychology-to-influence-or-exploit-children-for-commercial-purposes.

4. Susan Linn, "Commercializing Childhood: The Corporate Takeover of Kids' Lives," *Multinational Monitor*, Vol. 30. No. 1, July/August 2008. Accessed April 1, 2013: www.multinationalmonitor.org/mm2008/072008/interview-linn.html.

5. Joshua Brustein, "McDonalds Makes Subtle Play for Children Online," *New York Times*, April 20, 2011. Accessed April 1, 2013: http://bits.blogs.nytimes.com/2011/04/20/mcdonalds-makes-subtle-play-

for-children-online.

6. Jim Puzzanghera, "FTC Urged to Bolster Online Privacy Protection for Children," *Los Angeles Times*, August 2, 2012. Accessed April 1, 2013: http://articles.latimes.com/print/2012/aug/21/business/la-fi-ftc-children-marketing-20120822.

7. Ibid.

8. "Amusement Park Patrons 'Play and Pay' with RFID Smart Bands," *Texas Instruments RFID eNews*, No. 12 (September 2002). Accessed April 1, 2013: www.ti.com/rfid/docs/news/eNews/eNewsVol12.pdf.

9. Ibid.

10. Mary Madden, Sandra Cortesi, Urs Gasser, Amanda Lenhart and Maeve Duggan, "Parents, Teens and Online Privacy," Pew Research Center, The Berkman Center for Internet & Society at Harvard University, November 14, 2012, 2. Accessed April 1, 2013: http://pewinternet.org/~/media//Files/Reports/2012/PIP_ParentsTeensAndPrivacy.pdf.

11. Natasha Singer, "Apps for Children Fall Short on Disclosure to Parents, Report Says," *New York Times*, December 10, 2012. Accessed April 1, 2013: www.nytimes.com/2012/12/11/technology/many-mobile-apps-for-children-fall-short-on-disclosure-to-parents-ftc-report-says.html?pagewanted=all&.

12. Federal Trade Commission, Staff Report, "Mobile Apps for Kids: Disclosures Still Not Making the Grade," December 2012, 4. Accessed April 1, 2013: http://ftc.gov/os/2012/12/121210mobilekidsappreport.pdf.

13. Kevin J. O'Brien, "Data-Gathering via Apps Presents a Gray Legal Area," *New York Times*, October 28, 2012. Accessed April 1, 2013: www.nytimes.com/2012/10/29/technology/mobile-apps-have-a-ravenous-ability-to-collect-personal-.data.html?pagewanted=all&_r=0&gwh=476F54BBC11519BFD5D34E1EA1E22775.

14. Richard Lardner, "Cellphone Apps Erode Child Privacy Rights," *Portland Press Herald*, December 11, 2012. Accessed April 1, 2013: www.pressherald.com/business/cellphone-apps-erode-child-privacy-rights_2012-12-11.html.

15. *See* Case No. CV-11-03958 (U.S.D.C. for the N. D. of California).

16. "An Examination of Children's Privacy: New Technologies and the Children's Online Privacy Protection Act (COPPA)," before the Subcommittee on Consumer Protection, Product Safety, and Insurance, United States Senate, 111th Cong. (April 29, 2010) (Testimony and

Statement for the Record of Marc Rotenberg, Executive Director, EPIC, Adjunct Professor, Georgetown University Law Center). Accessed March 4, 2013: http://epic.org/privacy/kids/EPIC_COPPA_Testimony_042910.pdf.

17. Federal Trade Commission, "FTC Charges That Security Flaws in RockYou Game Site Exposed 32 Million Email Addresses and Passwords," news release, March 27, 2012. Accessed April 1, 2013: www.ftc.gov/opa/2012/03/rockyou.shtm.

18. "Testimony and Statement for the Record of Marc Rotenberg, director, Electronic Privacy Information Center on the Children's Privacy Protection and Parental Empowerment Act, H.R. 3508, Before the House of Representatives, Committee on the Judiciary, Subcommittee on Crime," September 12, 1996. Accessed March 4, 2013: http://epic.org/privacy/kids/EPIC_Testimony.html.

19. Shannon P. Duffy, "School District Accused of Spying on Students via Home Webcams," *The Legal Intelligencer*, February 19, 2010. Accessed April 1, 2013: www.law.com/jsp/article.jsp?id=1202443844888&School_District_Accused_of_Spying_on_Students_via_Home_Webcams&slreturn=20130220175616.

20. "Testimony and Statement for the Record of Marc Rotenberg, director Electronic Privacy Information Center, on the Children's Privacy Protection and Parental Empowerment Act, H.R. 3508 Before the House of Representatives, Committee on the Judiciary, Subcommittee on Crime," September 12, 1996. Accessed March 4, 2013: http://epic.org/privacy/kids/EPIC_Testimony.html.

21. Ibid.

22. Federal Trade Commission, Code of Federal Regulations, Children's Online Privacy Protection Rule: Final Rule Amendments and Statement of Basis and Purpose, title 16, Part 312, December 19, 2012. Accessed April 1, 2013: http://ftc.gov/os/2012/12/121219copparulefrn.pdf.

23. Ibid.

24. Comments of Electronic Privacy Information Center to the Department of Education, "Notice of Proposed Rulemaking," RIN 1880-AA86, May 23, 2011. Accessed April 1, 2013: http://epic.org/privacy/student/EPIC_FERPA_Comments.pdf.

25. Ibid., 14.

26. United States Department of Education, Privacy Technical Assistance Center, "Frequently Asked Questions—Cloud Computing,"

June 2012. Accessed March 4, 2012, http://ptac.ed.gov/sites/default/files/cloud-computing.pdf.

27. Ibid., 2.

CHAPTER 6

1. Gary T. Marx, *Undercover: Police Surveillance in America* (Berkeley: University of California Press, 1988), xv.
2. Rob Evans and Paul Lewis, "Undercover Police Had Children with Activists," *Guardian* (UK), January 20, 2012. Accessed April 1, 2013: www.guardian.co.uk/uk/2012/jan/20/undercover-police-children-activists.
3. Ibid.
4. Simon Hattenstone, "Mark Kennedy: Confessions of an Undercover Cop," *Guardian* (UK), March 25, 2011. Accessed April 1, 2013: www.guardian.co.uk/environment/2011/mar/26/mark-kennedy-undercover-cop-environmental-activist; Paul Lewis and Rob Evans, "Mark Kennedy: A Journey from Undercover Cop to 'Bona Fide' Activist," *Guardian* (UK), January 9, 2011. Accessed April 1, 2013: www.guardian.co.uk/environment/2011/jan/10/mark-kennedy-undercover-cop-activist.
5. Colin Moynihan, "New Twist in British Spy's Case Unravels in U.S.," *New York Times*, March 15, 2013. Accessed April 1, 2013: http://thelede.blogs.nytimes.com/2013/03/15/new-twist-in-british-spys-case-unravels-in-u-s.
6. Cosmo Garvin, "Conspiracy of Dunces," Sacramento newsreview.com, July 27, 2006. Accessed March 29, 2013: www.newsreview.com/sacramento/conspiracy-of-dunces/content?oid=80311.
7. *United States v. Eric McDavid*, Case No. 2:06-00035-MEC (2007). Memorandum of Points in Authorities Supporting Facts, December 19, 2006, 3.
8. Ibid., 3-4.
9. Ibid.
10. Ibid.
11. *United States v. Eric McDavid*, No. 2:06-CR-00035 MEC (2007). Judgment and Sentence, May 8, 2008.
12. *United States v. Eric McDavid*, No. 2:06-CR-00035 MEC (2007). Declaration of Juror Carol Runge in Support of Defense Sentencing Memorandum, May 8, 2008, 2-4.
13. *See generally* Natasha Lennard, "Who Gets to Be an FBI Threat?"

Salon, May 18, 2012. Accessed April 1, 2013: www.salon. com/2012/05/18/who_gets_to_be_an_fbi_threat.

14. Michael A. Sheehan, *Crush the Cell: How to Defeat Terrorism without Terrorizing Ourselves* (New York: Three Rivers Press, 2008), 102.

15. *Green Is the New Red*, blog by Will Potter, www.greenisthenewred. com/blog/.

16. "FBI File Reveals Discussion of Discrediting Animal Rights Activists by Planting Rumors," blog entry by Will Potter, *Green Is the New Red*. Accessed April 1, 2013: www.greenisthenewred.com/blog/ fbi-file-reveals-discussion-of-discrediting-animal-rights-activists-by-planting-rumors/3282, December 6, 2010. The file was from the FBI's Johnson City Resident Agency (part of the Knoxville field office) and was based on conversations between an FBI agent and "Source," identified as someone involved in "direct actions" willing to share information in exchange for immunity from prosecution.

17. *See generally Green Is the New Red*, blog by Will Potter. Accessed April 1, 2013: www.greenisthenewred.com/blog/.

18. "Hill & Knowlton Dirty Tricks," Center for Media and Democracy, SourceWatch. Accessed April 7, 2013: www.sourcewatch.org/index. php?title=Judi_Bari.

19. Ibid.

20. Ibid.

21. Ibid.

22. Laura W. Murphy, Devon Chaffee, "Homegrown Terrorism: The Threat to Military Communities inside the United States," Written Statement of the American Civil Liberties Union to the Senate Committee on Homeland Security and Governmental Affairs Committee and House Committee on Homeland Security, December 7, 2001. Accessed March 29, 2013: www.aclu.org/files/assets/2011-12-06_-_ aclu_statement_for_joint_hearing_on_homegrown_terrorism_-_final. pdf.

23. Ibid., 4.

24. Ibid.

25. Ibid.

26. Ibid.

27. Kera Abraham, "Is Eco-Sabotage Terrorism?," *Eugene Weekly*, December 21, 2006. Accessed April 1, 2013: www.eugeneweekly. com/2006/12/21/webextra1.html.

28. *See* Tex. Civ. Prac. & Rem. § 96.001 et seq.

29. "Oprah Accused of Whipping up Anti-Beef 'Lynch Mob': Food Defamation Trial Opens in Amarillo," *CNN*, January 21, 1998. Accessed April 1, 2013: www.cnn.com/US/9801/21/oprah.beef.

30. *See* Texas Beef Group v. Oprah Winfrey, 201 F.3d 680 (5th Cir. 2000).

31. 18 USC § 43.

32. Animal Enterprise Protection Act (AETA), Pub. L. 102-346, 106 Stat. 928 (1992).

33. *See* the ALEC website at www.alec.org/. Accessed April 1, 2013. ALEC has the support of more than three hundred large corporations in the tobacco, petroleum, pharmaceutical and transportation areas, among others. It forges working relationships with right-wing entities such as the National Rifle Association, the Family Research Council and the Koch, Scaife, Bradley, and Heritage Foundations in an attempt to further its agenda and to influence legislation to the benefit of its big business members and contributors.

34. Fla. Stat. § 776.013.

35. Andy Parker, "Beyond AETA: How Corporate-Crafted Legislation Brands Activists as Terrorists," White Paper, National Lawyers Guild (2009). Accessed April 1, 2013: www.nlg.org/beyond-aeta. See also: www.alec.org/about-alec/frequently-asked-questions//3.

36. Ibid, 3.

37. Center for Constitutional Rights, "Rights Group Condemns Dismissal of Animal Rights 'Terrorism' Case: Activists Will Appeal, Attorneys Say," news release, March 18, 2013. Accessed April 1, 2013: http://ccrjustice.org/newsroom/press-releases/rights-group-condemns-dismissal-of-animal-rights-%E2%80%9Cterrorism%E2%80%9D-case.

CHAPTER 7

1. Ann Fagan Ginger and Eugene M. Tobin, eds., *The National Lawyers Guild: From Roosevelt through Reagan* (Philadelphia: Temple University Press, 1988), 336.

2. FISA Amendments Act of 2008, also known as Foreign Intelligence Surveillance Act of 1978 Amendments Act of 2008, Pub. L. 110-261, 122 Stat. 2436 (2008).

3. "A History of the National Lawyers Guild 1937–1987)," National Lawyers Guild Foundation, 1987. On file with National Lawyers Guild, National Office, New York, NY, 7.

4. Ibid.
5. Ibid., 10.
6. *See generally* Arthur Kinoy, *Rights on Trial: The Odyssey of a People's Lawyer* (Cambridge, MA: Harvard University Press, 1983).
7. "A History of the National Lawyers Guild 1937–1987," National Lawyers Guild Foundation, 1987. On file with National Lawyers Guild, National Office, New York, NY, 56.
8. Ann Fagan Ginger and Eugene M. Tobin, eds., *The National Lawyers Guild: From Roosevelt through Reagan* (Philadelphia: Temple University Press, 1988), 226.
9. "A History of the National Lawyers Guild 1937–1987," National Lawyers Guild Foundation, 1987. On file with National Lawyers Guild, National Office, New York, NY, 56.
10. *See National Lawyers Guild v. Attorney General of the United States, et al.*, Case No.77 Civ. 999 (S.D.N.Y. 1977).
11. Colin Moynihan, "Trove of F.B.I. Files on Lawyers Guild Shows Scope of Secret Surveillance," *New York Times*, June 25, 2007.
12. *Heutsche v. United States*, 414 U.S. 898, 903 (1973) (Douglas, J., dissenting).
13. Weissenberger's Federal Evidence, Sec. 501.4.
14. Geoffrey C. Hazard Jr., "An Historical Perspective on the Lawyer-Client Privilege," 66 Cal. Law Review 1061 (1978), 1069-70. Retrieved from the Yale Law School Legal Scholarship Repository, March 29, 2013.
15. Geoffrey C. Hazard Jr., "An Historical Perspective on the Lawyer-Client Privilege," 66 Cal. Law Review 1061 (1978), 1069-70. Retrieved from the Yale Law School Legal Scholarship Repository. Accessed March 29, 2013: http://digitalcommons.law.yale.edu/cgi/viewcontent.cgi?article=3288&context=fss_papers.
16. Ibid.
17. Code of Federal Regulations, title 28, part 501.3(d) (2001).
18. Code of Federal Regulations, title 28, part 501.3(a) (2001).
19. "Special Administrative Measures for Prevention of Acts of Violence and Terrorism," 66 Fed. Reg. 55062 (October 31, 2001) (amending 28 C.F.R. Sec 501.3 (2001)).
20. Ibid.
21. United States Attorney, Southern District of New York, April 9, 2002, news release announcing the indictments of Ahmed Abdel Sattar, Yassir Al-Sirri, Lynne Stewart, and Mohammed Yousry. Accessed

March 29, 2013: http://cryptome.org/usa-v-4bad-ind.htm#Press%20 Release.

22. *Center for Constitutional Rights, et al. v. Obama, et al.* (formerly *Center for Constitutional Rights, et al. v. Bush et al.*), Case No. 07-cv-1115-VRW (N.D. Cal. 2007); see also http://ccrjustice.org/ourcases/current-cases/ccr-v.-bush.

23. Shayana Kadidal, interview by Heidi Boghosian and Michael Smith, WBAI, September 18, 2006. Accessed April 1, 2013: www.lawanddisorder.org/2006/09/law-and-disorder-september-18-2006.

24. Ibid.

25. Geoffrey C. Hazard Jr., "An Historical Perspective on the Lawyer-Client Privilege," 66 Cal. Law Review 1061 (1978), 1069–70. "The history of this privilege goes back to the reign of Elizabeth, where the privilege already appears as unquestioned. . . . The policy of the privilege has been plainly grounded, since the latter part of the 1700s. . . . In order to promote freedom of consultation of legal advisors by clients, the apprehension of compelled disclosure by the legal advisers must be removed; and hence the law must prohibit such disclosure except on the client's consent." [Citing 8 J. Wigmore EVIDENCE §§ 2290-91 (3d ed. 1940)]. Retrieved from the Yale Law School Legal Scholarship Repository. Accessed March 29, 2013: http://digitalcommons.law.yale.edu/cgi/viewcontent.cgi?article=3288&context=fss_papers.

26. Elaine Cassel, "The Lynne Stewart Case: When Representing an Accused Terrorist Can Mean the Lawyer Risks Jail, Too" *Counterpunch*, October 12, 2002. Accessed April 1, 2013: www.counterpunch.org/2002/10/12/the-lynne-stewart-case.

CHAPTER 8

1. Adam Liptak, "A High-Tech War on Leaks," *New York Times*, February 11, 2012. Accessed April 1, 2013: www.nytimes.com/2012/02/12/sunday-review/a-high-tech-war-on-leaks.html.

2. Marlena Telvick and Amy Rubin, "The Press and Subpoenas: An Overview," *Frontline*, PBS, February 27, 2007. Accessed April 1, 2013: www.pbs.org/wgbh/pages/frontline/newswar/part1/subpoenas.html. *Frontline* submitted Freedom of Information Act (FOIA) requests to obtain this information. Of these subpoenas, fewer than twenty were approved by the U.S. attorney general seeking reporters' confidential sources.

3. Ibid.
4. Reporters Without Borders, "Press Freedom Index 2013," accessed February 22, 2013: http://en.rsf.org/press-freedom-index-2013,1054. html.
5. *Final Report to the President by the Commission on CIA Activities within the United States* (Washington, D.C.: Superintendent of Documents, 1975), 164.
6. Ibid.
7. Ibid.
8. James Risen, *State of War: The Secret History of the CIA and the Bush Administration* (New York: Simon & Schuster, 2006).
9. Affadivit of James Risen, Document 115-2, *United States v. Jeffrey Alexander Sterling*, No. 1:10cr485 (LMB) (E.D. Va., 2011). Accessed March 29, 2013: www.fas.org/sgp/jud/sterling/062111-risen115.pdf.
10. Ibid.
11. "Book Causes Controversy for Author and Bush," *NBCNews.com*, January 10, 2006. Accessed March 29, 2013: www.nbcnews.com/id/10790497/ns/msnbc-hardball_with_chris_matthews/t/book-causes-controversy-author-bush/#.UUhuFBnhHJw.
12. Affadivit of James Risen, Document 115-2, *United States v. Jeffrey Alexander Sterling*, No. 1:10cr485 (LMB) (E.D. Va., 2011) 3. Accessed April , 2013: www.fas.org/sgp/jud/sterling/062111-risen115.pdf.
13. Clara Hogan, "Judge Explains Decision to Quash Risen Subpoena," Reporters Committee for Freedom of the Press, *Reporter's Privilege*, August 4, 2011. Accessed April 1, 2013: www.rcfp.org/browse-media-law-resources/news/judge-explains-decision-quash-risen-subpoena#sthash.bdUmmCpd.dpuf.
14. Walter Pincus, "Reporter's Ordeal Continues in Convoluted CIA Case," *Washington Post*, July 4, 2011. Accessed April 1, 2013: http://articles.washingtonpost.com/2011-07-04/national/35236615_1_grand-jury-cia-case-discrimination-case.
15. Brian Ross and Richard Esposito, "FBI Acknowledges: Journalists' Phone Records Are Fair Game," *ABC News*, May 16, 2006. Accessed April 1, 2013: http://abcnews.go.com/blogs/headlines/2006/05/fbi_acknowledge.
16. United States Attorneys' Manual (USAM) Title 9, 9:13.400. News Media Subpoenas; Subpoenas for Telephone Toll Records of News Media; Interrogation, Arrest, or Criminal Charging of Members of the News Media. Accessed March 6, 2013: www.justice.gov/usao/

eousa/foia_reading_room/usam/title9/13mcrm.htm#9-13.400. "In light of the intent of the regulation to protect freedom of the press, news gathering functions, and news media sources, the requirements of 28 C.F.R. § 50.10 do not apply to demands for purely commercial or financial information unrelated to the news gathering function." 28 C.F.R. § 50.10(m).

17. Transcript, House Hearing on the Hewlett-Packard Pretexting Scandal, *Washington Post*, September 28, 2006. Accessed April 1, 2013: www.washingtonpost.com/wp-srv/business/documents/HP_hearing09282006.html.

18. Ibid.

19. U.S. Attorney's Office, Northern District of California, "Owner, Employee and Contractor of Private Investigative Firm Sentenced in Connection with Pretexting," news release December 14, 2012. Accessed April 1, 2013: www.justice.gov/usao/can/news/2012/2012_12_13_wagner.sentenced.press.html.

20. Ibid.

21. Federal Trade Commission, "FTC Permanently Halts 'Pretexting' Scheme; Defendants Barred from Obtaining or Selling Consumers' Phone Records to Third Parties," news release, May 28, 2008. Accessed April 1, 2013: www.ftc.gov/opa/2008/05/arg.shtm.

22. *See* Telephone Records and Privacy Protection Act of 2006, Pub. L. 109-476, 120 Stat. 3568 (January 12, 2007). Accessed April 1, 2013: https://bulk.resource.org/gpo.gov/laws/109/publ476.109.pdf. The act forbids "pretexting" (pretending to be someone else) to buy, sell or obtain confidential telephone phone records or customer information. An exception is when pretexting is conducted by law enforcement or intelligence agencies.

23. *See* Stuart Benjamin, "Rethink Shield Laws," *New York Times*, December 12, 2011. Accessed April 1, 2013: www.nytimes.com/roomfordebate/2011/12/11/are-all-bloggers-journalists/should-we-rethink-shield-laws.

24. *See*, e.g., *Cohen v. Cowles Media Co.*, 501 U.S. 663 (1991).

25. 408 U.S. 665 (1972).

26. "Handbook for Safeguarding Sensitive Personally Identifiable Information," U.S. Department of Homeland Security, March 2012. Accessed March 6, 2013: www.dhs.gov/xlibrary/assets/privacy/dhs-privacy-safeguardingsensitivepiihandbook-march2012.pdf.

27. "Privacy Compliance Review of the NOC Media Monitoring Initia-

tive," U.S. Department of Homeland Security, November 15, 2011. Accessed March 6, 2013: www.dhs.gov/xlibrary/assets/privacy/privacy_privcomrev_ops_monitoring_initiative.pdf.

28. Ron Wyden, Senator for Oregon, "Wyden Places Hold on Intelligence Authorization Bill," news release, November 14, 2012. Accessed April 1, 2013: www.wyden.senate.gov/news/press-releases/wyden-places-hold-on-intelligence-authorization-bill-.

29. Ibid.

CHAPTER 9

1. Patrick Radden Keefe, "Don't Privatize Our Spies," Op-Ed, *New York Times*, June 25, 2007. Accessed April 1, 2013: www.nytimes.com/2007/06/25/opinion/25keefe.html.

2. *See*, e.g., Boeing, "Boeing Forms New Intelligence and Security Systems Division," news release, December 20, 2007. Accessed April 1, 2013: www.boeing.com/news/releases/2007/q4/071220b_nr.html. See also David Hubler, "Northrop Selects New VP of Command, Control and Intell Unit," *Washington Technology*, January 19, 2012. Accessed April 1, 2013: http://washingtontechnology.com/articles/2012/01/19/northrop-personnel-move.aspx. See also, "Intelligence Community: Supporting the US Intelligence Mission," Booz Allen Hamilton, accessed April 1, 2013: www.boozallen.com/consultants/defense-consulting/intelligence-community; "Intelligence Systems and Services," Lockheed Martin, accessed March 6, 2013: www.lockheedmartin.com/us/products/intelligence.html.

3. American Federation of Government Employees (AFGE), "AFGE Statement on Fiscal Year 2013 National Defense Authorization Act," news release, December 19, 2012. Accessed April 1, 2013: www.unions.org/home/union-blog/2012/12/19/afge-statement-on-fiscal-year-2013-national-defense-authorization-act.

4. Intelligence Authorization Act for Fiscal Year 2008, H.R. 2082 (110th). Accessed April 1, 2013: www.govtrack.us/congress/bills/110/hr2082.

5. Stop Outsourcing Security Act, H.R. 4102 (110th). Accessed April 1, 2013: http://act.janschakowsky.org/p/dia/action/public/?action_KEY=12.

6. Frank Naif, "Congress Demands Full Account of Intelligence Outsourcing Mess—and It's a Mess," *Huffington Post*, July 14, 2009. Accessed April 1, 2013: www.huffingtonpost.com/frank-naif/congress-

demands-full-acc_b_231584.html.

7. Ibid.

8. "HOMELAND SECURITY: Preliminary Results Show Federal Protective Service's Ability to Protect Federal Facilities Is Hampered by Weaknesses in Its Contract Security Guard Program," Mark L. Goldstein, Director Physical Infrastructure Issues, Testimony before the Senate Committee on Homelands Security and Governmental Affairs, U.S. Government Accounting Office, July 8, 2009. Accessed April 1, 2013: www.gao.gov/new.items/d09859t.pdf.

9. Ibid., 5.

10. Ibid.

11. New York City Police Department, NYPD SHIELD, Operation Nexus. Accessed March 6, 2013: www.nypdshield.org/public/nexus. aspx.

12. Whitney Gunter and Jason Kidwell, "Law Enforcement and Private Security Liaison: Partnerships for Cooperation," International Foundation for Protection Officers, June 2004. Accessed April 1, 2013: www.ifpo.org/articlebank/lawprivateliaison.html.

13. Matthew Harwood, "Private Contractors Make up More Than 25 Percent of Intelligence Community," *Security Management*, August 28, 2008. Accessed April 1, 2013: www.securitymanagement.com/news/private-contractors-make-more-25-percent-intelligence-community-004588.

14. Greg Miller, "Budget 2012: CIA/Intelligence agencies," *Washington Post*, February 14, 2011. Accessed April 1, 2013: http://voices.washingtonpost.com/44/2011/02/budget-2012-ciaintelligence-ag.html.

15. City of New York, "Mayor Bloomberg, Police Commissioner Kelly and Microsoft Unveil New, State-of-the-Art Law Enforcement Technology That Aggregates and Analyzes Existing Public Safety Data in Real Time to Provide a Comprehensive View of Potential Threats and Criminal Activity," August 8, 2012, press release. Accessed April 1, 2013: www.nyc.gov/html/om/html/2012b/pr291-12.html.

16. Bank of America, "Revitalizing Detroit One Police Officer at a Time," July 17, 2012. Accessed March 6, 2013: about.bankofamerica. com/en-us/partnering-locally/project-14.html.

17. JPMorgan Chase & Co., 2011 Corporate Responsibility Report, "Doing Our Part: Strengthening Our Communities, Growing the Economy," 24. Accessed February 23, 2013: www.jpmorganchase. com/corporate/Corporate-Responsibility/document/31700_JPMC_

CorpReport_ALL_062912a.pdf.

18. "How Are Innovations in Technology Transforming Policing?" Critical Issues in Policing Series, Police Executive Research Forum, January 2012. Accessed April 1, 2013: http://policeforum.org/library/critical-issues-in-policing-series/Technology_web2.pdf.

19. Firetide, "City of Chicago, Firetide Wireless Mesh Key to City-Wide Video Security Deployment," 2007. Accessed on April 1, 2013: www.firetide.com/pdf/CaseStudies/City_of_Chicago.pdf.

20. "Lessons from the Mumbai Terrorist Attacks," statement before the Committee on Homeland Security & Governmental Affairs, United States Senate, 111th Cong. (January 8, 2009) (Testimony of Raymond W. Kelly, Police Commissioner, City of New York). Accessed April 1, 2013: www.hsgac.senate.gov/download/010809kelly.

21. U.S. Secret Service, "Microsoft Announces Anti-Virus Reward Program," news release, November 5, 2003. Accessed April 1, 2013: www.secretservice.gov/press/ms_110503.pdf.

22. Aundreia Cameron, Elke Kolodinski, Heather May, and Nicholas Williams, "Measuring the Effects of Video Surveillance on Crime in Los Angeles," prepared for the California Research Bureau, University of Southern California School of Policy, Planning, and Development, May 5, 2008. Accessed April 1, 2013, www.library.ca.gov/crb/08/08-007.pdf.

CHAPTER 10

1. Acxiom, "PersonicX Cluster Perspectives," 22. Accessed April 1, 2013: www.acxiom.com/WorkArea/DownloadAsset.aspx?id=1410&LangType=1033&ekfxmen_noscript=1&ekfxmensel=e63f594de_6_72.

2. Ibid.

3. Natasha Singer, "Mapping, and Sharing, the Consumer Genome," *New York Times*, June 16, 2012. Accessed April 1, 2013: www.nytimes.com/2012/06/17/technology/acxiom-the-quiet-giant-of-consumer-database-marketing.html.

4. For an article describing some problems with fusion centers, *see* Robert O'Harrow Jr., "DHS 'Fusion Centers' Portrayed as Pools of Ineptitude, Civil Liberties Intrusions," *Washington Post*, October 2, 2012. Accessed April 1, 2013: http://articles.washingtonpost.com/2012-10-02/news/35500769_1_fusion-centers-investigators-report.

5. Privacy Act of 1974, 5 U.S.C. Sec. 552a.

6. Natasha Singer, "F.T.C. Opens an Inquiry into Data Brokers, *New York Times*, December 18, 2012. Accessed April 1, 2013: www.ny-times.com/2012/12/19/technology/ftc-opens-an-inquiry-into-data-brokers.html.

7. Michael Fischel and Lawrence Siegel, "Computer-Aided Techniques against Pubic Assistance Fraud: A Case Study of the Aid to Families with Dependent Children Program (AFDC)," MITRE Corporation (Prepared for the Law Enforcement Assistance Administration), January 1980. Accessed April 1, 2013: http://bjs.ojp.usdoj.gov/content/pub/pdf/catapaf.pdf.

8. U.S. Department of Agriculture, Computer Matching Projects Involving Individual Privacy Data, No. 3450-001, April 17, 1984. Accessed April 1, 2013: www.ocio.usda.gov/sites/default/files/docs/2012/DR3450-001.html.

9. *See* 5 U.S.C. 552a(o), et seq.

10. OMB's proposed guidelines on these amendments appear at 56 Fed. Reg. (No. 78), 18599-601 (Apr. 23, 1991). Accessed April 1, 2013: www.whitehouse.gov/sites/default/files/omb/assets/omb/inforeg/computer_amendments1991.pdf.

11. *See* Federal Bureau of Investigation, "FBI: National Crime Information Center." Accessed April 1, 2013: www.fbi.gov/about-us/cjis/ncic/ncic.

12. Experian, "Analytical Services." Accessed April 1, 2013: www.experian.com/marketing-services/analytical-services.html.

13. *See* "INSOURCE Data Contributes to Best Buy's Successful Customer Relationship Management (CRM) Strategy." Accessed April 13, 2013: www.experian.com/case_studies/best_buy.pdf.

14. www.experian.com/healthcare/revenue-cycle-management.html.

15. Deborah Pierce and Linda Ackerman, "Data Aggregators: A Study of Data Quality and Responsiveness," May 19, 2005. Accessed April 1, 2013: www.csun.edu/~dwm3265/IS312/DataAggregatorsStudy.pdf.

16. Grant Gross, "Senator Questions FBI over ChoicePoint Contract," *Infoworld*, April 5, 2006. Accessed April 1, 2013: http://podcasts.infoworld.com/t/platforms/senator-questions-fbi-over-choicepoint-contract-662?_kip_ipx=622934055-1363659906.

17. Ibid.

18. Ibid.

19. Federal Financial Institutions Examination Council, "Bank Secrecy Act Anti-Money Laundering Examination Manual." Accessed April

1, 2013: www.ffiec.gov/bsa_aml_infobase/pages_manual/OLM_015. htm.

20. Don Reisinger, "Congressional Privacy Caucus Takes Aim at Data Brokers," *CNet*, July 25, 2012. Accessed April 1, 2013: http://news. cnet.com/8301-1009_3-57479722-83/congressional-privacy-caucus-takes-aim-at-data-brokers.

21. *See* European Commission, "DGs–Home Affairs–What we do–... Police Cooperation–Data Retention." Accessed April 1, 2013: http:// ec.europa.eu/dgs/home-affairs/what-we-do/policies/police-cooper-ation/data-retention/index_en.htm. See also the Electronic Privacy Information Center. Accessed April 1, 2013: http://epic.org/privacy/ intl/data_retention.html.

22. Electronic Communications Privacy Act of 1986 (ECPA), Pub.L. 99–508, 100 Stat. 1848 (1986).

23. *See* "E-commerce Law and Policy: The E-commerce Newsletter for Lawyers," Vol. 15, No. 1, January 2013, 15. Accessed on April 1, 2013: www.ifrahlaw.com/wp-content/uploads/2013/01/ECLP-January-2013.pdf.

24. "House Judiciary Committee Debates Mandatory Data Retention Requirements," *The Secure Times* (an online forum of the American Bar Association Section of Antitrust Law's Privacy and Information Security Committee), January 26, 2011. Accessed April 1, 2013: www. thesecuretimes.com/2011/01/house_judiciary_committee_deba.php.

25. U.S. Department of Justice, Bureau of Justice Statistics, "Use and Management of Criminal History Record Information: A Comprehensive Report, 2001 Update," 21. Accessed April 1, 2013: http://bjs. ojp.usdoj.gov/content/pub/pdf/umchri01.pdf.

26. Letter from Marc Rotenberg and Marcia Hofman, Electronic Privacy Information Center, to Joshua B. Bolten, director, Office of Management and Budget, February 20, 2004. Accessed April 1, 2013: http:// epic.org/privacy/ncic/NCIC_letter.pdf.

27. Ibid.

28. Ibid.

29. For an overview of the Privacy Act of 1974 and the exemptions, *see* www.justice.gov/opcl/1974privacyact-overview.htm. Accessed April 1, 2013.

30. U.S. Department of Justice, Office of the Inspector General, Audit Division, "Review of the Terrorist Screening Center," Audit Report 05-27, June 2005. Accessed April 1, 2013: www.justice.gov/oig/re-

ports/FBI/a0527/final.pdf.

CHAPTER 11

1. Debra Cleghorn, "UAVForge Challenge: You Can Win $100,000!," *Model Airplane News*, July 14, 2011. Accessed April 1, 2013: www. modelairplanenews.com/blog/2011/07/14/uavforge-challenge-you-can-win-100000.

2. William A. Eddy, "Photographing from Kites," *The Century: A Popular Quarterly*, Vol. 54, No. 1 (May 1897), 91.

3. Radioplane OQ-19D, National Museum of the U.S. Air Force, fact sheet, May 29, 2007. Accessed April 1, 2013: www.nationalmuseum. af.mil/factsheets/factsheet.asp?id=4777.

4. U.S. Department of Defense, "Unmanned Aerial Vehicles." Accessed April 1, 2013: www.defense.gov/specials/uav2002.

5. "Case History: Unmanned and Dangerous," *The Economist*, December 6, 2007. Accessed April 1, 2013: www.economist.com/ node/10202603. See also William Wagner, *Lightning Bugs and other Reconnaissance Drones* (Fallbrook, CA: Aero, 1982).

6. Jim Garamone, "From U.S. Civil War to Afghanistan: A Short History of UAVs," U.S. Department of Defense, American Forces Press Service, April 16, 2002. Accessed April 1, 2013: www.defense.gov/ News/NewsArticle.aspx?ID=44164.

7. Jeremiah Gertler, "U.S. Unmanned Aerial Systems," Congressional Research Service, January 3, 2012. Accessed April 1, 2013: www.fas. org/sgp/crs/natsec/R42136.pdf.

8. Ibid.

9. Ibid.

10. James Hasik, *Arms and Innovation: Entrepreneurship and Alliances in the Twenty-First Century Defense Industry* (Chicago: University of Chicago Press, 2008), 33.

11. "Case History: Unmanned and Dangerous," *The Economist*, December 6, 2007. Accessed April 1, 2013: www.economist.com/ node/10202603.

12. James Hasik, *Arms and Innovation*, 33.

13. "Talk of Drones Patrolling U.S. Skies Spawns Anxiety," *USA Today*, June 19, 2012. Accessed April 1, 2013: http://usatoday30. usatoday.com/news/washington/story/2012-06-19/drone-back-lash/55682654/1.

14. Natasha Lennard, "Which Police Departments Want Drones?"

Salon, February 11, 2013. Accessed April 1, 2013: www.salon.com/2013/02/11/which_police_departments_want_drones.

15. Federal Aviation Administration, fact sheet, "Unmanned Aircraft Systems (UAS)," February 19, 2013. Accessed April 1, 2013: www.faa.gov/news/fact_sheets/news_story.cfm?newsId=14153.

16. Ibid.

17. Ibid.

18. Stephen Dean, "First Unmanned Police Drone in Texas Set to Launch North Of Houston," *Examiner.com*, October 29, 2011. Accessed on April 1, 2013: www.examiner.com/article/first-unmanned-police-drone-texas-set-to-launch-north-of-houston.

19. Jason Koebler, "Police to Use Drones for Spying on Citizens," *US News and World Report*, August 23, 2012. Accessed April 1, 2013: www.usnews.com/news/articles/2012/08/23/docs-law-enforcement-agencies-plan-to-use-domestic-drones-for-surveillance.

20. Hina Jilani (Special Representative of the Secretary General on the Status of Human Rights Defenders), "Promotion and Protection and Human Rights: Human Rights Defenders," United Nations, E/CN.4/2004/94/Add.3, March 23, 2004, 151, para. 476. Accessed August 1, 2004: www.unhchr.ch/pdf/chr60/94add3AV.pdf. See also Independent Review Panel (Jorge E. Reynardus, Esq., Chairperson, Civilian Oversight of Miami-Dade Police and Corrections and Rehabilitation Departments), Final Draft Report on the Free Trade Area of the Americas (FTAA) Inquiry, June 2004.

21. Public Law 112-95 (2012).

22. Spencer Ackerman, "Domestic-Drone Industry Prepares for Big Battle With Regulators," *Wired*, February 13, 2013. Accessed April 1, 2013: www.wired.com/dangerroom/2013/02/drone-regulation.

23. *See* "Camcopter S-100 Unmanned Air System" brochure. Accessed April 1, 2013: www.schiebel.net/File.aspx?Id=1979&Path=~%2fDownload%2fBrochures&Name=pdfDownload.

24. FAA Modernization and Reform Act of 2012, Pub. L. 111-95 (2012).

25. Trevor Timm, excerpt from talk at "Drone Summit: Killing and Spying by Remote Control," Washington, D.C., April 28–29, 2012, broadcast on *Law and Disorder*, WBAI, July 9, 2012. Accessed April 1, 2013: http://lawanddisorder.org/2012/07/law-and-disorder-july-9-2012.

26. Ibid.

27. Lee Fang, "Drone Lobby Group Brands Itself as 'Academic'

Organizations, but Funds Come Primarily From Weapons Makers," *Republic Report*, June 25, 2012. Accessed April 1, 2013: www. republicreport.org/2012/drones-academic-weapons; See also www. auvsi.org/Association for Unmanned Vehicle Systems International.

28. ManTech International Corporation, "ManTech Awarded $46 Million Contract to Provide Flight Test Support for NAVAIR Manned and Unmanned Air Vehicle Evaluation Division," news release, April 27, 2012. Accessed April 1, 2013: http://investor.mantech.com/releasedetail.cfm?ReleaseID=668033.

29. Johns Hopkins University, "Unraveling a Butterfly's Aerial Antics Could Help Builders of Bug-Size Flying Robots," news release, February 2, 2012. Accessed April 1, 2013: http://releases.jhu. edu/2012/02/01/butterfly-study-could-help-builders-of-bug-size-flying-robots.

30. Richard M. Thompson II, "Drones in Domestic Surveillance Operations: Fourth Amendment Implications and Legislative Responses," Congressional Research Service, September 6, 2012. Accessed April 1, 2013: www.fas.org/sgp/crs/natsec/R42701.pdf.

31. Ibid.,16.

32. Paul Rosenzweig, Steven P. Bucci, Charles "Cully" Stimson, and James Jay Carafano, "Drones in U.S. Airspace: Principles for Governance," Heritage Foundation, September 20, 2012. Accessed April 1, 2013: www.heritage.org/research/reports/2012/09/drones-in-us-airspace-principles-for-governance.

33. Ibid.

34. Thom Shanker, "A New Medal Honors Drone Pilots and Computer Experts, *New York Times*, February 13, 2013. Accessed April 1, 2013: www.nytimes.com/2013/02/14/us/new-medal-to-honor-drone-pilots-and-computer-experts.html?ref=thomshanker&gwh=0D6D87388E8 D39B4088115E67F3E2B06.

35. Ryan Gallagher, "Surveillance Drone Industry Plans PR Effort to Counter Negative Image," *The Guardian (UK)*, February 2, 2012. Accessed April 1, 2013: www.guardian.co.uk/uk/2012/feb/02/surveillance-drone-industy-pr-effort.

36. Jefferson Morley, "A Drone Near-Disaster? An Airplane Pilot Reports a Near Collision with a 'Remotely Controlled Aircraft' Over Denver," *Salon*, May 18, 2012. Accessed April 1, 2013: www.salon. com/2012/05/18/denvers_drone_near_disaster.

37. Brian Bennett, "Police Employ Predator Drone Spy Planes on Home

Front," *Los Angeles Times*, December 10, 2011. Accessed April 1, 2013: http://articles.latimes.com/2011/dec/10/nation/la-na-drone-arrest-20111211.

CHAPTER 12

1. Mohammed Jamjoom, "Saudi Arabia's Unsolicited Monitoring of Women's Travels Draws Activists' Outrage," *CNN*, November 26, 2012. Accessed April 1, 2013: www.cnn.com/2012/11/25/world/meast/saudi-arabia-women.

2. Eric Lichtblau, "Wireless Firms Are Flooded by Requests to Aid Surveillance," *New York Times*, July 8, 2012. Accessed April 1, 2013: www.nytimes.com/2012/07/09/us/cell-carriers-see-uptick-in-requests-to-aid-surveillance.html.

3. Kevin J. O'Brien, "Smartphone Sales Taking Toll on G.P.S. Devices," *New York Times*, November 14, 2010. Accessed April 1, 2013: www.nytimes.com/2010/11/15/technology/15iht-navigate.html. See also, Verizon Wireless, "E911 Compliance FAQs," accessed on April 1, 2013: http://support.verizonwireless.com/faqs/Wireless%20Issues/faq_e911_compliance.html. "Because the FCC requires that carriers convert nearly all of their handsets to GPS capability, Verizon Wireless will no longer allow non-GPS-capable phones to be on the network. Older phones that are not GPS-capable cannot assist in estimating their location. If a non-GPS-capable phone that is currently active is disconnected for any reason, it will not be reactivated. If you purchased your handset in 2001 or earlier, it will not be GPS-capable and you should upgrade it. Even if you bought your phone in 2002 or later, it may not be GPS-capable and if so you should upgrade it."

4. 18 U.S.C. ch. 121. It requires Internet providers to retain any "record" in their possession for ninety days "upon the request of a governmental entity." See also Federal Communications Commission, "Guide Protecting Your Telephone Calling Records." Accessed April 1, 2013: www.fcc.gov/guides/protecting-your-telephone-calling-records.

5. *See*, e.g., "Providing Senior Safety with GPS Tracking," Tracking System Direct, October 20, 2012. Accessed April 1, 2013: www.tracking-system.com/for-consumers/gps-elderly-tracking-system/1171-gps-locator-watch-for-seniors.html.

6. Michael Winter, "Judge Estimates 30K Secret Spying Orders Approved Yearly," *USA Today*, June 05, 2012. Accessed April 1, 2013:

http://content.usatoday.com/communities/ondeadline/post/2012/06/ judge-estimates-30k-secret-spying-orders-approved-each-year/1.

7. Location Privacy Protection Act of 2012, S. 1223, 112th Cong. (The bill died on December 13, 2012.)

8. Bob Violino, "The History of RFID Technology," *RFID Journal*, January 16, 2005. Accessed April 1, 2013: www.rfidjournal.com/articles/view?1338#sthash.APH9kOe3.dpuf.

9. Katherine Albrecht and Liz McIntyre, *Spychips: How Major Corporations and Government Plan to Track Your Every Purchase and Watch Your Every Move* (New York: Plume, 2006), 23.

10. The Uniform Code Council is now known as GS1 US, manager of the GS1 System in the USA which assigns Company Prefixes to companies/organizations. The most common use of a GS1 US assigned GS1 Company Prefix is the creation of Universal Product Codes or U.P.C.s, which contain a 12-digit Global Trade Item Number.

11. Ibid.

12. Katherine Albrecht and Liz McIntyre, *Spychips: How Major Corporations and Government Plan to Track Your Every Purchase and Watch Your Every Move* (New York: Plume, 2006), 24–25.

13. Nicole Ozer, "'Chipping' Students Creates More Problems than It Solves," ACLU of Northern California, September 1, 2010. Accessed April 1, 2013: www.aclunc.org/issues/technology/blog/chipping_students_creates_more_problems_than_it_solves.shtml.

14. "Texas Schools Track Students with RFID," *RFID News*, October 11, 2010. Accessed April 1, 2013: www.rfidnews.org/2010/10/11/texas-schools-track-students-with-rfid#top.

15. David Kravets, "Tracking School Children with RFID Tags? It's All about the Benjamins," *Wired*, September 7, 2012. Accessed April 1, 2013: www.wired.com/threatlevel/2012/09/rfid-chip-student-monitoring.

16. Jack Kelly, "Washington County Students Carry Devices to Help Pitt Monitor Spread of Flu," *Pittsburgh Post-Gazette*, November 5, 2012. Accessed April 1, 2013: www.post-gazette.com/stories/news/science/ washington-county-students-carry-devices-to-help-pitt-monitor-spread-of-flu-660701.

17. Ibid.

18. *See*, e.g., TokenWorks, ID Scanner Solutions for age verification, lead capture, access control. Accessed April 1, 2013: www.idscanner.com/.

19. John Coté, "Calif. Cops Want More Cameras, ID Scanners in

Nightclubs," *San Francisco Chronicle*, September 17, 2010. Reprinted and accessed April 1, 2013: www.policeone.com/news/2679165-Calif-cops-want-more-cameras-ID-scanners-in-nightclubs.

20. Jamie Schram, "Furor as NYPD Squeezes Clubs for ID Scanners," *New York Post*, June 7, 2011. Accessed April 1, 2013: www.nypost.com/p/news/local/manhattan/furor_as_nypd_squeezes_clubs_for_q24kgG4jJAbhQ6aRv00XSP.

21. Simon Morton, "Barcelona Clubbers Get Chipped," *BBC News*, September 29, 2004. Accessed April 1, 2013: http://news.bbc.co.uk/2/hi/technology/3697940.stm.

22. *See* University of Reading, Professor Kevin Warwick, "I, Cyborg," accessed April 1, 2013: www.kevinwarwick.com/ICyborg.htm.

23. Alexandra Leo, "RFID Tags: Convenient Technology or Path to Government Monitoring?" *ABC News*, May 2, 2006. Accessed April 1, 2013: http://abcnews.go.com/Technology/story?id=1913574&page=1.

24. Andy Greenberg, "Want an RFID Chip Implanted into Your Hand? Here's What the DIY Surgery Looks Like," *Forbes*, August 13, 2012. Accessed April 1, 2013: www.forbes.com/sites/andygreenberg/2012/08/13/want-an-rfid-chip-implanted-into-your-hand-heres-what-the-diy-surgery-looks-like-video/?commentId=comment_blogAndPostId/blog/comment/948-7565-5783.

25. Katherine Albrecht and Liz McIntyre, *Spychips: How Major Corporations and Government Plan to Track Your Every Purchase and Watch Your Every Move* (New York: Plume, 2006), 179.

26. Claire Swedberg, "Alzheimer's Care Center to Carry Out VeriChip Pilot," *RFID Journal*, May 25, 2007. Accessed April 1, 2013: www.rfidjournal.com/articles/view?3340#sthash.V3eSX8vd.dpuf.

27. "VeriChip Corporation Enters into Development and Supply Agreement with Medical Components, Inc., Valued at More Than $3 Million," *Business Wire*, March 18, 2009. Accessed April 1, 2013: www.businesswire.com/news/home/20090318005363/en/VeriChip-Corporation-Enters-Development-Supply-Agreement-Medical.

28. Jim Edwards, "Down with the Chip: PositiveID Axes Its Scary Medical Records Implant," *CBS News*, July 15, 2010. Accessed April 1, 2013: www.cbsnews.com/8301-505123_162-42845130/down-with-the-chip-positiveid-axes-its-scary-medical-records-implant.

29. VeriTeQ Acquisition Corporation, "VeriTeQ Acquisition Corporation's VeriChip Technology Is the Original Universal Patient

Identifier to Address National Need for Rapid, Accurate Access to Critical Patient Data," press release, January 25, 2012. Accessed April 1, 2013: www.reuters.com/article/2012/01/25/idUS120140+25-Jan-2012+BW20120125.

30. Katherine Albrecht, interview by Heidi Boghosian, Michael Ratner and Michael Smith, *Law and Disorder*, WBAI, July 2, 2012. Accessed April 1, 2013: http://lawanddisorder.org/2012/07/law-and-disorder-july-2-2012.

31. Ibid.

32. *See generally*, Andrew J. Blumberg and Peter Eckersley, "On Locational Privacy, and How to Avoid Losing It Forever, Electronic Frontier Foundation," August 3, 2009. Accessed April 1, 2013: www.eff.org/wp/locational-privacy.

CHAPTER 13

1. *See Garcia, et al., v. Bloomberg, et al.*, 11 Civ. 6957 (JSR) (S.D.N.Y, June 7, 2012), Document 25, Opinion and Order, 1. Accessed April 1, 2013: www.justiceonline.org/docs/garcia-v-bloomberg-et-al.pdf.

2. Lisa W. Foderaro, "Privately Owned Park, Open to the Public, May Make Its Own Rules," *New York Times*, October 13, 2011. Accessed April 1, 2013: www.nytimes.com/2011/10/14/nyregion/zuccotti-park-is-privately-owned-but-open-to-the-public.html.

3. National Lawyers Guild, "Lawyers Challenge Occupy Evictions," news release, November 21, 2011. Accessed April 1, 2013: www.nlg.org/news/lawyers-challenge-occupy-evictions.

4. *See, e.g.*, Michael S. Schmidt and Colin Moynihan, "F.B.I. Counter-terrorism Agents Monitored Occupy Movement, Records Show," *New York Times*, December 24, 2012. Accessed April 1, 2013: www.nytimes.com/2012/12/25/nyregion/occupy-movement-was-investigated-by-fbi-counterterrorism-agents-records-show.html. Documents obtained through Freedom of Information Act requests are available on the Partnership for Civil Justice Fund website. Accessed April 1, 2013: www.justiceonline.org/our-work/ows-foia.html.

5. Mara Verheyden-Hilliard, interview by Heidi Boghosian and Michael Smith, *Law and Disorder*, WBAI, January 7, 2013. Accessed April 1, 2013: http://lawanddisorder.org/2013/01/law-and-disorder-january-7-2013/.

6. Ibid. "FBI Documents Reveal Secret Nationwide Occupy Monitoring," Partnership for Civil Justice Fund, www.justiceonline.org/com-

mentary/fbi-files-ows.html.

7. Partnership for Civil Justice Fund, www.justiceonline.org/.

8. Mara Verheyden-Hilliard, interview by Heidi Boghosian and Michael Smith, *Law and Disorder*, WBAI, New York City, January 7, 2013. Accessed: www.lawanddisorder.org/2013/01/law-and-disorder-january-7-2013.

9. When only handcuffs are used, the police can easily use bolt cutters to arrest and remove the protesters. The sleeping dragon prolongs the process of arrests by forcing the police to expend greater time and effort to separate individuals from the group.

10. Greg Gladden, email on file with the author, February 14, 2013.

11. Ibid.

12. Thoma J. Sheeran and Kantele Franko, "FBI: 5 Men Charged in Ohio Bridge Bomb Plot," Associated Press, May 1, 2012. Accessed April 1, 2013: www.boston.com/news/nation/articles/2012/05/01/ap_source_5_arrested_in_alleged_bombing_plot.

13. Lee Klawans, "Lawyers Guild Claims NATO Activists Entrapped by Police Informants," *Examiner.com*, May 22, 2012. Accessed April 1, 2013: www.examiner.com/article/lawyers-guild-claims-nato-activists-entrapped-by-police-informant-photo.

14. Michael Martinez and Paul Vercammen, "Police: 3 Terror Suspects at NATO Summit Were Plotting to Hit Obama's Campaign HQs," *CNN*, May 19, 2012. Accessed April 1, 2013: www.cnn.com/2012/05/19/us/nato-terror-suspects.

15. Michael Tarm, "NATO Protesters Indicted on 11 Counts in Chicago," Associated Press, June 20, 2012. Accessed on April 1, 2013: http://bigstory.ap.org/article/apnewsbreak-nato-protesters-indicted-11-counts.

16. Sarah Gelsomino, interview by Heidi Boghosian, Michael Ratner, and Michael Smith, *Law and Disorder*, WBAI, May 28, 2012. Accessed April 1, 2013: http://lawanddisorder.org/2012/05/law-and-disorder-may-28-2012.

17. Kris Hermes, "The NATO 5: Manufactured Crimes Used to Paint Political Dissidents as Terrorists," *Huffington Post*, January 25, 2013. Accessed April 1, 2013: www.huffingtonpost.com/kris-hermes/the-nato-5-terrorism-charges_b_2552554.html.

18. Mara Verheyden-Hilliard, interview by Heidi Boghosian and Michael Smith, *Law and Disorder*, WBAI, January 7, 2013. Accessed April 1, 2013: www.lawanddisorder.org/2013/01/law-and-disorder-janu-

ary-7-2013.

CONCLUSION

1. James Bamford, *The Shadow Factory* (New York: Anchor Books, 2009), 341.
2. Ibid., 340.
3. Ibid., 345.
4. James X. Dempsey and David Cole, *Terrorism & The Constitution: Sacrificing Civil Liberties in the Name of National Security* (Washington, D.C.: First Amendment Foundation, 2002), 175.
5. Tim Weiner, *Enemies: A History of the FBI* (New York: Random House, 2012), 371.
6. Eric Lichtblau, David Johnston, and Ron Nixon, "FBI Officials Struggle to Handle Wave of Financial Fraud Cases," *New York Times*, October 19, 2008. Accessed April 1, 2013: www.nytimes.com/2008/10/19/world/americas/19iht-19fbi.17066845.html.
7. Ibid.
8. Paul Wallis, Op-Ed: "White Collar Crime: FBI Investigations Trashed by Spreadsheet Politics," *Digital Journal*, October 29, 2008. Accessed April 1, 2013: www.digitaljournal.com/article/261341#ixzz2KQWCyDIs.
9. "Foreclosure Crisis Pushes More Americans out of Their Homes," PBS, October 22, 2010. Accessed April 1, 2013: www.pbs.org/newshour/extra/features/economics/july-dec10/Foreclosure_10-22.html.
10. New York University, "NYU Researchers Question Effectiveness of Surveillance Cameras in Reducing Crime," news release, February 26, 2009. Accessed April 1, 2013: www.nyu.edu/about/news-publications/news/2009/02/26/nyu_researchers_question.html.
11. Jennifer King, Deirdre K. Mulligan, and Steven Raphael, "CITRIS Report: The San Francisco Community Safety Camera Program: An Evaluation of the Effectiveness of San Francisco's Community Safety Cameras," University of California, Berkeley, December 17, 2008. Accessed April 1, 2013: http://fedgeno.com/documents/citris-report-on-community-safety-camera-program.pdf.
12. Jennifer 8. Lee, "Study Questions whether Cameras Cut Crime," *New York Times*, March 3, 2009. Accessed April 1, 2013: http://cityroom.blogs.nytimes.com/2009/03/03/study-questions-whether-cameras-cut-crime.
13. Edward L. Bernays, *Propaganda* (Brooklyn, NY: Ig, 2005), 37.

14. "Calif. 1 of 11 States Seeking to Limit Use of Drones by Police," *ABC News10 (CA)*, February 5, 2013. Accessed April 1, 2013: www.news10.net/news/california/article/228731/430/Calif-1-of-9-states-seeking-to-limit-use-of-drones-by-police.

15. *See A.H. v. Northside Independent School District*, Civil No. SA-12-CA-1113-OG (W.D. TX 2013).

16. *See Rutherford Institute*, "VICTORY: Maryland School District Agrees to Cease Implementation of Biometric Palm Reader Program After Rutherford Institute Voices Concerns," news release, December 13, 2013. Accessed April 1, 2013: www.rutherford.org/publications_resources/on_the_front_lines/victory_maryland_school_district_agrees_to_cease_implementation_of_biometri.

17. "Palm Scanners to Pay For School Lunch at Moss Bluff Elementary Has Parents up in Arms, Call It 'Mark of the Beast,'" *Huffington Post*, August 19, 2012. Accessed April 1, 2013: www.huffingtonpost.com/2012/08/17/palm-scanners-to-pay-for-_n_1799735.html.

18. *See* "History and Highlights: Campaign for a Commercial Free Childhood." Accessed April 1, 2013: www.commercialfreechildhood.org/history-and-highlights.

19. Ibid.

20. Ibid.

21. Ibid.

22. Ibid.

23. Ryan Gallagher, "FBI Documents Shine Light on Clandestine Cellphone Tracking Tool," *Slate*, January 11, 2013. Accessed April 1, 2013: www.slate.com/blogs/future_tense/2013/01/10/stingray_imsi_catcher_fbi_documents_shine_light_on_controversial_cellphone.html.

24. Ibid.

25. Michael Kelley, "FBI Concerned about the Legality of Its Own Portable Surveillance Technology," *Business Insider*, January 11, 2013. Accessed April 1, 2013: www.businessinsider.com/fbi-stingray-technology-2013-1.

26. Andrew Levine, "Boston Overkill," Communications Assistance for Law Enforcement Act (CALEA), Pub. L. No. 103-414, 108 Stat. 4279, codified at 47 USC 1001 et seq.

27. Andrew Levine, "Boston Overkill," *Counterpunch*, April 23, 2013. Accessed May 2, 2013: www.counterpunch.org/2013/04/23/boston-overkill/.

28. "Surveillance's Dark Downside," *New York Daily News*, April 28, 2013. Accessed May 2, 2013: www.nydailynews.com/opinion/surveillance-dark-downside-article-1.1328574.

29. Liberty Was Also Attacked in Boston," April 29, 2013. Accessed May 2, 2013: www.dailypaul.com/283917/ron-paul-liberty-was-also-attacked-in-boston-april-29-2013.

30. "Surveillance State No Answer to Terror," CNN, April 23, 2013. Accessed May 2: 2013: www.cnn.com/2013/04/23/opinion/richards-surveillance-state.

31. James Bamford, "The NSA Is Building the Country's Biggest Spy Center (Watch What You Say)," *Wired*, March 15, 2012. Accessed April 1, 2013: www.wired.com/threatlevel/2012/03/ff_nsadatacenter/.

32. Richard A. Posner, *Uncertain Shield: The U.S. Intelligence System in the Throes of Reform* (Lanham, MD: Rowman & Littlefield, 2006), 119–139.

33. Report to the President by the Commission on CIA Activities within the United States, June 1975, Vice President Nelson A. Rockefeller, Chairman, 5.

INDEX

Page numbers in *italic* refer to illustrations. "Passim" (literally "scattered") indicates intermittent discussion of a topic over a cluster of pages.

Heidi Boghosian is the executive director of the National Lawyers Guild, a progressive bar association established in 1937 as an alternative to the American Bar Association. She cohosts the weekly civil liberties radio program *Law and Disorder*, which airs on Pacifica's WBAI in New York and on more than fifty national affiliate stations around the country. A former editor of the independent community newspaper the *East Villager*, she has resided in Manhattan's East Village since 1986.

"Heidi Boghosian's *Spying on Democracy is the answer to the question, 'If you're not doing anything wrong, why should you care if someone's watching you?' It's chock-full of stories about how innocent people's lives were turned upside-down by public and private sector surveillance programs. But more important, it shows how this unrestrained spying is inevitably used to suppress the most essential tools of democracy: the press, political activists, civil rights advocates and conscientious insiders who blow the whistle on corporate malfeasance and government abuse."*

MICHAEL GERMAN, former FBI agent, ACLU Senior Policy Counsel

Spying on Democracy **reveals how technology is used** to categorize and monitor people based on their activities, their associations, their movements, their purchases, and their perceived political beliefs. Corporations gather information from sources as diverse as surveillance cameras to iris scans and medical records, while combing websites, email, phone records, and social media for personal data to aggregate and sell to third parties, including U.S. government intelligence agencies.

PQ057956S

OPEN MEDIA
CITY LIGHTS BOOKS
www.citylights.com
ARM YOURSELF WITH INFORMATION

ISBN 978-0-87286-599-0

51895 >

9 780872 865990   US$18.95